THE CIVILIZATION OF THE AMERICAN INDIAN SERIES

FEB 2006

FEB 2006

THE
KANSA
INDIANS

UNIVERSITY OF OKLAHOMA PRESS : NORMAN

THE KANSA INDIANS

A HISTORY OF THE WIND PEOPLE, 1673-1873

by William E. Unrau

foreword by R. David Edmunds

A PLAINS REPRINT

The University of Oklahoma Press is committed to keeping its best works in print. By utilizing digital technology, we can reprint titles for which demand is steady but too small to justify printing by conventional methods. All textual content is identical to that of previous printings. Illustration quality may vary from the originals.

By William E. Unrau

The Kansa Indians: A History of the Wind People 1673–1873 (Norman, 1971)
The Kaw People (Phoenix, Ariz., 1975)
The End of Indian Kansas (with H. Craig Miner) (Lawrence, Kans., 1978)
Tending the Talking Wire (Salt Lake City, Utah, 1979)
The Emigrant Indians of Kansas (Bloomington, Ind., 1979)
Tribal Dispossession and the Ottawa Indian University Fraud (with H. Craig Miner) (Norman, 1985)

Library of Congress Cataloging-in-Publication Data

Unrau, William E., 1929–
The Kansa Indians : a history of the Wind People, 1673–1873.

(The Civilization of the American Indian series ; v. 114)
Bibliography : p.
Includes index.
1. Kansa Indians—History. 2. Indians of North America—Kansas—History.
I. Title. II. Series.
E99.K2U75   1986   978.1'00497   85–26535
International Standard Book Number: 0–8061–1965–9

The Kansa Indians: A History of the Wind People, 1673–1873 is
Volume 114 in The Civilization of the American Indian Series.

Copyright © 1971 by the University of Oklahoma Press, Norman, Publishing Division of the University. All rights reserved. Manufactured in the U.S.A.

4 5 6 7 8 9 10 11 12 13

978.1 U58k 1986
Unrau, William E., 1929-
The Kansa Indians : a history
of the Wind People, 1673-1873

For Millie

CONTENTS

ILLUSTRATIONS

MAPS

FOREWORD
by R. David Edmunds

If asked to describe or discuss American Indians, most Americans will mention tribes such as the Cherokees, Sioux, Navajos, or Apaches: large tribes whose history and culture have enjoyed considerable investigation. Indeed, most Americans' knowledge of Indian people is circumscribed by the image of Native Americans projected through the popular media (novels, movies, and television), or by their limited contacts with Indian communities during vacation excursions in the American Southwest. They have watched Apache and Sioux war parties thunder across the screens of their television sets or marveled at the craftsmanship of Navajo and Hopi artisans. Yet if asked to discuss the history and culture of the tribes which once occupied their local region, many non-Indians would be hard pressed to supply such information.

Many of the smaller tribes fought no monumental military engagements, left no stirring oratory, produced no "patriot chiefs," yet their quiet struggles to maintain their traditions in the face of overwhelming odds is more indicative of the Indian experience than the more publicized accounts of Indian-white warfare. The Kansa or Kaw Indians are certainly representative of these smaller, less conspicuous tribes.

Prior to the 1970's most of the Siouan-speaking people of the Middle Border—the Kansas, Quapaws, Poncas, and Omahas, who all speak the Dhegihan dialect, and the Chiwerian-speaking

Iowas and Otoe-Missourias—had received only nominal attention from both historians and the American reading public. Only the Dhegihan-speaking Osages, an oil-rich tribe who attracted considerable attention during the first third of the twentieth century, were the subject of any long-term historical inquiry, and much of the writing focusing upon Osage history and culture was produced by John Joseph Mathews, a member of the tribe.

In contrast, in the decade between 1971 and 1981, the University of Oklahoma Press published three volumes which chronicled the history of the Siouan-speaking tribes: Martha Royce Blaine's *The Ioway Indians* (1979); W. David Baird's *The Quapaw Indians: A History of the Downstream People* (1980); and William E. Unrau's *The Kansa Indians: A History of the Wind People, 1673-1873* (1971). Of the three volumes, *The Kansa Indians* focuses upon a smaller chronological period and therefore provides a more detailed study of the tribe.

In *The Kansa Indians*, William Unrau presents a classic account of an Indian tribe surrounded by more powerful neighbors and forced to struggle for its existence. Never a populous people, the Kansas occupied the mid-Missouri Valley, near the junctures of the Missouri and Kansas rivers. Forced westward by more powerful tribes, the Kansas relocated along the lower Kansas Valley, concentrating their villages between the mouth of the Big Blue River and Stranger Creek. Although they remained in eastern Kansas during most of the nineteenth century, their tenure in the region seemed perennially in doubt. Threatened on their eastern borders by successive waves of emigrant Indians and American settlers, their westward retreat was blocked by the more numerous and nomadic Plains tribes. Ceding their homeland, they sought refuge on a·series of shrinking reservations, until in 1872 they surrendered their lands in the fertile Neosho Valley. By 1873 most of the Kansas had removed to northern Oklahoma.

Like numerous other tribes, many of the Kansas' problems resulted from their growing economic dependency upon first the Europeans, then the Americans. Enmeshed in the fur trade, the Kansas not only lost their traditional self-sufficiency, they also were drawn into competition with the Osages, the Pawnees, and other tribes for the steadily dwindling supply of pelts. As the fur bearers declined, the Kansas no longer had the wherewithal to purchase the trade goods that once had been luxuries but now were necessities. In consequence they parceled away their homeland, citing their reservations for government payments and annuities. Meanwhile their weakened condition made them particularly vulnerable to the series of epidemics which swept through the plains during the nineteenth century.

They remained more resistant to the government's attempts to force them to live like white men. Catholic, Presbyterian, and Methodist missionaries all labored mightily in the Kansa villages, but their harvest was spare. Most of the Kansas expressed little interest in mission schools, and both missionaries and federal agents repeatedly failed in their efforts to turn the Indians into small yoeman farmers. Like many other Indian peoples, the Kansas clung tenaciously to their traditional ways. If federal agents expected them to make major changes, they were sorely disappointed.

Tragically, the Kansa saga also presents a classic case study in the all too familiar annals of inefficiency, fraud, and corruption surrounding the administration of Indian affairs in the nineteenth century. Fortunes were made in the "Indian business," and like many other tribes the Kansas played an important, if unwilling, role. Meanwhile, opportunistic frontiersmen trespassed upon Kansa lands, denuding the reservation of valuable timber. Anticipating the Kansas' removal, other groups of squatters and land speculators fought among themselves over who would control the prime farmland along the Neosho River after the Indians had been removed to Oklahoma.

And yet perhaps the most pervasive theme in Unrau's volume is that the Kansas persisted. Although outnumbered by their Indian enemies, they fought back against the Pawnees, Osages, and Cheyennes. Retaining their traditions, they refused to walk the white man's road and stubbornly clung to their Indian values, even in the face of the government's most dogged attempts to force their acculturation. Obviously they suffered, but like many small tribes they triumphed over what seemed to be unsurmountable odds. Today they still take pride in their Kansa heritage.

Historians of the American frontier, of American Indians, and of the Middle Border have touted this volume as a solid contribution in its field. It is well researched, and in these times of pervading anthropological jargon, remarkably well written. Although it has emerged as the standard authoritative study of Kansa history, its appeal transcends professional historians to include anyone interested in the American West. In addition to being reliable history, *The Kansa: A History of the Wind People* is "good reading."

PREFACE TO THE PAPERBACK EDITION

Since the first publication of this volume a decade and a half ago only a modest amount of new research has been published to document the tragic history of the Kansa people prior to their removal from Kansas in 1873. Post-1971 additions to the bibliography of this reprint indicate some of the more important studies and opportunities for additional research in the future. Particular mention should be made of Louise Barry's monumental compilation, *The Beginning of the West: Annals of the Kansas Gateway to the American West,* 1540–1854 (1972), which provides additional details regarding demography, political, and social organization and tribal movements prior to the opening of the Kansas Territory in 1854. While these data, some of which correct my earlier research, enrich our understanding of the Kansas, they complement rather than contradict the basic generalizations I arrived at in 1971.

My own work since then indicates that several themes warrant greater emphasis. First and foremost is the divisive and destructive impact of the St. Louis Treaty of 1825. Article 6 of that treaty, which granted one-mile-square "reservations" to the twenty-three so-called "half breeds of the Kanzas nation," wrecked the traditional political and social leadership of the Kansas and provided the principal mechanism whereby white land jobbers, government agents, and the many other champions of tribal dispossession could manipulate the Kansas almost at will. That the ultimate ownership of these valuable lands is still being litigated

xix

in the federal courts, and that blood quantum as a prerequisite for bona fide tribal membership is still one of the most volatile issues in contemporary Kansa politics, confirms the grave importance of this treaty.

In light of recent scholarship in historical demography, and more evidence regarding the government's inconsequential efforts to control contagion and malnutrition among the Kansas, the impact of epidemic disease also warrants greater attention than was given initially in this volume. Certainly a examination of the few health and medical records for the period surviving after 1873 confirms the long-standing consequences of biological decimation. Traditional clan cohesion disintegrated, family life was severely weakened, and a kind of cynical, unproductive factionalism became a commonplace feature of Kansa life. Indeed, to fully comprehend the ultimate tragedy of tribal dissolution in the early twentieth century, the careful student of Kansa history needs to understand that virtually uninterrupted biosocial destruction served as the backdrop to a continuum of government ineptitude and white land-grabbing, extending from the 1825 Treaty to President Theodore Roosevelt's signing of the Kansa (Kaw) Allotment Bill of 1902.

What is needed, of course, is a well-documented account of the Kansa-Kaw experience since 1873. *The Kaw People*, a slender volume I published in 1975, provides a possible outline and implied suggestions for further research. Because of shoddy government record maintenance and bureaucratic snarls after about 1880, the research problems are legion. For example, Charles Curtis, the vice-president during the Hoover administration, was a distinguished Kaw mixed-blood whose powerful role in national tribal politics dated back to the immediate post-Dawes era, yet even Curtis's accomplishments remain clouded with those assimilationist biases so characteristic of uncritical Indian historiography at the turn of the century. The same can be said for events during much of the five decades subsequent to allotment, until in the 1950's efforts to reorganize the Kaw Tribe of Oklahoma as a legal corporate body finally succeeded. In short, a great deal of research into the history of the Kansa-Kaw people remains to be done, and it is hoped that the reissue of *The Kansa Indians* will serve as an impetus toward that objective.

WILLIAM E. UNRAU

Flagstaff, Arizona

PREFACE TO THE FIRST EDITION

W<small>HEN</small> I first embarked on this study, a good friend and practicing historian suggested that, while the Kansa story needed to be told, there probably was not enough information to develop a comprehensive narrative. Others advised me that the absence of a highly publicized massacre or battlefield encounter between the Kansas and the white man constituted a formidable obstacle to lay-reader interest and perhaps to some members of the scholarly community as well. Notably absent also, I was told, were adequate archaeological guidelines for the prehistoric period, spectacular flights in the face of overwhelming odds, quotable pronouncements by tribal dignitaries, and strategic intertribal alliances that for a time might have left the conflict in doubt. In short, I was led to believe that the Kansa story lacked the kind of vibrancy readers have come to expect in the history of the American Indian.

On the other hand, a cursory survey of some of the sources convinced me that the devious tactics employed by the squatters and land jobbers on the Kansa domain, together with the tenacious determinism with which traders, missionaries, and government officials instigated a cultural revolution, were important aspects of social history that the historian could ill afford to ignore. Taken in conjunction with the ravages of epidemic disease and the seemingly calculated destruction of the tribe's means of natural subsistence, evidence of these distressing developments finally prompted me to raise a fundamental question: How was it that the Kansas were able to maintain even a modified form of their traditional culture for as long as they did?

Seeking answers to this and other significant questions seemed all the more appropriate in view of current efforts to encourage a sense of "Indianness" among the heirs of those who first inhabited parts of the Western Hemisphere. Thus in spite of an anticipated paucity of information and the unhappy prospect that the finished product might be considered dull and lackluster, this study was undertaken. I hope the reader will decide that it was worth while.

No book is the work of one person, and I am happy to acknowledge the contributions of those who came to my assistance. I hasten to add, of course, that all errors in fact and interpretation are my responsibility.

Karl Schlesier, William Bass, and Thomas A. Witty helped me lessen the distance between history and anthropology. Raymond J. DeMallie, of the Smithsonian Institution's Anthropology Office, read parts of the manuscript and made some important suggestions. Laura E. Kelsay, of the National Archives, and Frances H. Stadler, of the Missouri Historical Society, were exceedingly helpful in the procurement of maps and documents.

Nyle Miller's exceptionally competent staff at the Kansas State Historical Society deserves a special word of thanks. In that impressive depository, across from the statehouse in Topeka, Robert Richmond, Joseph Snell, Eugene Decker, and Joseph Gambone gave freely of their time and talents. Paul W. Gates, John J. Mathews, and Harry Kelsey offered encouragement and advice at various stages in the research. My colleagues in the history department at Wichita State University, especially John Harnsberger, James Gray, John D. Born, Jr., Phillip D. Thomas, and James Duram, came to my assistance when needed. John Rydjord, whose sound judgment and knowledge of the American Indian are difficult to match, read parts of the manuscript and made a number of significant suggestions. In the procurement of source material Thoburn Taggert, Jr., and Michael Heaston cooperated beyond the call of duty, while Lou Beck, Charles W. Sloan, Jr., and

Michael Sievers furnished dependable clerical assistance. I would also like to thank the Faculty Research Committee at Wichita State University for providing financial support for this project.

Finally, I would like to acknowledge the large debts I owe to Robert G. Athearn and Robert Heffley, who, in different ways and from different perspectives, have taught me a great deal of what history is all about.

WILLIAM E. UNRAU

Wichita, Kansas

THE
KANSA
INDIANS

CHAPTER 1 ORIGINS
AND EARLY MIGRATIONS

A pervading theme in cultural history is man's quest for knowledge about himself and the people about him. In this regard the Kansa Indians were no exception. Like the several groups comprising what ethnologists have classified as the Dhegiha (or Ȼegiha) branch of the Siouan-speaking peoples,[1] the Kansas sustained a variety of legends concerning the nature of the universe and the origin of their ancestors. Since nothing approaching a written Kansa language was extant until the nineteenth century,[2] these accounts were preserved as oral traditions until interested white men in historical times translated some of them into English and recorded them as important facets of Siouan culture. Understandably, the personal biases of narrators and certain errors in transmission from one generation to another may have exaggerated or even radically altered the earlier Kansa concepts of being and time; yet the general character of these native accounts clearly establishes the existence of a viable culture in the prehistoric period.

[1] W. J. McGee, "The Siouan Indians," *Fifteenth Annual Report of the Bureau of Ethnology to the Secretary of the Smithsonian Institution*, 159–64 (the *Bureau of Ethnology* is cited hereafter as BE). *Dh* (or Ȼ) is pronounced *th*, as in *them*; hence *Dhegiha* (or Ȼegiha) is pronounced *They-gee'-hah*.

[2] For a rudimentary example of nineteenth-century written Kansa, see Manuscript No. 4800 (Kansa), James Owen Dorsey Papers, Office of Anthropology Archives, Smithsonian Institution, Washington, D. C. Dorsey prepared his Kansa dictionary in 1883 from material he collected in Indian Territory from November, 1882, to February, 1883.

Thomas Say, who accompanied the Stephen H. Long expedition to the Central Plains in the summer of 1819, spent four days at the principal Kansa village, then located near the confluence of the Blue Earth (presently the Blue in north-central Kansas) and Kansas rivers. The inquisitive scientist was surprised, perhaps, to learn that the Kansas entertained a rather orthodox view concerning the origin of their progenitors. Say was told the "Master of Life" had simply formed man, who was placed on earth. With the passing of time, man cried out about his solitary existence, and so the "Master . . . sent him down a woman." The son and daughter born to this first union eventually married and located their lodge apart from that of their parents. From this union, Say learned, "all the nations proceeded." Significantly, and unlike certain later accounts, the "nations" included only Indians, for the Kansas claimed to have no knowledge concerning the origin of other races.[3]

Other more detailed origin accounts have been preserved by George P. Morehouse. Unlike Say, whose information was based on limited personal contacts with these people, Morehouse became rather intimately acquainted with a number of the Kansas while they were confined to the Upper Neosho Reservation during the middle years of the nineteenth century. In fact, he enjoyed such a degree of popularity with at least some tribal leaders that in 1908 he was elected "Historian of the Kansa or Kaw Tribe" by the Old Kaw Tribal Council.[4]

In his voluminous and somewhat repetitious records Morehouse emphasized that the Kansas had a variety of traditions regarding the creation of earth and man. Some believed that "hundreds and hundreds of snows" after the earth had come into existence, the human family (apparently including all races), as well as all plant and lower animal life, had simply "emerged" from the earth. Other

[3] *James' Account of S. H. Long's Expedition, 1819–1820* (Vols. XIV–XVII in Reuben Gold Thwaites [ed.], *Early Western Travels*), XIV, 12, 194–95; Waldo R. Wedel, "The Kansa Indians," *Transactions of the Kansas Academy of Science,* XLIX (1946), 4.
[4] Copy of "Appointment as Historian of the Kansa or Kaw Tribe," Kaw Indian Agency, Washunga, Oklahoma, July 4, 1908, George Pierson Morehouse Papers, Manuscript Division, Kansas State Historical Society (the Kansas State Historical Society is cited hereafter as KSHS).

Kansa informants recalled that at one time there had been only red men. Among other things, these people were especially proud of their "long tails." When the "Great Spirit" became offended at the excessive pride displayed by these men, he punished them by removing their tails and creating women from them. At the same time swarms of mosquitoes were sent down, perhaps to torment man and remind him that an overabundance of pride was undesirable.[5]

A more popular legend held that man and woman were created by the Great Spirit before the creation of "the main part of the earth." The two were placed on a very small island surrounded by "leagues and leagues of water." Quarrels ensued as children were born to this and subsequent unions, with the result that the family of man began of necessity to push its excessive population into the sea. Indian man was then tempted to seek additional means of destroying some of his increasing progeny, but woman, apparently endowed with compassion and love for her children, "prayed to the Great Spirit to save them from destruction by giving them more room." The benevolent Master listened with pity and sent down a large number of beavers, muskrats, and turtles, whose task it was to enlarge the area of the island and thus make it suitable for all life. For years these animals industriously gathered material from the bottom of the great waters, which they used to expand the outer boundaries of the island. The ultimate result was the present size and shape of the earth. Dying autumn leaves from the trees that grew naturally along the new rivers were used by the Master to create exotic birds; deer, buffalo, and other animals were created to eat the luxurious grass and provide food for Indian man. With fruit and flower attractive to the eye and pleasing to the taste, "the entire circle of the world was filled with life and beauty."[6]

That these creation myths validated the culture as it existed and that they satisfied the basic needs of a people confronted with the beginning, development, and end of earthly life as they understood it cannot be disputed. The legends (or legend fragments) are more difficult to appraise than subsequent events based on more precise

---

[5] Copy of "The Creation," Morehouse Papers.
[6] *Ibid.*

written documents. Nevertheless, they reflect a sincere attempt at cosmological inquiry and, as will be seen,[7] are of considerable importance in explaining why the Kansas were never particularly receptive to the work of Christian missionaries in the nineteenth century.

Evidence concerning the development of their language, together with the orthography of tribal designation, constitutes another approach to understanding the Kansas as they may have viewed themselves in prehistoric times. As has been noted, ethnologists have classified these people as members of the Dhegiha division of the Siouans. The principal consideration in this method of classification is the genetic relationship of languages, reflecting a common ancestry, as well as similar modes of economic activity and a general cultural affinity in prehistoric times. Indeed, the migration pattern alleged to have taken place sometime before 1763 supports the case for linguistic conformity and genetic unity among the Dhegiha Siouans.[8]

The crudely constructed and dimly outlined map based on Père Jacques Marquette's journey down the Mississippi River in 1673 still stands as the oldest extant historical document that indisputably makes reference to the people under consideration.[9] Since there is no evidence that Marquette's party experienced personal contact with this tribe, it must be assumed that the entry of the name Kansa on the map was based on information obtained from one of the Illinois tribes or some other friendly source. In either case this French record includes no supplementary information concerning the origin and meaning of the Kansa designation. It simply provides a rough location for a group of people at a given time.

It may be argued that an endemic belief concerning the origin of *Kansa* might provide one means of understanding certain crucial aspects of the tribe's prehistory and migratory pattern, especially since ethnologists now recognize that languages are meaningful and wholly adequate to the needs of the people who speak them and

[7] See Chap. 5, pp. 130–37.

[8] David I. Bushnell, Jr., "Villages of the Algonquian, Siouan and Caddoan Tribes West of the Mississippi," Bureau of American Ethnology *Bulletin 83*, 77 (the Bureau of American Ethnology is cited hereafter as BAE).

that basic concepts can be translated if they are not at variance with other aspects of the alien culture as a whole.[10] Scholars, explorers, government officials, and other interested persons have addressed themselves to the Kansa linguistic question, and elaborate arguments can be found to support endemic, nonendemic, or European nomenclature theories.

More than half a century ago William E. Connelley, a former president of the Kansas State Historical Society, stated unequivocally that *Kansa* was an old Siouan term. While admitting that "the full meaning of the word Kansa may never be known," Connelley argued that it could not have evolved from any European language, since its use and application could be traced directly to the political and social organization of the Siouan linguistic family.[11] Apparently Connelley's conclusion was based on the analyses of certain ethnologists who had determined that the Kansas, like the Omahas and Osages, recognized a separate Kansa gen within their own ranks, even though they were unable to prove that it had a precise or necessary relationship with the tribal organization.[12]

Connelley's seemingly plausible appraisal was challenged by Morehouse, whose studies in the early twentieth century remain the principal source for those who hold that the name Kansa was first used by European explorers, perhaps the Spaniards, in the early years of the seventeenth century. On the basis of what he termed an exhaustive consideration of the nomenclature question, Morehouse announced in 1907 that he had discovered more than 125 different spellings of the tribal name. Included in his list were what he called the "simplest" forms, such as *Can, Caw, Kan,* and *Kaw;* the "longer" forms, *Ka-anzou, Kancez, Kanissi, Kansies,* and *Kantha;*

[9] Sara Jones Tucker (comp.), "Indian Villages of the Illinois Country," Illinois State Museum *Scientific Papers,* II, Pt. 1 (1942), Plate V.

[10] Franz Boas, *Handbook of American Indian Languages,* BAE *Bulletin 40,* Pt. I, 6–14, 53–56. For an earlier and mostly conflicting view, especially as it relates to the Siouan language, see McGee, "The Siouan Indians," 168.

[11] William E. Connelley, *A Standard History of Kansas and Kansans,* I, 196.

[12] Alice C. Fletcher and Francis La Flesche, "The Omaha Tribe," *Twenty-seventh Annual Report of the Bureau of American Ethnology to the Smithsonian Institution,* 39–40; James Owen Dorsey, "Migrations of Siouan Tribes," *American Naturalist,* XXX (1886), 215.

the "odd" forms, *Caugh*, *Kensier*, and *Quans*; and the "most complicated" forms, *Escansaques*, *Escanzaques*, *Excanjaques*, and *Excansaquex*. Some notable aspects of Morehouse's reasoning suggested that forms with *Kah*, *Kaw*, or *Kau* in the first syllable were French in origin, while those with *Can* or *Kan* in the first syllable were the earlier and more authentic Spanish variations. Thus, concluded Morehouse, "Cansa or Kansa [were] first used by the Spanish ... then by Father Marquette and finally by French explorers and writers for 125 years after his time. This would seem to establish beyond any doubt, even from French sources, that this form of the name was by far the older."[13]

Morehouse was persuaded that *Kansa* was a form of *Escansaques*, the Spanish name given to a group of Indians presumably encountered by Juan de Oñate in his expedition to the Quivira region of south-central Kansas in 1601. However, the morphological technique used to bridge the linguistic chasm between the two names is somewhat less than convincing or, as one ethnologist has described it, "more ingenious than convincing."[14] Perhaps there is some reason to conclude, as did Morehouse, that a combination of the Spanish verb *cansar*, "to molest, to stir up, to harass," and the noun *cansado*, "a troublesome fellow, a disturber,"[15] logically evolved into *Escansaques*. But an emphasis of this sort detracts from a prior and perhaps more crucial question. Were the Indians whom Oñate encountered on the plains actually the Kansas? The editors of the Oñate manuscripts state that the Escansaques "may have been Kansa or Osage," but they then describe the Indians' homes and economy in a manner quite contrary to subsequent and more careful appraisals of these important characteristics. They also note that the word *Escanjaques* (or *Escansaques*, *Escanxaques*) was uttered by these Indians as they placed their hands on their breasts to make the traditional sign of peace, a gesture which obviously conflicts with the emphasis Morehouse placed on the alleged belli-

---

[13] George P. Morehouse, "History of the Kansa or Kaw Indians," *Transactions of the Kansas State Historical Society* (cited hereafter as *TKSHS*), X (1907–1908), 333–34.

[14] Wedel, "The Kansa Indians," 4.

[15] Morehouse, "History of the Kansa," 335.

gerence of the Kansas.[16] Additional evidence, based on careful anthropological studies of the Escansaques, particularly their economy, further qualifies the assertion that they were the Kansas noted by Marquette some seven decades later.[17]

The rejection of a Spanish—and by extension, French—theory concerning *Kansa* as a group designation suggests that a focus on endemic beliefs relative to the question might provide important clues about these people before their contact with European culture. Regrettably, the evidence is scanty and inconclusive. Connelley was probably correct when he complained that the name was so old "that its full signification was lost even to the tribes of the Siouan family when they first met white men."[18] It is known that Kansa, Osage, and Ponca are considerably older than the Kwapa (Quapaw) and Omaha tribal designations that comprise the Dhegiha Siouan group.[19] As a linguistic division these five tribes may have existed for centuries without having, or needing, any particular designation for themselves. They may have referred to themselves simply as "Men," as "People of the Parent Speech," or as individuals "from the land itself."[20]

Of considerable importance to the nomenclature question is a late-seventeenth-century French report. According to this account, several of the Illinois tribes of the Lower Ohio Valley referred to the five Dhegiha tribes as "Arkansa[s]" or "Alkansa[s]." Though suggestive in terms of Marquette's use of *Kansa*, the origin and meaning of these designations are not known.[21] Later evidence that

---

[16] George P. Hammond and Agapito Rey (eds.), *Don Juan de Oñate, Colonizer of New Mexico, 1595–1628* (Vols. V–VI in George P. Hammond [ed.], *Coronado Cuarto Centennial Publications*), V, 25, 751–52, 865.

[17] France V. Scholes and H. P. Mera, "Some Aspects of the Jumano Problem," *Contributions to American Anthropology and History*, VI (1940), 273–75; Wedel, "The Kansa Indians," 8.

[18] Connelley, *A Standard History*, I, 194.

[19] Dorsey, "Migrations of Siouan Tribes," 215.

[20] McGee, "The Siouan Indians," 167; Elliott Coues (ed.), *The Expeditions of Zebulon Montgomery Pike*, II, 559. With regard to the "primitive names given by the savages themselves," Pike used *Kansa*, as opposed to the English version *Kans*. See his "Statistical Abstract of 1808" in Donald Jackson (ed.), *The Journals of Zebulon Montgomery Pike With Letters and Related Documents*, II, 40–41.

[21] Dorsey, "Migrations of Siouan Tribes," 215.

the Kansas did recognize the tribal name customary in historical times is found in a report by Baptist missionary and government surveyor Isaac McCoy, who informed the secretary of war in 1831 that the "authentic" pronunciation was "Kan'zau." In substance his report agreed with that of Lewis Henry Morgan nearly thirty years later.[22] However, Addison W. Stubbs, for many years a Kansa interpreter, reported in 1896 that the word closest to *Kansa* in their spoken language was *Konza*, which to them meant "plum." Stubbs emphasized that Kansa was what others called them, but to them "it was simply a name with no meaning."[23]

All things considered, it seems plausible to conclude that the name Kansa probably evolved into the language of the European invader from some endemic source, Siouan or otherwise. It reflected, perhaps, a legend or event of considerable importance, one that became increasingly vague but no less significant with the passing of time. By the nineteenth century, when serious efforts were made to inquire into the traditional meaning or meanings of the name (and other Kansa words), reliable information was, as Stubbs learned, virtually unobtainable. Nevertheless, the importance of summarizing what the name may have meant at given times is readily apparent.

In 1839 it was reported that James G. Pratt, a Baptist missionary-printer assigned to work among the Kansas, had printed, with the assistance of other missionaries stationed at the Shawanoe Mission, near the mouth of the Kansas River, a 24-page "Kauzas Book" composed in the Kansa language. Reported to have contained 7,200 words, it was lost almost immediately, and efforts to recover it have been unsuccessful.[24] The Kansa vocabulary compiled in 1878 by Albert S. Gatschet and Addison W. Stubbs is of little help in defining Kansa words. It simply lists and translates into English

[22] Isaac McCoy to John Eaton, January 31, 1831, Isaac McCoy Papers, Manuscript Division, KSHS; Lewis Henry Morgan (ed.), *The Indian Journals, 1859–1862*, 204.

[23] Addison W. Stubbs to T. G. Adams, May 23, 1896, Addison Woodward Stubbs Papers, Manuscript Division, KSHS.

[24] "Missions in North America," *Baptist Missionary Magazine*, XIX (1839), 125; copy of "The Kansas Language Never Reduced to Writing," Morehouse Papers.

about 150 words, including *Kónsa* ("Kaw") and *tádshe ńika-shínga* ("Wind gens"). Of course, the latter phrase is of some importance in understanding the less than precise relationship between oral tradition and the tribal designation.[25] More significant is James Owen Dorsey's list of 604 Kansa words, compiled as part of a general Dhegiha Siouan vocabulary, which underscored the relationship between *Kansa* and *wind* (or *south wind*).[26]

According to Dorsey, who interviewed a number of Kansas in the 1870's, these people had close and meaningful relationships with the Omahas in prehistoric times. As a fairly exclusive clan or as groups of clans, they broke away from the Omahas before the Europeans arrived, for reasons long forgotten. At the time of the disruption, also in prehistoric times, the Kansas divided into at least two principal gentes, "the Keepers of the Pipe," and "the Wind People." Subsequently, there was maintained within the structure of Kansa society a Kansa gens, which was subdivided into two distinct gentes, "the Wind People, or Southwind People," and "the Small Wind People or Makes-a-Breeze-near-the-Ground." Significantly, this social order was recognized in the formal organization of the tribal camp circle, with the Kansa gens always enjoying a specific position in what Dorsey refers to as the Ictunga (or Ishtuñga) moiety. Since the rites pertaining to the winds and deities belonged to this moiety and gens—a practice common among the other Dhegiha Siouan groups who recognized a Kansa gens (the Omahas, for example)—it seems logical to conclude that *Kansa* as a designation in tribal tradition had a fairly specific association with wind; more precisely, as Rydjord has recently concluded, the association was probably with the south wind.[27]

[25] Copy of "Vocabulary of the Kansas or Kaw Indians recorded by Albert S. Gatschet, March, 1878, from A. W. Stubbs, Kaw Interpreter," Morehouse Papers.

[26] James Owen Dorsey, "A Study of Siouan Cults," *Eleventh Annual Report of the Bureau of Ethnology to the Secretary of the Smithsonian Institution*, xxi–xxii. Dorsey made about 25,000 entries for a general Kansa-English dictionary, preserved in the Dorsey Papers.

[27] James Owen Dorsey, "Siouan Sociology," *Fifteenth Annual Report of the Bureau of Ethnology to the Secretary of the Smithsonian Institution*, 226–30; James O. Dorsey, "Mourning and War Customs of the Kansas," *American Naturalist*, XIX (1885), 676; Dorsey, "A Study of Siouan Cults," 537; Dorsey,

The temptation, of course, is to conclude that this endemic engrossment with winds establishes a prehistoric Kansa residence in a region where strong winds (perhaps south winds) predominated, as, for example, in the prairie-plains of the Middle West. The determinative factor, however, is too subjective to be of definitive significance. Its importance lies mainly in the manner in which it complements the larger framework of Kansa migratory traditions and the few historical facts that can be brought to bear on the question.

The known Kansa legends suggest vague recollections of a westward movement from an undefined area east of the Mississippi River, where, according to native accounts collected in the 1880's, the Kansas, Quapaws, Omahas, Osages, and Poncas once lived together as one nation.[28] Several theories have been proposed to explain the forces which led to the westward migration: (1) long before the arrival of the Europeans, gentile vanity and an inherent sense of independence within contending groups constituted the seeds of disintegration and the rationale for seeking new homes west of the Mississippi;[29] (2) the Siouan-speaking peoples (or their ancestors) may have followed straggling buffalo herds through the cis-Mississippi habitat;[30] (3) the migration resulted from no concerted action, but rather was a consequence of accidental circumstances or conflicts between ambitious chiefs;[31] (4) a semi-sedentary people may have found the fertile river bottoms and terrace-lined valleys between the Mississippi River and the High Plains a distinct attraction for the cultivation of corn;[32] and (5) it

"Migrations of Siouan Tribes," 215; Fletcher and La Flesche, "The Omaha Tribe," 29–40, 66; William E. Connelley, "Notes on the Early Indian Occupancy of the Great Plains," *Collections of the Kansas State Historical Society* (cited hereafter as CKSHS), XIV (1915–18), 456–58. The most recent and exhaustive study of the nomenclature question states that "Kansa means the 'wind people.'" See John Rydjord, *Indian Place-Names*, 13–19.

[28] Dorsey, "Migrations of Siouan Tribes," 215.

[29] John Joseph Mathews, *The Osages: Children of the Middle Waters*, 341–42.

[30] McGee, "The Siouan Indians," 187.

[31] Fletcher and La Flesche, "The Omaha Tribe," 37–38.

[32] Waldo R. Wedel, *Prehistoric Man on the Great Plains*, 80–81.

is possible that some of the Siouan tribes indigenous to the Lower Wabash Valley were subjected to attacks by alien and more powerful tribes from the northeast.[33] A combination of these factors may have precipitated the migration, or it may have resulted from other conditions long forgotten. In any case, the westward trek of the Kansas must have taken place sometime before 1673.[34] The date can be pushed back to the mid-sixteenth century on the basis of a report by Hernando de Soto, who claimed to have met the Quapaw splinter group on the Lower Mississippi as a separate and distinct tribe in 1540.[35]

As they drove other people before them, tradition has it, there occurred a major separation among the Dhegiha Siouans at the mouth of the Ohio River. Those who journeyed down the Mississippi took the name Kwapa, meaning "the downstream people," while those who ascended the river came to be known as the Omahas, or "those going against the wind or current." Of crucial importance is the fact that both *Kwapa* and *Omaha* came into use as tribal designations after the names *Kansa, Osage,* and *Ponca.* Leaving the Quapaws, the remaining groups followed the Mississippi to its confluence with the Missouri near the present site of St. Louis, where, according to native informants, they remained "for some time." Eventually they continued their migration by ascending the Missouri Valley to a place characterized by "an extensive peninsula . . . having a high mountain as a landmark," where the four tribes "dwelt together." Later they journeyed to the mouth of the Osage River, where a final separation took place. The Omahas and Poncas crossed the Missouri to continue their wanderings in a northwesterly direction. The Osages ascended the Osage River to the southwest, while the Kansas continued up the Missouri to the area just above the mouth of the Kansas River. Since further movement up the Missouri was blocked by inimical peoples, the Kansas retreated to the Lower Kansas Valley, where, accord-

[33] George E. Hyde, *Indians of the Woodlands from Prehistoric Times to 1725,* 62.
[34] Tucker, "Indian Villages of the Illinois Country," II, Pt. I, Plate V.
[35] Dorsey, "Migrations of Siouan Tribes," 215.

Kansa migration

ing to historical evidence, they were first encountered by European traders and trappers in the early eighteenth century.[36]

There is at least a scrap of historical evidence that adds credence to some aspects of this archaic version of Kansa migration. Bacqueville de La Potherie's *History of the Savage People Who Are Allies of New France* (1718), believed to be based on the first-hand observations of Nicholas Perrot, French commandant in the Northwest during the last years of the seventeenth century, stated that "as the [Illinois tribes] were not willing to remain thus in inaction, they marched, to the number of twelve hundred warriors, against the Ozages and the Accances (who are in the lower Missisipi country), and carried away captive the people of a village there."[37] This report, dated no later than 1698 and apparently based on an earlier action against a group that may have been the Kansas, thus makes the Marquette map more credible and perhaps adds some basic historical insight into the legendary version of Kansa migration.[38]

If it can be accepted that sometime before the last third of the seventeenth century the Kansas were living east of the Mississippi River, perhaps in the Lower Wabash Valley, the question remains, How much farther east might they have been before that time? Recalling the rather widespread dispersal of the Siouan-speaking peoples, including such groups as the Catawbas of North Carolina, is it possible that the Kansas (or their ancestors) may have resided in the Upper Ohio Valley, in eastern Kentucky or Tennessee, or even east of the Appalachians, perhaps within a stone's throw of the Atlantic Coast?

These questions cannot be ruled out as completely irrelevant, for during the course of an interview at the Kansas' reservation in the 1880's, Waqube-k'i[n] told Dorsey that the tribe's sacred objects,

[36] *Ibid.*, 215–18; McGee, "The Siouan Indians," 191–93; Wedel, "The Kansa Indians," 6–10; Bushnell, "Villages of the Algonquian, Siouan and Caddoan Tribes," 77; Henri Folmer, "De Bourgmont's Expedition to the Padoucas in 1724," *Colorado Magazine*, XIV (1937), 119–28.

[37] Emma H. Blair (trans. and ed.), *The Indian Tribes of the Upper Mississippi Valley and Region of the Great Lakes as Described by Nicholas Perrot*, II, 36.

[38] Hyde, *Indians of the Woodlands*, 62.

including the medicines, the pipes, and the clam shell, "were brought from the shore of the great water at the east." Ali^{n}kawahu, one of the oldest Kansas, said: "On the other side [of the Mississippi River?] by the *tciyeta*^{n} which is at Nyu Yak, dwelt the people at the very first." While "Nyu Yak" may have referred to New York, it was Dorsey's opinion that *tciyeta*^{n} was probably intended to have been *dje tange*, or "great lake." Thus, concluded Dorsey, Ali^{n}kawahu and Waqube-k'i^n were in fact referring to Lake Michigan, not the Atlantic Ocean.[39]

One anthropological appraisal of Ponca and Omaha legends concludes that the Dhegiha Siouan tribes once lived together as a group in the "southeast."[40] Since the generally accepted route of migration was to the north and west, the location may refer to the traditional site near the confluence of the Wabash and Ohio rivers. On the other hand, a recent comparison of Southern Cult (or Oneota) shell gorgets with a native drawing of the clam shell used in Kansa religious ceremonies reveals a rather remarkable similarity between the two. Taken from the pear-shaped section of the outer whorl of the whelk shell (*Busycou perversum*) and generally in the form of a human face, the gorgets are known to be indigenous only to the South Atlantic and Gulf coasts, although they have been carried as far north as Manitoba and Saskatchewan.[41] If the Kansa shell was in fact a Southern Cult gorget, then Waqube-k'i^n's statement that it came "from the shore of the great water at the east" may take on new significance. He may well have been referring, not to one of the Great Lakes, but to the Atlantic Ocean, thus indicating the possibility of a Kansa habitation east or southeast of the traditional Wabash Valley site. In any case the question should remain open, for additional information about the pattern of Kansa mobility and migration may be available. Barring the discovery of additional historical manuscripts, the situation will probably be

[39] Manuscript No. 1429, Dorsey Papers. Citing Stephen R. Riggs, *A Dakota-English Dictionary*, one recent study suggests that *Hútañga*, a term used by the Kansas to refer to themselves, closely resembles *hu-tam-ya*, meaning "by the edge of the shore." See Rydjord, *Indian Place-Names*, 14.

[40] James H. Howard, "The Ponca Tribe," BAE *Bulletin 195*, 14.

[41] James H. Howard, "The Persistence of Southern Cult Gorgets among the Historic Kansa," *American Antiquity*, XXI (1956), 301–302.

clarified to some extent by the results of archaeological investigation, much of which has been under way for some time.

Systematic archaeological field work relating directly to the Kansas was inaugurated in 1937 by Waldo R. Wedel, of the United States National Museum, although excavations by local archaeologists (mostly amateurs) date back to the work of Isaac McCoy in 1830. McCoy, a Baptist missionary charged with surveying the official boundary of the Delaware Indian Reservation, opened, on October 4, 1830, several burial mounds located about one mile west of Fort Leavenworth. Composed of stones and earth, they yielded fragmentary bones of partially burned adults and children. A few years later another mound was opened in the same vicinity, this time by men garrisoned at Fort Leavenworth. According to Lieutenant J. Henry Carleton, director of the group, it contained a limited quantity of bone fragments.

Inconclusive at best, these initial excavations were significant primarily because they were discovered in the general area above the mouth of the Kansas River where Étienne Veniard de Bourgmont visited a major Kansa village in 1724 and where Lewis and Clark observed some village ruins at a much later date. Corroborative evidence for the existence of the "Grand Village des Canzes," which probably stood near the site of present Doniphan, Kansas, is the Guillaume Delisle map of 1718. It notes a village of "les Cansez" at the mouth of a local stream called the "Petite Riv. des Cansez." In juxtaposition to the general pattern of the Missouri River drainage system in the area, this little stream was probably the one Lewis and Clark named "Independence Creek" in the early nineteenth century. Whether a direct relationship can be established between this particular village and the rather vague reference to the Kansas on the Marquette map of 1673 remains uncertain, but that the village at Doniphan was inhabited by the Kansas in the early eighteenth century appears certain. Wedel's conclusion is firm when he states: "The tribal identity of the principal historic Indian remains at Doniphan thus seems settled beyond question."[42]

42 Waldo R. Wedel, *An Introduction to Kansas Archeology*, BAE Bulletin 174, 83–84, 98–102; Kate L. Gregg (ed.), "The Missouri Reader, Explorers

Additional excavation was performed by the early residents of Doniphan, established in 1853, and by George J. Remsburg in the early twentieth century. Remsburg reported the recovery of charcoal, pottery, and various stone objects, but unfortunately he failed to make or retain a careful description of the artifacts. He also located what he thought was another abandoned Kansa village site downstream from Doniphan near the mouth of Salt Creek just above Fort Leavenworth. Since Bourgmont apparently traveled through the area but made no mention of the village, it may have been established sometime during the second quarter of the eighteenth century. Regrettably, a collection of hand stones and hammer stones recovered from the site is nondiagnostic and thus of limited archaeological significance. Whether comprehensive work here by trained field workers will shed additional light on Kansa prehistory remains questionable. The only professional study of artifacts points to an earlier cultural affiliation.[43]

On a broader scale, careful investigation has shown that preceding the arrival of tribes such as the Kansas, successive waves of earlier peoples inhabited the Central Plains west of the Missouri River. For example, charcoal secured by Marvin F. Kivett from the second of four levels at the Logan Creek site in Burt County, Nebraska, has been radiocarbon-dated at 3674 B.C. and termed a pre-pottery, "ancient hunter" culture. A later Plains Woodland culture, which had pottery and which has been dated from 1872 B.C. to A.D. 828, was apparently related to the Hopewellian people, a corn-growing group whose Kansas City sites have yielded radiocarbon dates ranging all the way from 122 B.C. to A.D. 828. Around A.D. 1000, or soon after, these two groups probably gave way to other cultures characterized by hunting, fishing, rudimentary horticulture, pottery manufacturing, and a fairly extensive artifact inventory. Among the groups that collectively comprised these people were what archaeologists have referred to as the Upper

in the Valley, Part II," *Missouri Historical Review*, XXXIX (1944–45), 522–23; Tucker, "Indian Villages of the Illinois Country," II, Pt. I, Plate XV.

[43] Wedel, *An Introduction to Kansas Archeology*, 94, 101–102; Roscoe Wilmeth, "Present Status of the Archaeology of the Kansa Indians," Kansas Anthropological Association *Newsletter*, IV (1959), 7, 54–56.

Republican, Dismal River, Great Bend, Nebraska, and Oneota aspects. The latter two are of particular importance to an understanding of what professional investigation can tell us about certain characteristics of Kansa prehistory.[44]

National Museum excavations directed by Wedel from 1937 to 1940 did much to clarify the less scientific conclusions of earlier archaeologists. Three major sites, all in Kansas, were partially investigated: the Doniphan site (14DP2), where the "Grande Villages des Canzes" was once located; the Fanning site (14DP1), on Wolf Creek about one mile north of the Fanning townsite; and the Blue River site (14 PO24), near the Kansas River about two miles east of Manhattan. Among other things it was hoped that material evidence recovered—pottery, shells, bones, foodstuffs, worked stone, and the like—would in the aggregate constitute the basis for confirming the existence of a Kansa cultural complex during the late prehistoric period.[45]

Although somewhat disappointing as an archaeological breakthrough, the results of these excavations are of considerable interest to the Kansa question. The paucity of material found at the three sites militated against the recognition of a definable Kansa cultural complex. At Doniphan, Wedel determined the presence of at least two earlier, perhaps distinctive communities. One was correlated with certain older Nebraska Aspect sites known to have existed in western Iowa and eastern Nebraska; the other was a later, post-white Kansa community which in all probability was the one visited by the French in the early eighteenth century. The Fanning site yielded material, especially pottery, that placed it in the Oneota Aspect. This was a rather late cultural manifestation which possibly developed after A.D. 1600 but which some scholars believe may have preceded this date "by some time." Yet no satisfactory answer to the knotty question of tribal designation at Fanning was possible. Some pits contained post-white material which could have been deposited by itinerant European traders at a much later date; others did not. Consequently, no certain relationships with the historic

[44] Wedel, *Prehistoric Man on the Great Plains*, 87–120.
[45] Wedel, *An Introduction to Kansas Archeology*, 98ff., 131ff., 187ff.

village at Doniphan could be established. Wedel's guarded conclusion was that the Oneota-Fanning site was abandoned by the time Bourgmont reached the Kansa village at Doniphan in 1724; perhaps it was deserted even before 1700. Thus the failure at Doniphan to uncover more material evidence for comparative purposes and the absence of contemporary artifacts attributable to the Osages (with whom the Kansas had close contacts) suggest that any categorical tribal designation for the Fanning people is premature. Nevertheless, Wedel concluded, "with some reservations," that "the Kansa were probably responsible for the Fanning site."[46] Even the pre-1700 abandonment date must be considered of some historical significance, since it is well within the time limits of Marquette's map entry of 1673. At least it provides an additional argument for a seventeenth-century Kansa penetration of the Trans-Missouri West.[47]

Excavation at the historic Blue River site near Manhattan failed to establish a cultural complex related to the Doniphan and Fanning sites and thus was of little or no importance in shedding further light on the Kansa migration problem.[48] Whether additional work at either Doniphan or Fanning will yield more remains to be seen. An official of the Kansas State Historical Society has suggested that additional investigation of the village at Salt Creek, which for a time was contemporary with the Doniphan occupation, might yield important artifacts. However, Remsburg's earlier non-diagnostic work at this location stands alone, and more recent attempts to find the site of the French fort built there in 1744 have been unsuccessful.[49]

In 1964 a group of teachers from St. Benedict's College in Atchison, Kansas, headed by Dennis McCarthy, an art instructor, discovered four additional burial pits at the old Doniphan site. The

[46] Ibid., 127–31, 167–72; Wedel, Prehistoric Man on the Great Plains, 120.

[47] George R. Brooks (ed.), "George C. Sibley's Journal of a Trip to the Salines in 1811," Missouri Historical Society Bulletin, XXI (1965), 172.

[48] Wedel, An Introduction to Kansas Archeology, 197.

[49] Wilmeth, "Present Status of the Archaeology of the Kansas Indians," 54–56; Charles E. Hoffhaus, "Fort de Cavagnial," Kansas Historical Quarterly (cited hereafter as KHQ), XXX (1964), 425–26, 453–54.

skeletal remains of three adults and one child were uncovered in the same general area where Wedel excavated two earth lodges and several burial sites in 1937. According to Thomas A. Witty, Jr., archaeologist on the staff of the Kansas State Historical Society, these newly discovered skeletal remains were those of Kansa Indians. In addition, "five small triangular-shaped points" were found in a rodent burrow beneath some of the bones. Some of the bones were removed for an appraisal by William M. Bass, physical anthropologist at the University of Kansas, who concluded they were "definitely Kansa Indian burials [dating] from the period of the mid-1800s." Perhaps this rather late date at Doniphan may be explained by the not unusual Kansa practice of returning to earlier village sites to bury their dead.[50]

The precise date the Kansas abandoned the Missouri River villages in favor of new locations on the Kansas River to the south and west cannot be determined on the basis of evidence available at this writing, but there is reason to believe that the removal took place before the turn of the century. The Bellin map of 1743, the Delisle map of 1750, and the Du Pratz map of 1757 all placed at least some of the Kansas at or near the mouth of the Kansas River,[51] yet these notations are at best inconclusive. As late as 1758, Louis Billouart de Kerlerec, governor of Louisiana, reported the Kansas were situated farther up the Missouri River, near the old French military installation at Cavagnial.[52] By 1796 the Collot map noted the Kansas as far west as the confluence of the Blue and Kansas rivers,[53] while Jean Baptiste Trudeau in 1798 reported a more eastern village on the banks of the Kansas River.[54]

In addition to the Collot map, a variety of historical evidence

[50] Thomas A. Witty, Jr., "Newly Discovered Burials at the Doniphan Site, 14DP1," Kansas Anthropological Association *Newsletter*, IX (1964), 6–7; William M. Bass to the author, December 9, 1968; William M. Bass and Donald F. Nelson, "The Identification of an Adult Kansa Male from the Doniphan Site, 14DP2, Doniphan County, Kansas," Kansas Anthropological Association *Newsletter*, XIII (1968), 4–10.

[51] Wedel, "The Kansa Indians," 11, citing C. O. Paullin, *Atlas of the Historical Geography of the United States*, Plates 23 B–C.

[52] Abraham P. Nasatir (ed.), *Before Lewis and Clark*, I, 52.

[53] Wedel, "The Kansa Indians," 12.

[54] Louis Houck (ed.), *The Spanish Regime in Missouri*, II, 251–52.

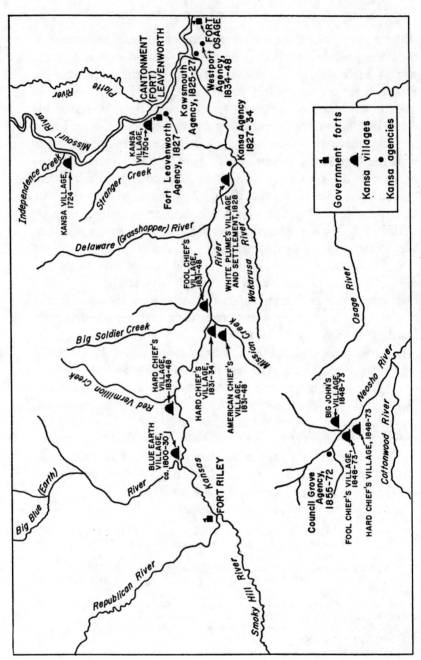

Kansa villages and agencies, 1724–1873

supports the archaeological record concerning Kansa settlement at the mouth of the Blue River by about 1800. The reports of William Clark, Zebulon M. Pike, and George C. Sibley and an account in the *Missouri Gazette* described the chief characteristics of this settlement, as well as the Kansas' confinement to the Kansas River Valley.[55] Soon after 1800 the Kansas began to stake out substantial portions of the lucrative bison plains of the Upper Arkansas Valley which they had earlier visited on an occasional basis but which until then had been largely monopolized by the Osages. Although this action forced them into a sometimes violent competition with more powerful, wide-ranging tribes of the High Plains, the need for food and the profitable character of the fur trade were attractive considerations. Obviously, the western hunting country was more accessible from the Blue River location than from the old Missouri River villages.[56]

Other factors may have encouraged migration to the Kansas River Valley. As early as 1698, when the British-sponsored tribes of the Illinois country sent powerful raiding parties against the Kansas and Osages in quest of pelts and human captives, military encounters with the better-armed Sauks (Sacs) and Iowas did much to discourage further movement up the Missouri River.[57] Subsequent confrontations with the Pawnees, complicated by the outbreak of smallpox on the Middle and Lower Missouri,[58] and the

[55] Wedel, "The Kansa Indians," 12–13; Ernest S. Osgood (ed.), *The Field Notes of Captain William Clark, 1803–1805*, 71; Coues, *The Expeditions of Zebulon Montgomery Pike*, II, map; Brooks, "George C. Sibley's Journal," 174; *Missouri Gazette*, November 16, 1809, cited in Albert Watkins (ed.), "Notes on the Early History of the Nebraska Country," *Publications of the Nebraska Historical Society*, XX (1922), 3.

[56] James B. Wilkinson to General James Wilkinson, October 28, 1806, cited in Herbert E. Bolton (ed.), "Papers of Zebulon M. Pike," *American Historical Review*, XIII (1907), 817; Noel M. Loomis and Abraham P. Nasatir, *Pedro Vial and the Roads to Santa Fe*, 376–78.

[57] Blair, *The Indian Tribes of the Upper Mississippi Valley*, II, 36, 199, 234; Nasatir, *Before Lewis and Clark*, II, 52, 185; John C. McCoy, "Survey of Kansas Indian Lands," *TKSHS*, IV (1886–88), 303; Donald Jackson (ed.), "Journey to the Mandans, 1809: The Lost Narrative of Dr. Thomas," Missouri Historical Society *Bulletin*, XX (1964), 184; *Bradbury's Travels in the Interior of North America* (Vol. V in Reuben Gold Thwaites [ed.], *Early Western Travels*), 67.

[58] See E. Wagner Stearn and Allen E. Stearn, *The Effect of Smallpox on the Destiny of the Amerindian*, especially Chap. 3.

23

commercial opportunities afforded by Franco-Spanish merchants working out of St. Louis and at stations near the mouth of the Kansas River forced the Kansas to seek new homes. In addition, British traders from the north also encouraged the southwestern migration. Thus by the beginning of the nineteenth century, when they came under the influence and finally the control of the United States, these people were beginning to look upon the Kansas Valley and the hunting grounds to the west as their permanent homes.

Here they lived until 1846, when the increasing pressure of white settlers and land jobbers forced them to negotiate a major cession treaty with the United States and accept a greatly reduced reservation in the Upper Neosho Valley. New villages were located a few miles southeast of the small white settlement at Council Grove, where government agents, missionaries, and teachers were unable to contain the social and economic pressure brought to bear on the Kansas by a combination of merchants, itinerant Santa Fe traders, squatters, land speculators, and railroad promoters. The final migration of these people as a group took place in 1873, when they were forced to leave the Neosho Valley and accept a new reservation in the northern part of Indian Territory. By this time their tribal traditions and organization had been so radically altered that they were almost wholly dependent upon whatever benevolence the federal government and private groups wished to bestow on them.

CHAPTER 2 THE KANSA
WAY OF LIFE

As a distinctive group of people in historical times, the Kansas
were forced to live in poverty and exist mainly as a survival culture.
Starting in the seventeenth century and continuing for nearly two
hundred years, they encountered a superior number of alien people
and difficult conditions that militated against any natural increase
in population. A refinement of their traditional way of life was
virtually impossible. By the time they had experienced their final
forced removal to Indian Territory in 1873, the Kansas had been
reduced to less than half their original number; meanwhile, their
culture had been so radically modified as to be almost unrecogniz-
able in terms of the past.

In one of the earliest accounts dealing specifically with the
Kansas, Sieur de Iberville (Pierre Lemoyne), a French colonial
official, reported on June 20, 1702, that the tribe numbered about
1,500 persons.[1] There was little increase during the course of the
next century, for in 1806 Lieutenant Zebulon M. Pike recorded 465
warriors, 500 women, and 600 children, or a total of 1,565.[2]

Population statistics for the next three generations fluctuated
considerably and ultimately documented a radical decline. Isaac
McCoy estimated the tribe's population to be 1,500 in 1831, 1,200

[1] Mémoire of June 20, 1702, cited in Nasatir, *Before Lewis and Clark*, I, 8.
[2] Coues, *The Expeditions of Zebulon Montgomery Pike*, II, 590; Jackson,
The Journals of Zebulon Montgomery Pike, II, 40-41.

25

in 1832, and 1,750 in 1840.[3] In spite of widespread malnutrition and chronic illness, McCoy's 1832 count is a conservative figure, perhaps because entire families fled to the buffalo plains to escape the dreaded smallpox; moreover, his figure for 1840 appears exaggerated when compared to the official report of Indian Agent Richard W. Cummins, who in 1839 counted 1,602 men, women, and children.[4] Three years later a report issued by the Society of Friends placed the total population at about 1,600,[5] which appears to have been very close to the maximum for the nineteenth century. After the Kansas were placed on the greatly reduced reservation near Council Grove, a substantial decline occurred. For example, in 1855—the year their agent described them as "a poor, degraded, superstitious, thievish, indigent"[6] type of people—the Commissioner of Indian Affairs reported their number at 1,375.[7] By 1859 it was down to 1,035[8] and in 1868 to 825.[9] Finally, while this "improvident class of people" made plans for permanent removal to Indian Territory, an official Indian Bureau count placed their number at "about 600."[10] Clearly, the long-range trend appeared to be one of eventual obliteration.

For the Kansas, survival became increasingly uncertain because of several factors. An almost uninterrupted migration from one region to another brought them face to face with more powerful tribes who often objected to even a temporary Kansa encroach-

[3] Isaac McCoy to John H. Eaton, April 20, 1831, Letters Received by the Office of Indian Affairs, Fort Leavenworth Agency (M 234, R 300), National Archives (cited hereafter as LR, OIA, Fort Leavenworth Agency); Isaac McCoy, *History of Baptist Indian Missions*, 565.

[4] Richard W. Cummins to Joshua Pilcher, October, n.d., 1839, Letters Received by the Office of Indian Affairs, St. Louis Superintendency (M 234, R 752), National Archives (cited hereafter as LR, OIA, St. Louis Superintendency).

[5] John D. Lang and Samuel Taylor, Jr., *Report of a Visit to Some Tribes of Indians, Located West of the Mississippi River*, 21.

[6] John Montgomery to A. Cumming, cited in *Report of the Commissioner of Indian Affairs* (1855), 434.

[7] Wedel, "The Kansa Indians," 16.

[8] *Kansas Press* (Council Grove), October 10, 1859.

[9] E. S. Stover to Thomas Murphy, January 25, 1868, Letters Received by the Office of Indian Affairs, Kansas Agency (M 234, R 367), National Archives (cited hereafter as LR, OIA, Kansas Agency).

[10] *Report of the Commissioner of Indian Affairs* (1869), 476.

ment upon what they considered their traditional hunting grounds. The result was recurrent warfare with such groups as the Sacs and Foxes, Omahas, Osages, Iowas, Otoes, Pawnees, and Cheyennes in which many Kansas were killed at an early age.[11] Raids to seize captives and horses were common, in some cases necessary to prove male maturity and achieve economic status in the Kansa social order. Ironically, the festive celebration of military victory and recently achieved manhood was often accompanied by a new widow's mourning wail. Moreover, pressure from other sources— first from Spanish, French, and English traders and then from American merchants and land speculators—severely undermined the Kansas' traditional reliance on a subsistence economy. And a seemingly calculated destruction of the natural buffalo supply, together with the federal government's failure to provide adequate economic assistance, led to increasing malnutrition and, in some cases, death by starvation.[12] Finally, the introduction of cholera, smallpox, and other communicable diseases common to white society, especially in the nineteenth century, accounted for a mortality rate of alarming proportions.[13] Under these circumstances, then, it is not surprising that most Kansas developed cynical, almost fatalistic attitudes toward public and private promises to aid them along the so-called orderly road of progress.

As the Kansas fell under the domination of the white man's culture, their physical characteristics and social habits engaged the attention of several western travelers. F. M. Perrin Du Lac, a French aristocrat who visited one of the Kansas villages in 1802, de-

[11] William E. Dunn, "Spanish Reaction Against the French Advance Toward New Mexico, 1717–1727," *Mississippi Valley Historical Review*, II (1915), 351; Pierre Margry, *Explorations of the Tributaries of the Mississippi and Discovery of the Rocky Mountains, 1697–1754*, 25; Blair, *The Indian Tribes of the Upper Mississippi Valley*, 36; Nasatir, *Before Lewis and Clark*, I, 16, 185; *ibid.*, II, 517; Richard W. Cummins to Joshua Pilcher, October, n.d., 1839, LR, OIA, St. Louis Superintendency; John Dougherty Papers, Manuscript Division, KSHS; *Emporia News*, November 20, 1868.

[12] William Clark to T. L. McKenney, April 1, 1828, LR, OIA, St. Louis Superintendency.

[13] Archives Nationales (Paris), Colonies, C134, XL, folios 135–40, 142–44, cited in Nasatir, *Before Lewis and Clark*, I, 52; Isaac McCoy to War Department, January 31, 1831, and October 15, 1832, Isaac McCoy Papers.

scribed the males as "tall, handsome, vigorous and brave."[14] A few years later, Thomas Say commented favorably on their coppery color, straight black hair, high cheek bones, and large "symmetrically well formed bodies." Say was particularly impressed by the hair plucking so scrupulously practiced by most of the chiefs and warriors. Using a wire apparatus often carried as an article of dress, most Kansa men carefully plucked their arms, chins, eyebrows, and most of the scalp, leaving only a narrow strip of hair on the top and back portions of the head, apparently for the scalping honor of an enemy warrior. The strip was sometimes colored with vermilion or decorated with the tail feather of a war eagle; an important chief might attach a deer tail at the base.

The clothing of an average male included a blue or red breechcloth secured with a girdle, plus leggings and moccasins of dressed deer skins. A blanket, discarded in hot weather, rounded out his simple but utilitarian wardrobe. Of striking interest were the beads, tin trinkets, or porcelain sticks suspended from a slash in the outer cartilage of the ear, and the colorful tattoos on various parts of the body.[15] Warriors were variously armed with lances, naked swords suspended from their waists, and the traditional bow and arrows; some wore a collar of bear claws or metal buttons about their necks or fastened to their leggings.[16] Even as late as 1855 the carriage of a typical Kansa warrior was described as "erect, dignified and proud; sometimes even scornful."[17]

Reflecting, perhaps, a preconceived and largely romantic notion about the alleged beauty of Indian women, western travelers generally described the typical Kansa female in somewhat less than complimentary terms. Say viewed them as "small and homely, with

14 F. M. Perrin Du Lac, *Travels through the Two Louisianas, and Among the Savage Nations of the Missouri*, 50–51.

15 *James' Account of S. H. Long's Expedition*, XIV, 195–98; Friedrich Paul Wilhelm, Duke of Württemberg, "First Journey to North America in the Years 1822 to 1824," *South Dakota Historical Collections*, XIX (1938), 316. See the portrait of Mon-chonsia in Thomas L. McKenney and James Hall, *The Indian Tribes of North America*, III, 48.

16 Hiram M. Chittenden and Alfred T. Richardson (eds.), *Life, Letters and Travels of Father Pierre-Jean De Smet, S. J., 1801–1873*, I, 280–81.

17 Rev. C. B. Boynton and T. B. Mason, *A Journey through Kansas; with Sketches of Nebraska*, 123.

broad faces."[18] Edwin Bryant described them as deficient in intelligence and "miserable-looking objects in their features, figures and clothing,"[19] while John T. Irving, Jr., nephew of Washington Irving, complained: "We had heard of Indian beauties, but she [a Kansa woman] was not one of them . . . ; she engrossed in her own person a concentration of ugliness, which would have more than satisfied a dozen ordinary females."[20] On the other hand, Victor Tixier, who traveled across the plains in 1839–40, concluded that the Kansa girls he met were "much prettier" than their Osage counterparts.[21]

The fact that Kansa women generally were undernourished, shabbily dressed, and obligated to perform most of the manual labor about the village probably contributed to their crude and somewhat unkempt personal appearance.[22] A Kansa woman wore moccasins, leggings, a coarse cloth secured to her waist with a crude belt, a loosely attached shoulder garment that was often laid aside to expose her from the waist up, and long, braided hair tinged with vermilion. Thus her clothing and general appearance were hardly designed to appeal to the largely Victorian tastes of eastern observers.[23] Surely the sight of naked children and young adolescents in company with their mothers added a further dimension to the negative and even disgusting appraisals made of the average Kansa female.[24]

Among the distinguishing characteristics of Kansa society were the patriarchal organization and strong sense of fraternity at the family level. A few examples of clan development through the female line are extant,[25] but the prevailing custom required that no

[18] *James' Account of S. H. Long's Expedition*, XIV, 195.

[19] Edwin Bryant, *What I Saw in California*, 39.

[20] John T. Irving, Jr., *Indian Sketches Taken During an Expedition to the Pawnee Tribes*, 57.

[21] John Francis McDermott (ed.), *Tixier's Travels on the Osage Prairies*, 201, 203.

[22] Bryant, *What I Saw in California*, 51; Boynton and Mason, *A Journey through Kansas*, 122; Morehouse, "History of the Kansa," 362.

[23] *James' Account of S. H. Long's Expedition*, XIV, 197.

[24] Wilhelm, "First Journey to North America," 316.

[25] McGee, "The Siouan Indians," 187.

male could take a wife from his side of the gens; nor could he marry a kinswoman, no matter how remote the relationship might be.[26] It was also traditional that marriages be consummated between opposite clans in accordance with the arrangement of the tribal camp circle, as, for example, between the Raccoon People and the Deer People. Although the principal chiefs had little or no arbitrary power to enforce such customs, the practice of inheritance through the male line and a powerful sense of family identity—which one observer described as stronger than that of contemporary white society—regulated the matter to such a firm degree that outside authority was not generally required.[27]

A rather complex hierarchy of social organization prevailed above the family level. At the top were two moieties, or half-tribes, which, in terms of their initial relationship to the parent Dhegiha Siouan group, evolved from the Hañga-Cenu (Tents of the Buffalo and Cultivation of the Soil) phratry of the Omaha-Sioux camp circle. The emergent Kansa moieties, again reflecting the pattern of the camp circle, were the Uata and Ictunga, probably descending from common female ancestors. In turn, these half-tribes (Keepers of the Pipe and Wind People) were divided into at least seven or eight gentes, which were further divided into the various family units. As the result of extended interplay between clan and gentile organization, kin names were thus partly natural and partly artificial; they served to commemorate and perpetuate both family relationships and those involving the constituent elements of the total tribe.[28]

Indicative of the importance attached to the gens within the larger framework of Kansa society were the ceremonial responsibilities and exclusive rites deemed a matter of sacred privilege or taboo. Included in the fifteen or sixteen Kansa gentes were the Earth People, the Thunder People, the Buffalo People, the Ghost

26 Dorsey, "Siouan Sociology," 232.
27 Morgan, *The Indian Journals*, 35; *James' Account of S. H. Long's Expedition*, XIV, 193.
28 McGee, "The Siouan Indians," 177–78; Dorsey, "Siouan Sociology," 226–32; Alanson Skinner, "Societies of the Iowa, Kansa and Ponca Indians," *Anthropological Papers of the American Museum of Natural History*, XI (1915), 761.

People, and so on. According to the reminiscences of the elderly Wam'o^{n}ike, collected in the early twentieth century, the Earth People, after consulting with the Buffalo and Deer People, were allowed to announce the moving of the camp; they also enjoyed the honor of being the first to pitch their tents at a new campsite. However, they were never allowed to eat roasted maize until all the other gentes had taken their fill. The Thunder People were permitted to burn the prairie to cause rain and to throw cedar leaves on the fire, which was traditionally accepted as a means of moderating the violence of thunderstorms. The Buffalo People could not eat buffalo meat during a hunt until all others had finished, while the Ghost People had the responsibility of accepting a horse from the relatives of a deceased person; it was used to pay for a feast at which the Ghost People ate first. Each gens had its own particular type of sacred bundle—perhaps a clam shell or pipestone—and its exclusive origin myth. Individual titles, as opposed to the male and female gentile names, were given in order of birth on a rotation basis and apparently had some meaningful reference to the eponymous object (or objects) of the gens. Additional names, based on outstanding accomplishment on the field of battle or some other act of bravery, could be added, although they were not mandatory.[29]

It is not surprising that marriage was a fairly elaborate institution in a society where the family played such an important role. Largely as a result of parental negotiations and under the possible threat of social ostracism—or even heavier penalty—gentile exogamy prevailed.[30] According to Say's observations in 1819, the father of a prospective groom gave a feast for a few old men to acquaint them with the marriage plan; they then visited the prospective bride, who feigned unwillingness to accept the proposal. After repeated visits and an exchange of presents between both families, the parents of the young woman dressed her in her finest and led her through the village on a horse, escorted by an official crier who announced the upcoming marriage. The groom's parents then stripped the bride,

[29] Skinner, "Societies of the Iowa, Kansa and Ponca Indians," 762–69; Dorsey, "Siouan Sociology," 230–32.
[30] McGee, "The Siouan Indians," 178.

31

dressed her in the finest clothes available, gave her horses and other gifts, and sent her back to her parents. The ceremony was concluded with a feast for all at the bride's lodge, at which time it was customary for the father of the bride to direct a ranting speech at his son-in-law, complaining especially about his assuming command of his lodge and ownership of the valuable peltry belonging to himself and his daughter. "In every respect," reported Say, both parents became "subservient" to the young man.[31]

Later accounts emphasized that the marriage ceremony was primarily a business affair, an arrangement in which the prospective bride and groom had virtually no voice.[32] A young girl, perhaps no older than twelve or fourteen, would be ornately dressed and then paraded through the village by her mother or guardian. According to Thomas Huffaker, a Kansa trader and missionary at Council Grove in the 1850's and 1860's, this meant "that her parents [were] ready to barter her for ponies or other property to any man not objectionable to them."[33] If she were not of "mature age," she simply became a member of the groom's family until she was old enough to assume the duties of her own lodge.[34]

A modified type of polygamy, closely related to the marriage rite, was acceptable in Kansa society. Not only did the newly married daughter enjoy a considerable degree of social and economic authority over her immediate family, but her younger sisters, at the apparent discretion of the husband, could become his wives when they reached the proper age. In some instances the practice of polygamy extended beyond the scope of the two immediate families, but the inevitable absence of harmonious relations probably kept this type of arrangement at a minimum.

An accepted practice among other Dhegiha Siouan peoples, sodomy was permissible among the Kansas and appeared not to arouse disgust; however, its incidence in the tribe remains unknown. On the other hand, chastity among unmarried females was guarded

[31] *James' Account of S. H. Long's Expedition*, XIV, 191–93.
[32] Morgan, *The Indian Journals*, 35.
[33] Rev. Joab Spencer, "The Kaw or Kansas Indians: Their Customs, Manners and Folk-lore," *TKSHS*, X (1907–1908), 374.
[34] *Ibid.*

by the mother with great care. Since she knew too well that a violation of this taboo could render her daughter unacceptable to a chief, warrior, or outstanding hunter, its occurrence was understandably rare. If caught in an act of adultery, the woman might be whipped or even killed by her spouse, whose parents had no accepted means of obtaining redress. A male adulterer might be killed by the irate husband without fear of penalty.

Divorce was a relatively uncomplicated affair. The couple often reached a mutual agreement with no outside counsel or interference. If this was impossible, the husband returned to his parents, while the wife's parents sent a female envoy to attempt a reconciliation. When such action succeeded in resolving the differences, the husband's parents were required to send presents to the wife's family; if it failed, however, nothing more was done and the divorce became final. Both husband and wife were free to marry again.[35]

There were occasional intertribal marriages involving the Kansas before 1800, but apparently this was not a very common practice until after the peace settlement arranged by Pike in 1806.[36] Sibley observed in 1811: "Within the last three or four years they [the Kansas] have formed such extensive connections with the Osages by intermarriages that it is scarcely probable that any serious difference will ever occur again between them."[37] Eight years later Say reported the Kansas had so "freely intermarried" with the Osages that "their features more and more approach those of the Osages."[38]

Perhaps of greater historical significance were marriages involving French fur traders, particularly with the daughters of

[35] *Ibid.*; Morgan, *The Indian Journals*, 35, 82; *James' Account of S. H. Long's Expedition*, XIV, 191–93, 198; McGee, "The Siouan Indians," 178; Dorsey, "Siouan Sociology," 232; Skinner, "Societies of the Iowa, Kansa and Ponca Indians," 770–72; Franklin G. Adams, "Reminiscences of Frederick Chouteau," *TKSHS*, VIII (1903–1904), 430; Dorsey, "A Study of Siouan Cults," 379; P. L. Gray, *Gray's Doniphan County History*, 9.

[36] Coues, *The Expeditions of Zebulon Montgomery Pike*, II, 584.

[37] "Extracts from the Diary of Major Sibley," *Chronicles of Oklahoma*, V (1927), 199.

[38] *James' Account of S. H. Long's Expedition*, XIV, 195.

prominent chiefs or warriors. That certain tribal leaders openly solicited physical relationships (and in some cases the formality of the marriage rite) is apparent from the experience of Perrin Du Lac in 1802. "They feasted me by turns," he wrote, "and, according to their customs, offered me their daughters. I accepted those of the great chief, whom I was afraid of displeasing by a refusal."[39] He also noted that "to accept" the daughters of a chief was a pre-requisite to negotiations for Kansa furs.[40]

Traders thus tended to rationalize their relationships with Kansa women on economic grounds, but the practice did not go unchallenged by other white men, especially those with a vested interest in the ultimate destiny of the tribe. Father Joseph Anthony Lutz, a Catholic priest who failed in his attempt to establish a mission among the Kansas, was highly critical of French Catholics who were leading what he viewed as a sinful life among the Kansas. "They are 'slothful bellies,'" he complained, "[and] not much different from the Cretans, addicted to drink and much talking, ignorant to pass over in silence the rest of their vices. . . . Some of them live with Indian concubines, refusing the grace offered to them by my ministry. Only two could I prevail upon to dismiss their concubines and contract in legitimate marriages."[41] An example of the latter arrangement and its long-range implications was the experience of Louis Gonville, French interpreter and trader, who married a daughter of White Plume, the principal Kansa chief in the early nineteenth century. Three daughters born to this union —Josette, Julia, and Victoire—subsequently married the sons of Louis Pappan, a prominent St. Louis fur jobber with interests among the Kansas and Osages. In 1825 the Gonville sisters were among twenty-three Kansa half-bloods who received certain Lower Kansas Valley land grants that became objects of widespread land speculation and chronic dissension within the tribe. Animosity

[39] Perrin Du Lac, *Travels through the Two Louisianas*, 51; Perrin Du Lac, *Voyages dans les Deux Amériques*, Chap. X, cited in Nasatir, *Before Lewis and Clark*, II, 708.
[40] Perrin Du Lac, *Voyages dans les Deux Amériques*, Chap. X, cited in Nasatir, *Before Lewis and Clark*, II, 708.
[41] Rev. John Rothensteiner, "Early Missionary Efforts Among the Indians in the Diocese of St. Louis," *St. Louis Catholic Historical Review*, II (1920), 79.

between rival warriors and incipient chiefs increased to such a degree by 1827 that White Plume, in order to maintain his leadership, found it necessary to whip them into submission and seek outside support from government officials in St. Louis.[42]

Childbirth was a wholly natural and rather uneventful affair for the typical Kansa family, especially the mother. An unidentified "gentleman" traveling with a detachment of the Yellowstone Expedition in 1819 reported (with some exaggeration):

> The little inconvenience suffered by [Kansa] women in childbirth is really remarkable. No diminution of their usual laborious occupation takes place; on the contrary the only assistant or remedy they make use of, is exercise; which they always use freely when in this situation. A woman following the roving excursions of her tribe, carrying a bundle on her head or back, will step aside, bring forth her infant, wrap it in a piece of buffalo skin, resume her load, placing the infant on the top of it, and continue her route, without occasioning the least halt or delay to the party. At the first water she bathes herself and her child, or during the winter if no water is near, she washes it in the snow, or breaks the ice of the stream; at the evening's camp she assists as usual in putting up the lodge &c.[43]

Like their mothers and older sisters, Kansa girls were trained to work hard at an early age. Even seasoned French military officers, accustomed to the rigors of frontier travel, were astonished at the hundred-pound loads carried up to three leagues at a time by ten- to twelve-year-old girls.[44] With boys it was a different matter. Girls were expected to accept their role as domestic servants, but boys were encouraged to be willfully obstinate. Apparently this quality was highly pleasing to the parents, for to them it was

[42] McCoy, *History of Baptist Indian Missions*, 393; William W. Cone, *Historical Sketch of Shawnee County, Kansas*, 6–7; George W. Clark to A. Cumming, November 7, 1854, Letters Received by the Office of Indian Affairs, Potawatomie Agency (M 234, R 679), National Archives (cited hereafter as LR, OIA, Potawatomie Agency); B. O'Fallon to George C. Sibley, August 25, 1819, George C. Sibley Papers, Manuscript Division, Missouri Historical Society, St. Louis (the Missouri Historical Society is cited hereafter as MHS); Transcript of White Plume's speech to William Clark, St. Louis, May 17, 1827, LR, OIA, St. Louis Superintendency.

[43] "Notes on the Missouri River, and Some of the Native Tribes in its Neighborhood," *Analectic Magazine*, I (1820), 308.

[44] Margry, *Explorations of the Tributaries of the Mississippi*, 37.

indicative of their son's maturing into a brave hunter and warrior.[45] In either case, however, the fundamental relationship between parent and child was strong and affectionate, even after the off-spring had left to establish his or her own lodge. Severe forms of discipline were frowned upon, especially for young boys, since this might hamper the development of a headstrong character.[46]

While the adolescent period for the Kansa female meant hard labor in and about the village, the young male was expected to attend to the achievement of manhood through a technique known as the vision quest. At the age of about twelve or thirteen, the father would instruct his son to seek a lonely spot where he would remain without food or water for at least four days. During this time he was to invoke the spirits by introspection, wailing, and in some cases self-infliction of bodily torture. Any dreams experienced were believed to depict coming exploits and endow the young man with war powers. Animals and supernatural phenomena that appeared were expected to recur in subsequent dreams and, as a means of personal identification and a continuous reminder, were painted on war shields and tipi covers.[47]

Evidence dating back to the beginning of the nineteenth century suggests that the village domicile of the Kansas was functional and mainly eclectic in style. There is some reason to assume that at an early date, when they may have resided in the heavily timbered valleys of the Lower Ohio and Missouri rivers, their lodges were patterned after the Eastern Woodland style and constructed mainly of a pole frame covered with a thick, matlike fabric of leaves, bark, and branches. As the Kansas migrated westward into an area deficient in timber, they tended to substitute earth or sod for at least the lower walls of their conical huts. Buffalo and deer skins for constructing the utilitarian tipis used during periodic hunting excursions to the High Plains also appear to have been used in erecting the more permanent village lodges. Some evidence suggests that the

---

[45] *James' Account of S. H. Long's Expedition*, XIV, 193; "Notes on the Missouri River," 309–10.

[46] "Notes on the Missouri River," 311.

[47] Skinner, "Societies of the Iowa, Kansa and Ponca Indians," 767; Wedel, "The Kansa Indians," 32.

repeated relocation of core villages and the indiscriminate timber-cutting practices of white squatters ultimately forced the Kansas to rely almost exclusively on sod as their primary building material.[48]

The most detailed description of what probably was a fairly standard nineteenth-century lodge was based on an observation at the Blue Earth River site. The village was, in the words of one white visitor, "a confusing assemblage of lodges" placed close together, with diameters ranging from thirty to sixty feet. Timber piles were driven into the ground in the form of a circle and left extending four or five feet above the ground. At these several points, pole rafters were attached at an elevation of six or seven degrees and joined together at the apex of the circle, leaving a small aperture to allow smoke to escape from interior fireplaces.[49] Another observer noted that a number of the 128 lodges at the same location were more rectangular in form, generally sixty feet long and twenty-five feet wide; these "commodious and comfortable" dwellings were constructed of "stout saplings and poles, arranged in [the] form of a common garden arbour and covered with skins, bark and mats." Along the interior walls were wood platforms, raised about two feet from the ground, on which were placed the skins, food, weapons, and other personal property belonging to the three to five families living under one roof. Adjacent to the platforms were the family fireplaces, which were simply holes in the earth situated to allow smoke an easy passage out of the common opening in the roof.[50]

The obvious lack of family privacy apparently did not bother the Indians, but it left an indelible impression on some white visitors. The Reverend Isaac McCoy complained in 1828 that "half the village" appeared to crowd into the lodge assigned to him; children cried without interruption, adults screamed wildly, and the air was so saturated with smoke from the fireplaces and tobacco pipes that

---

[48] Bushnell, "Villages of the Algonquian, Siouan and Caddoan Tribes," 77; R. W. Cummins to J. Pilcher, October, n.d., 1839, LR, OIA, St. Louis Superintendency; Hiram W. Farnsworth to William Dole, January 27, 1861 (1862?), LR, OIA, Kansas Agency.

[49] "Notes on the Missouri River," 305–306.

[50] Brooks, "George C. Sibley's Journal," 174–75.

he was forced to punch a hole in the wall in order to breathe. George Sibley predicted that because of its fragile construction the average Kansa lodge was "incapable of any long duration." In general, however, the village presented a rather "neat and cleanly appearance," and, Sibley concluded, "[the Kansas] are by no means insensible to the virtue and importance of cleanliness."[51]

The eating habits of the Kansas were dictated by the subsistence character of their economy, the ever increasing competition with other tribes for the natural supply of buffalo, and changes wrought by the practices of white traders and farmers. Beans, pumpkins, prairie potatoes, melon, and especially corn were the principal crops cultivated in a rudimentary manner before the federal government's largely abortive attempt to instruct the Kansas in the more scientific techniques of horticulture. Corn was either roasted on the cob or cooked in a soup that included strips of buffalo meat; occasionally it was dried and wrapped in skins, to be stored in underground caches for future use. The curing process was usually performed in early fall just before the semiannual trip to the western buffalo country. However, since the Kansas eagerly shared this commodity with virtually any friendly tribe or traveler, the curing and accumulation of a corn surplus was not particularly motivated by the anticipation of lean months in the future. Repeated efforts by government agents to encourage their commitment to a horticultural economy were largely ineffective, mainly because of forced acceptance of the fur trader's mercantile economy. In addition, the fraudulent practices of squatters, land jobbers, and some Indian Bureau officials, coupled with reliance on buffalo hunting as the cornerstone of economic survival, also acted as powerful obstacles to the acceptance of commercial agriculture.[52]

[51] McCoy, *History of Baptist Indian Missions*, 346; Brooks, "George C. Sibley's Journal," 175.

[52] Brooks, "George C. Sibley's Journal," 176; "Notes on the Missouri River," 305; Wedel, "The Kansa Indians," 18; Bryant, *What I Saw in California*, 54; *Farnham's Travels in the Great Western Prairies, etc., May 21–October 16, 1839* (Vol. XXVIII in Reuben Gold Thwaites [ed.], *Early Western Travels*), 140; Morehouse, "History of the Kansa," 362–63; William Clark's Instructions to the Kansa Agriculturist, n.m., n.d., 1827, R. W. Cummins to Joshua Pilcher, October n.d., 1839, LR, OIA, St. Louis Superintendency; Hiram Farnsworth to William Dole, July 22, 1861, LR, OIA, Kansas Agency.

Fish, fowl, venison, and dog meat were important elements in the Kansa diet, but buffalo meat easily rated the dominant position. With the known availability of the horse in the Lower Missouri Valley by the early eighteenth century,[53] buffalo became so important that by about 1800 it was customary for the whole tribe to make two trips to the buffalo country each year, especially to the area north of the Arkansas River between Pawnee Fork and the Little Arkansas. One trip was made in early spring and the other in early fall, not long after federal agents had issued the annuity payment as authorized by the several treaties negotiated after 1825. The hunts yielded valuable robes used for clothing, shelter, and lucrative trade with St. Louis and Kawsmouth merchants, and the meat obtained served as an important staple in the Kansa diet. While the men killed the animals and discussed their more daring exploits, the women dressed the carcasses and preserved the meat for transportation back to the main villages.

Preservation techniques involved cutting the meat into long strips, plaiting it, and drying it, either on crude scaffolds or simply by wrapping it around short poles driven into the ground. Later it was cured with salt, most of which was obtained from the Grand Saline south of the Arkansas River. Even the fat was used, being preserved in casings fashioned out of the buffalo's intestines.

All things considered, the hunt was a happy and meaningful experience for all concerned. The excitement of the chase, the realization that a bountiful nature had assured a measure of economic security for the months ahead, and the satisfying character of these expeditions in general acted as powerful deterrents to the later acceptance of a sedentary existence. Such was the situation even after the buffalo supply was radically diminished and more powerful nomadic tribes contested the tribe's practice of hunting in the Smoky Hill and Arkansas valleys.[54]

[53] Frank Gilbert Roe, *The Indian and the Horse*, 72–92; Francis Haines, "The Northward Spread of Horses Among the Plains Indians," *American Anthropologist*, XL (1938), 431–33; Wedel, "The Kansa Indians," 19.

[54] *Farnham's Travels*, 85–86, 90; Morgan, *The Indian Journals*, 82; "Extracts from the Diary of Major Sibley," 210; *James' Account of S. H. Long's Expedition*, XIV, 195; R. M. Cummins to Elbert Herring, January 15, 1835, LR, OIA, Fort Leavenworth Agency.

39

At the conclusion of Kansa hunting expeditions, the consumption of food was excessive, at least by white standards. Clearly, this was the experience of one white party that visited the Blue Earth village in 1819:

> We were invited to a feast by one of the head men; we accompanied him to his lodge and were invited to seat ourselves on a mat; two wooden bowls, filled with Buffaloe meat, soup and corn were placed before us, with spoons made of the Buffaloe horn; we found the dish very palatable, and although we had just risen from eating, we ate heartily again. As soon as we had finished, we aroused and left the lodge; we were immediately, however, invited to another feast, and conducted to another lodge; we seated ourselves again on the mat; and corn, prepared in a manner new to us, was again set before us; we thought it good, and took our leave in the same unceremonious manner as before; we were invited again to a feast, that consisted of water melons; during the course of the day, we were invited to partake of nine or ten feasts.[55]

In the two decades after 1829, the forced removal of hundreds of eastern Indians to an area comprising roughly the eastern third of present-day Kansas, together with the repeated encroachments of the white man, made it ever more difficult for the Kansas to maintain their traditional level of economic abundance. Circumstances largely beyond their control dictated that begging and a degrading reliance on the inadequate assistance provided by the federal government would characterize their economy by the 1830's. In 1831, for example, Isaac McCoy was so shocked by their "remarkable improvidence" that he demanded an immediate government payment of $500;[56] three years later, John Townsend was impressed with their propensity for "asking unhesitatingly, and without fear of refusal, for any article that happen[ed] to take their fancy."[57] In 1835 Agent Richard W. Cummins reported starvation conditions among the Kansas, with less than twenty bushels of corn remaining for the whole tribe;[58] his report was the rule, not the

---

[55] "Notes on the Missouri River," 305.
[56] Isaac McCoy to John Eaton, January 31, 1831, Isaac McCoy Papers.
[57] *Townsend's Narrative of a Journey Across the Rocky Mountains, to the Columbia River, and a Visit to the Sandwich Islands, Chile, etc.* (Vol. XXI in Reuben Gold Thwaites [ed.], *Early Western Travels*), 145–46.

exception. Even as late as March, 1872, Agent Mahlon Stubbs advised the Indian Bureau that the Kansas were "absolutely destitute [and] living on [the] little corn and dead animals they [could] find lying around."[59]

As chronic malnutrition and starvation became a normal part of their day-to-day existence, the Kansas grew increasingly more susceptible to the ravages of cholera and smallpox. The spread of the latter disease among several Sioux bands at Quebec and other frontier posts during the course of the French and Indian War probably explains why Louis Billouart de Kerlerec reported in 1758 that "smallpox and wars with the Pawnees" had substantially reduced the Kansas, then frequenting the vicinity of Fort Cavagnolle on the Lower Missouri.[60] There is no evidence of a large-scale epidemic among the Kansas for the next seven decades, but in 1827 and 1828 the fatal disease struck with tragic force. Superintendent William Clark reported on October 20, 1827, that fully two-thirds of the tribe were sick "and a number [had] died before relief could be afforded."[61] Six months later he again reported a fatal "malignant disease," which in all probability was smallpox, then raging among the Osages and breaking out among the Pawnees shortly thereafter.[62] Father Joseph Anthony Lutz, the Catholic missionary who visited the Kansa villages in the fall of 1828, estimated that 180 deaths, including the two sons and principal wife of Chief White Plume, had occurred since September of the previous year.[63]

Another smallpox epidemic broke out in 1831, this time accompanied by chronic cholera, which lasted until at least 1833. It may have caused the death of no fewer than 300 people, since McCoy's statistics showed a population decline from 1,500 to 1,200

[58] Richard W. Cummins to William Clark, March 24, 1835, LR, OIA, Fort Leavenworth Agency.

[59] Mahlon Stubbs to Enoch Hoag, March 18, 1872, LR, OIA, Kansas Agency.

[60] Archives Nationales (Paris), Colonies, C13A, XL, folios 135–50, 142–44, cited in Nasatir, Before Lewis and Clark, I, 52.

[61] Report of William Clark, October 20, 1827, LR, OIA, St. Louis Superintendency.

[62] William Clark to Col. T. L. McKenney, April 1, 1828, LR, OIA, St. Louis Superintendency; Stearn and Stearn, The Effect of Smallpox, 78–79.

[63] Rothensteiner, "Early Missionary Efforts Among the Indians," 79.

between January 31, 1831, and October 15, 1832. Widespread panic was the order of the day, so much so that by September, 1833, Agent Marston G. Clark informed Superintendent William Clark in St. Louis that the majority of the tribe had fled to the plains to escape the dreaded epidemic; moreover, of the few who remained near the agency headquarters, only two were not suffering from a high fever.[64] Not until the spring of 1838 were most of the Kansas vaccinated, but because of ineffective or contaminated vaccine or failure to vaccinate those listed on the official report, the effort was largely ineffective. Smallpox again returned with great force in the middle 1850's, and before it had run its course, nearly 400 more Kansas lost their lives.[65]

The tragic impact of these epidemics contributed to the undermining of family cohesion and individual commitment to the traditions of Kansa society. In turn, these changes were aggravated by the widespread (and illicit) distribution of whiskey among their ranks. As early as 1743, French officials forbade all traders authorized to operate among the Missouri River tribes to use "wines, brandy, or other intoxicating liquors" as exchange for pelts obtained from the Indians.[66] A Louisiana territorial law of 1806 prohibited the "giving or selling" of ardent spirits without the permission of the Indian superintendent,[67] and a federal statute of July 9, 1832, held that "under no pretense" were intoxicating liquors to be introduced into Indian country.[68] The underlying logic was that a strong federal law would halt or perhaps severely limit the extensive whiskey traffic which had been authorized earlier, theoretically for the benefit of fur company employees

[64] Isaac McCoy to War Department, January 31, 1831, and October 15, 1832, Isaac McCoy Papers; Marston Clark to William Clark, September 1, 1833, LR, OIA, Fort Leavenworth Agency.

[65] Register of Kansas Indians Vaccinated by Dr. [A.] Chute, May and June, 1838, LR, OIA, Fort Leavenworth Agency; John Montgomery to A. Cumming, August 31, 1855, LR, OIA, Kansas Agency; typed copy of "Neosho Valley Villages at Council Grove," Morehouse Papers.

[66] Charter of M. Deruisseau, 1843, cited in Nasatir, *Before Lewis and Clark*, I, 38.

[67] Francis Paul Prucha, *American Indian Policy in the Formative Years*, 107.

[68] *U.S. Statutes at Large*, IV, 564.

but in practice for profitable disposal among the various tribes.[69]

Contrary to popular belief, a number of reports indicate the Kansas had no innate attraction to intoxicating beverages. Thomas Say noted in 1819 that drunkenness was rare and that whiskey was a "much ridiculed" commodity; a drunken person was considered "bereft of his reason" and generally avoided by his family and friends.[70] A few years later, Friedrich Paul Wilhelm, Duke of Württemberg, was impressed with Stand Black Man's polite refusal to sample some brandy; it was the Duke's considered conclusion that such a display of moderation was a rarity in Indian country.[71] Within a decade, however, things had changed. Realizing the Kansas had substantial buying power based on the regular receipt of government annuities, white settlers living near the mouth of the Kansas River (in Missouri, outside the legal jurisdiction of Indian Territory) established distilleries that provided the villages with an almost unlimited supply of the illicit commodity.[72] Some peddlers brazenly erected dramshops immediately adjacent to the Lower Kansas River villages,[73] while others simply joined Mexican freighters and distributed the liquor on an itinerant basis.[74] After the tribe moved to the Upper Neosho Reservation, whiskey was obtained with little difficulty from soldiers stationed at nearby Fort Riley or from merchants at Council Grove. Complaints from the few government agents who were honestly concerned were either ignored or dismissed on grounds that it was virtually impossible to police the situation.[75]

It should be emphasized that not all the Kansas' leisure time was given to the consumption of intoxicating beverages. Following

---

[69] William Clark to Lewis Cass, November 21, 1831, LR, OIA, St. Louis Superintendency; Prucha, *American Indian Policy*, 115, 136.

[70] *James' Account of S. H. Long's Expedition*, XIV, 194; XV, 49.

[71] Wilhelm, "First Journey to North America," 316.

[72] Marston Clark to William Clark, September 30, 1833, LR, OIA, St. Louis Superintendency.

[73] Richard Cummins to C. A. Harris, September 30, 1836, LR, OIA, Fort Leavenworth Agency.

[74] Richard Cummins to Thomas Harvey, December 21, 1847, LR, OIA, Fort Leavenworth Agency.

[75] John Montgomery to Alexander Cumming, November 1, 1855, and Hiram Farnsworth to William Dole, July 1, 1861, LR, OIA, Kansas Agency.

a particularly successful hunting expedition, there was feasting and dancing, sometimes lasting two weeks. These were tumultuous and exciting days, a time to forget the lean times of the past and enjoy the present.[76] Gambling, too, was a popular diversion, especially for men with substantial wealth in horses, robes, guns, and other articles available as stakes. Meetings for these games, which included a rudimentary form of dice, were usually held in the lodge of a chief, and for the relatively affluent warrior to ignore an invitation was to lose favor and suffer possible permanent exclusion from the chief's lodge.[77] Other forms of adult entertainment involved the display of physical prowess, including such activity as leaping, racing, and wrestling. Warriors often spent long hours decorating their garments or tipi skins or aesthetically modifying their weapons and ceremonial badges.[78] Continued erosion of the economic foundations of Kansa society contributed to the practice of begging in and around the settlements and military posts, but as one white visitor to Fort Leavenworth noted in 1833, some apparently well-provisioned parties spent much of their spare time begging "for mere amusement."[79]

What little leisure time young Kansa girls had was spent playing with crude dolls and playhouses they fashioned themselves or enjoying similar kinds of domestically related activity. Small boys had more time to practice archery, running, lance throwing, and a sort of mimic hunting that soon involved the actual chase of small birds and animals. Popular indoor guessing games for young people probably led to the development of an adult interest in gambling. During the months between hunting expeditions and military campaigns, young and old alike enjoyed listening to detailed descriptions of recent encounters with the Pawnees, Cheyennes, or some other tribe, or the recounting of archaic tribal stories. Included in these were confrontations involving mice, wolves, turkeys, buffalo, raccoons, crawfish, and turtles, with the general theme centering

[76] Rothensteiner, "Early Missionary Efforts Among the Indians," 82.
[77] Adams, "Reminiscences of Frederick Chouteau," 431; McGee, "The Siouan Indians," 175.
[78] McGee, "The Siouan Indians," 174.
[79] Irving, *Indian Sketches*, 69.

around the idea that a physically inferior animal could often over-power his adversary by planning, courageous acts, and a high degree of individual adaptability. Other tales recalled the awesome *Mialueka*, a mythological race with long beaks whose members enticed unsuspecting Indians to their solitary and dangerous places. Still others dealt with the regrettable consequences of domestic difficulties between husband and wife.[80]

Music was an important aspect of Kansa culture and held great importance in the performance of the various tribal dances. A dominant feature was rhythm, although a precise metrical pattern was not fully developed; harmonic form, by white standards of the time, was virtually unknown. Songs were simple and relatively unemotional chants intended to narrate a significant historical event and were often composed by the singers during the performance. According to one observer, the repeated expression *high-e-ye-ye* had no particular meaning, but was used as a device to maintain the sound between parts of the narrative. To the accompaniment of drums—made of wooden frames covered with prepared buffalo hides—deer's-foot rattles tied to strings, and crude flutes fashioned of wood, a lively chant was both a source of great personal enjoy-ment and a vital part of the dances.[81]

The Kansas performed at least seventeen different dances, including some reserved exclusively for women and others for men. Family, thanksgiving, medicine, track-finding, hide, calumet, war, and death dances were exceedingly popular affairs. However, the one that aroused the most interest and excitement, especially among white visitors, was the Dog Dance. It was usually performed at night, about the time visitors were retiring to their assigned lodges. Whether it was intended primarily for their entertainment or was simply a modified version of one of their war dances is not known; more certain was its abrupt, unannounced beginning. Without the slightest warning, a group of armed, screaming warriors would rush into the guest lodge, beating their drums and shaking their

[80] Dorsey Papers; Wedel, "The Kansa Indians," 28.

[81] McGee, "The Siouan Indians," 176; Spencer, "The Kaw or Kansas Indians," 376–77; George P. Morehouse, "Along the Kaw Trail," *TKSHS*, VIII (1903–1904), 210.

rattles in a defiant manner. After chanting a number of shrill songs, a leader would leap forward to strike a post, which signaled the beginning of a circular dance that might continue for hours, until the dancers were virtually exhausted. Finally, with yells "frightful to hear," they would depart as abruptly as they came. On some occasions they resumed the music, yelling, and dancing in other parts of the village and continued throughout the night. Whether the Dog Dance might extend over a period of several weeks, as in the case of some war and scalp dances, is not known.[82]

As in the case of other Dhegiha Siouans, evidence concerning the indigenous religious beliefs and practices of the Kansas is sketchy, probably because they were reluctant to discuss such matters with individuals outside their own community. The paucity of information is further complicated by the highly subjective appraisals made by missionaries, who were understandably anxious to convert and enroll them as members of a Christian denomination. Nevertheless, it is highly probable that Kansa beliefs were more theistic than pantheistic, more polytheistic than monotheistic, and were practiced in terms of propitiation rather than worship per se.

The Kansas' *waucondahs*, or mysterious spirits, varied in rank and power and existed throughout the universe—in the sun, light, darkness, heat, cold, seasons, thunder, rivers, woods, plains, islands, hunting, and the "underworld." References to the Great Spirit, the Master of Life, or a "Great Ghost of Life" are at best abstruse and are often accompanied by statements denying any claim by individuals to have seen, known, or precisely understood this most powerful deity. Perhaps it is appropriate, as one scholar has noted, to conclude that to the Kansas, Waucondah was more a quality than a definite entity, so that thunder was Waucondah, as opposed to being *a waucondah* or *the* Waucondah.[83]

To invoke Waucondah the Kansas consecrated some of their

[82] Morehouse, "Along the Kaw Trail"; *James' Account of S. H. Long's Expedition*, XIV, 208–209; Spencer, "The Kaw or Kansas Indians," 376; Morgan, *The Indian Journals*, 35; Skinner, "Societies of the Iowa, Kansa and Ponca Indians," 761–67; *Western Christian Advocate*, VII (1841), 193, typed copy in Morehouse Papers.

[83] Dorsey, "A Study of Siouan Cults," 521; McGee, "The Siouan Indians," 182–83.

fireplaces when erecting new lodges; they also assigned sacred qualities to such objects as white horses, war pipes, clam shells and various roots used by the tribal shamans. In some instances, hearts that had been removed from enemies killed in battle were sacrificed to the four winds, while bits of their own flesh were sometimes offered to the various *waucondahs.*

Of special religious importance was a salt spring located near the fork of the Solomon River near present Cawker City, Kansas. This unique deposit, about 170 feet in circumference at the base and 30 feet high, with a pool 55 feet in diameter, was named Nepaholla by the Kansas, meaning "water on the hill." According to Isaac McCoy's account of 1830, the bubbling fountain (or spring) in the center was known as Ne Wôh'Kôn'daga, meaning he said, "spirit Water." It was repeatedly visited by the Kansas, who threw valuable "conjuring charms" in the water, either to placate or invoke the power of Waucondah.[84] The pervading influence of white culture during the course of the nineteenth century brought about confusion and an increasingly more eclectic concept of the mysterious spirits, as was illustrated in a statement by Hard Hart to Indian Commissioner James W. Denver in 1857. While making a passionate plea for more supplies, the Kansa chief stated: "You are the same to me as God [Waucondah]. You can do everything like one. You can do anything you like."[85]

In a society like that of the Kansas, in which premature death was commonplace, it is not surprising that burial and mourning customs were developed to a degree of considerable complexity. Preparation of the corpse for burial was largely the responsibility of the women, especially members of the deceased's gens. After the face had been painted and the body covered with bark and a buffalo robe, an old man might talk to the corpse, giving directions to the world of the dead; then the body was placed in a shallow individual

[84] Wedel, "The Kansa Indians," 32–33; *James' Account of S. H. Long's Expedition,* XIV, 194–95; Dorsey, "A Study of Siouan Cults," 365–80, 415, 522; Mathews, *The Osages,* 266; McCoy, *History of Baptist Indian Missions,* 411; McGee, "The Siouan Indians," 182–83; Morehouse, "History of the Kansa," 359; Connelley, "Early Indian Occupancy," 458.

[85] Speech of Hard Hart (written transcript), July 22, 1857, LR, OIA, Kansas Agency.

47

grave, usually located on a hill or bluff near the village. Some evidence suggests it was placed in a horizontal position, with the head facing what may have been considered the life-giving east; other reports tell of the corpse being placed in a sitting posture, facing west, with arms crossed and knees flexed. In either case, the deceased person's garments, weapons, utensils, pipe, and a supply of corn, beans, and dried buffalo meat were deposited in the burial pit, apparently for use by the deceased during the journey ahead. Finally, after earth and rock slabs had been placed over the grave, the dead man's horse might be killed (usually by strangulation) and left on top of the grave. Understandably, the nature of the deceased's subsequent journey was never stated with any degree of precision. References to the "hereafter," the "good path," and a kind of "reanimation" are even more vague than accounts dealing with "spirit villages," which were believed to be located at or near the site of the village occupied immediately preceding the present one. Thus, from the Kansa point of view, the spirits of deceased persons were expected to return to a succession of earthly habitations extending back in time and place from the Neosho to the Kansas, Missouri, Ohio, Wabash, and other valleys, some of them long forgotten.[86]

Mourning customs were rigid and involved both the immediate family and the tribe as a whole. A widow fasted, scarified her face and hands, covered her person with clay, and became negligent in her dressing habits for one year. Then, without ceremony, she usually became the wife of her deceased husband's eldest brother. However, if the deceased left no brother, the widow was free to marry whom she pleased. In the case of the wife's death, the husband was expected to undergo a lengthy period of mourning, in some instances up to eighteen months; fasting from sunrise to sunset, wailing, scarifying the body, and rubbing mud on the face

[86] Dorsey, "A Study of Siouan Cults," 377, 422; Connelley, "Early Indian Occupancy," 459; Morgan, The Indian Journals, 82–83; Wedel, "The Kansa Indians," 27; Council Grove Press, May 19, 1861; Bushnell, "Villages of the Algonquian, Siouan and Caddoan Tribes," 53–55; Edward King, "The Great South: The New Route to the Gulf," Scribner's Monthly, VI (1873), 268; "Letters of Rev. James M. Jameson," CKSHS, XVI (1925), 263.

were mandatory obligations on his part. Those who could afford it hired professional mourners to visit the new grave regularly for a period of not less than two weeks, during which time they were to fast and not communicate with anyone; the less affluent relied on their immediate relatives to perform these rites. The death of a warrior or prominent person often precipitated an expedition against a tribal enemy, apparently to place the Kansas—as opposed to the enemy—on an equal footing with the Great Spirit. Generally speaking, then, the collective rationale underlying the mourning rites appears to have been the desire to arrange a propitiatory settlement with Waucondah.[87]

The pervading experience of Kansa society in the two hundred years after French explorers first noted their existence was an almost uninterrupted cultural modification forced upon them by vested-interest groups and aggressive individuals. During the short intervals when they were able to resume their semisedentary way of life in comparative isolation, only the most minor changes took place. However, these brief respites were of little importance, since traders, merchants, government agents, missionaries, and white settlers quickly and easily overwhelmed them. Clearly, it was an unfair match, and in the process the Kansa political leadership was unable to maintain the respect and authority it had once exercised.

Traditionally, the political arrangement of Kansa society centered around a number of separate villages held together only by the loosest form of political confederation. Although a particularly brave or capable leader might enjoy, at least for a limited time, the position of principal chief over all the villages, the more common practice was for the rank and file to recognize a head chief at each of the several villages. On occasion these leaders might be elected by a "common council" composed "of the people," but wisdom, bravery, and distinguished acts were equally, if not more, important factors. Reflecting the apparent influence of white culture, the position of village chief eventually became mainly heredi-

[87] Bushnell, "Villages of the Algonquian, Siouan and Caddoan Tribes," 54; Skinner, "Societies of the Iowa, Kansa and Ponca Indians," 772–73; *James' Account of S. H. Long's Expedition*, XIV, 193; Spencer, "The Kaw or Kansas Indians," 378; Adams, "Reminiscences of Frederick Chouteau," 429.

tary, with the office normally going to the eldest son of the ruling chief. On the other hand, this did not necessarily preclude the deposition of a hereditary leader, as was the case in 1867 when Kah-he-gah-wah-ti-an-gah (Fool Chief the Younger) killed a Kansa warrior without good cause and was, by tribal action, replaced by Al-le-ga-wa-ho.[88]

In the eighteenth and nineteenth centuries the number of chiefs varied considerably. According to Bourgmont there were seven "chiefs" and twelve "war chiefs" (or hunting leaders) in 1724, suggesting that in matters of war and certain internal affairs the village headman could be forced to assume a position subordinate to brave men and established warriors.[89] In 1811 Sibley reported that Kansa war councils were "much distracted by jealousies arising from the ambition and turbulent disposition of some of the warriors and minor chiefs."[90] By 1833 it was necessary for Commissioner Henry L. Ellsworth to obtain the signature of seven chiefs—White Plume, Fool Chief the Elder, Hard Chief, Little White Bear, White Hair Striker, The Man Charles, and Little Old Man—in order to bind the Kansas to an informal peace treaty with several other tribes at Fort Leavenworth.[91] Meanwhile, White Plume, who in the 1820's and 1830's still exercised some authority over all the villages, complained bitterly of tribal factionalism and repeated attempts by minor chiefs and council members to undermine his political position.[92] From this power struggle there eventually emerged a triumvirate of brothers, Kah-he-ge-wah-che-ha (Hard Chief), Peg-gah-hosh-she (Big John), and Ish-tah-lesh-yeh

---

[88] Skinner, "Societies of the Iowa, Kansa and Ponca Indians," 746; Wilhelm, "First Journey to North America," 313; Morgan, *The Indian Journals*, 35; Thomas M. Marshall (ed.), "The Journals of Jules De Mun," Missouri Historical Society *Collections*, V (1928), 321–22; Thomas Murphy to N. G. Taylor, July 29, 1867, LR, OIA, Kansas Agency.

[89] Margry, *Explorations of the Tributaries of the Mississippi*, 23, 29.

[90] Brooks, "George C. Sibley's Journal," 176–77.

[91] Copy of peace agreement, 1833, n.d., Letters Received by the Office of Indian Affairs, Western Superintendency (M 234, R 921), National Archives (cited hereafter as LR, OIA, Western Superintendency).

[92] Transcript of White Plume's speech to William Clark, St. Louis, May 17, 1827, LR, OIA, St. Louis Superintendency; Marshall, "Journals of Jules De Mun," 325–26.

(Speckled Eye), sometimes referred to as the more conservative "old crowd," who were nearly always at odds with the younger, more aggressive rank-and-file warriors.[93]

Thus by 1862, when Kansa Agent Hiram Farnsworth complained to the Commissioner of Indian Affairs that factionalism and internal bickering militated against any meaningful administration of the government's policies,[94] the failure—indeed the demise—of the Kansa political leadership was not only indicative of that policy's shortcomings, but was also symptomatic of the revolutionary changes and corroding socio-economic effects begun earlier by profit-minded European traders.

[93] R. A. Cummins to C. A. Harris, September 25, 1838, LR, OIA, Fort Leavenworth Agency; copy of "Neosho Valley Villages at Council Grove," Morehouse Papers.

[94] Hiram Farnsworth to Commissioner of Indian Affairs, April 16, 1862, LR, OIA, Kansas Agency.

CHAPTER **3** THE IMPACT OF
THE EUROPEAN FUR TRADE

AMONG the developments that led to personal contact between the Kansa Indians and the mercantile community of Western Europe, none was more significant than the increasing demand for fur products in the sixteenth and seventeenth centuries. Stylish hats and elegant robes, particularly those fashioned from highly valued beaver pelts, were proudly displayed by the religious and secular aristocracy of Europe during the late medieval and early modern periods; from a utilitarian point of view, they were a source of great comfort for a civilization lacking a satisfactory means of heating homes, churches, and public buildings during the cold winter months. Deer, beaver, marten, otter, and fox had once been fairly abundant in Europe, but the capricious character of high fashion, the ever increasing population, and a rising demand for fur products among the middle and lower classes brought about a shortage of critical proportions. Happily, at least for the enterprising merchant classes of England, France, and the Netherlands, this shortage coincided with European occupation of substantial parts of North America and the discovery that its forests and river valleys were literally teeming with fur-bearing animals.[1]

Following the arrival of English traders along the Acadian coast soon after 1600 and the French founding of Quebec in 1608, there developed between the two powers a rivalry over the St.

[1] Paul C. Phillips, *The Fur Trade*, I, 3–7.

52

Lawrence Valley fur kingdom and the area east of the Great Lakes. It was mainly Louis de Bade, Comte de Frontenac, who championed the plan to extend French influence into the vast fur reserves of interior North America. Appointed governor of New France in 1672, Frontenac looked inland, to the lower lake country, where he hoped to expand the fur trade, enhance the economic and political power of France, and add to his personal fortune as well. Together with his associates, among them Réné Robert Cavelier, later Sieur de La Salle, Frontenac also directed French attention to the Mississippi Valley, a move which became increasingly vital to French interests when England seized New Netherland and established a dominant position in the Hudson Bay area after 1660. Coming in the wake of Marquette's Mississippi journey of 1673, La Salle's interior voyage to the Gulf in 1682—which established France's claim to the Mississippi Valley—was of great importance to the beginning of regular white contacts with the Kansas. Not only did La Salle inaugurate a movement contrary to the interest of monopoly-minded French merchants in Montreal and Quebec, he encouraged an understanding with the various Illinois tribes and, from the standpoint of the Kansas and other tribes then located on the Lower Missouri, helped usher in the era in which aggressive French *coureurs de bois* wandered into the Trans-Mississippi West in quest of pelts, skins, and buffalo wool. While these men cultivated profitable relationships with the Missouri River tribes on an informal basis, the establishment of French posts at the mouth of the Arkansas River in 1686 and at Cahokia in 1699 represented the formal beginning of a commercial wedge driven between the English colonies to the east and Spanish possessions to the southwest.[2]

Other considerations encouraged French movement into the area west of the Mississippi. On the basis of Coronado's expedition and those of other conquistadors in the seventeenth century, Spain claimed a large region northeast of Santa Fe and Taos, although the topographical character and precise limits of this region remained exceedingly vague. England's claim was based on the sea-to-sea provisions in the several colonial charters, while France could point

2 *Ibid.*, 204–205, 228–39; Nasatir, *Before Lewis and Clark*, I, 2.

to the explorations of Marquette, Louis Hennepin, and La Salle. Clearly, the region occupied by the Kansas when they first encountered the advance guard of European culture was a vast domain subject to considerable—and often confused—diplomatic contention. Rumors of the long-sought passage to the western waters and somewhat more tenable accounts concerning the mines of northern New Spain acted as catalytic forces to draw French attention west of the Mississippi. As early as 1683 La Salle tried to convince the Marquis de Seignelay that colonization of the Mississippi Valley was a first strategic step in the conquest of the Spanish mining country,[3] and in 1702 Governor Iberville of Louisiana reported that twenty "Canadians" had left the Tamarois mission at Cahokia to trade in New Mexico and determine whether the mines reported by the "savages" really existed.[4]

By the end of the seventeenth century, Spanish authorities in New Mexico were concerned over increasing French influence among the tribes west of the Mississippi. Following the disastrous Pueblo Revolt of 1680, Governor Diego de Vargas attempted to reestablish Spanish authority in New Mexico, which, in terms of the delicate diplomatic balance in Europe, required the containment of French influence wherever it appeared. By 1697, after the Peace of Ryswick, France was in a better position to pursue her interests in the Trans-Mississippi West, but slow communication between officials here and abroad, plus events unfolding in the New World, dictated that her encounter with Spain in the vast Indian country would have to proceed in something less than an orderly manner.

Particularly distressing to Governor Vargas in 1695 was information obtained from a group of Apaches trading at Picurís, a pueblo just south of Taos. They reported that a number of Frenchmen were advancing toward the Central Plains and arming some of the Indians with whom they were trading. Three years later other Indians brought more unwelcome news about French traders among the tribes west of the Missouri.[5] Although these reports

[3] Henri Folmer, *Franco-Spanish Rivalry in North America, 1524-1763*, 145.
[4] Mémoire Sur le Pays du Mississippi, June 20, 1702, cited in Nasatir, *Before Lewis and Clark*, I, 8.

probably were exaggerated, there is no doubt that the French were determined, as a countervailing measure, to establish a commercial foothold among the Kansas, Osages, and Pawnees. On July 10, 1700, Father Gabriel Marest of the Kaskaskia mission wrote Governor Iberville that the Kansas and Pawnees of the Missouri Valley were carrying on an extensive commerce in horses with the Spaniards; this he considered dangerous and detrimental to French colonial policy.[6] Shortly thereafter Iberville dispatched a long memorial to Seignelay, outlining the importance of counteracting the increasing economic activity of Spanish and English traders in Upper Louisiana.[7]

Iberville's report contained a number of recommendations, some of which were to have important consequences for the Kansas. Spain and England must be driven from Louisiana; a government post to encourage the fur trade must be established somewhere west of the Mississippi; and the Indians must be armed, especially to help contain the English, who by then were sending traders as far southwest as the Arkansas Valley. Above all, Iberville advised, much more freedom should be granted to the *coureurs de bois*; the vast quantities of skins obtained from the Indians could be processed at government-operated tanneries on the various tributaries west of the Mississippi and then shipped abroad. Although Iberville's ambitious suggestions were not unacceptable to Seignelay and French authorities in Paris, financial pressure brought on by the War of the Spanish Succession militated against any immediate implementation of his program.[8] The enterprising *coureurs de bois* and rowdy *voyageurs* were thus left to compete with the Spanish and English traders as best they could, although on the basis of Pennsylvania Governor William Keith's report to the British Board of Trade in 1719 and the findings of a convocation called by the Marquis de Valero, viceroy of New Spain, in 1720 there is every reason to believe they did quite well and that through them the

---

[5] Folmer, *Franco-Spanish Rivalry*, 277–78.
[6] Archives du Service Hydrographique de la Marine (Paris), Vol. 115, No. 15, cited in Nasatir, *Before Lewis and Clark*, I, 6.
[7] Phillips, *The Fur Trade*, I, 364–65.
[8] *Ibid.*, 364–69.

French began to enjoy a dominant position in the Kansa fur trade.[9]

Spanish officials in New Mexico decided to take military action in the face of this distressing French influence with the Indians west of the Missouri River. When news of the War of the Quadruple Alliance reached New Spain in June, 1719, the French threat seemed all the more pressing. One month earlier the Louisiana Council of Commerce had in fact decided to seize at least some of the Mexican mines, and shortly thereafter Philip V of Spain ordered Viceroy de Valero to "force the French to abandon the territory they unjustly [held]," which included, of course, the area where the Kansas then resided. However, peace negotiations, which began in Madrid in October, 1720, forced the Spanish monarch to revise his instructions to Valero, who was now ordered to "wage only a defensive war in case the French should invade."[10]

This, then, was the international background to Lieutenant General Pedro de Villasur's expedition to the plains in the summer of 1720 and the Kansas' more direct involvement in the fast-changing colonial struggle between France and Spain. For these two powers, it was a matter of empire and commercial monopoly in a vast, mostly unexplored region; for the Kansas and their Indian allies, it was a question of dependable markets for furs and skins, as well as the threshold to a new way of life based on the cultural paraphernalia of European civilization.

There is no better example of French influence among the Pawnees, Otoes, Missouris, and Kansas in the early eighteenth century than the disaster that soon befell Villasur near the mouth of the Loup River in present east-central Nebraska. Following a January, 1720, decision by the War Council in Mexico City to "block the French penetration," Governor Don Antonio Valverde y Cosío of New Mexico was ordered to build a presidio at El Cuartelejo on the Upper Arkansas (about fifty miles east of present-day Pueblo, Colorado), but for some unexplained reason, he failed to carry out the order. Instead he sent Villasur with about

[9] *Ibid.*, 283; Charles W. Hackett (ed.), *Pichardo's Treatise on the Limits of Louisiana and Texas*, III, 204.

[10] Folmer, *Franco-Spanish Rivalry*, 251, 265-69.

fifty troops and sixty friendly Indians to reconnoiter the Gallic threat. Leaving Santa Fe sometime in late June or early July, Villasur advanced northeast to the site of El Cuartelejo. He then moved on to the Platte Valley, which he reached in early August. By the tenth of that month he had encountered a number of suspicious Pawnees and possibly Missouris, Otoes, and Kansas. From the Indian point of view, which was obviously encouraged by the French traders, suspicion gave way to outright fear. Early on the morning of August 14 in the Lower Platte Valley, the combined Indian force surprised and killed twenty-five Spaniards, including Villasur, and eleven of their Pueblo allies. Thus, in what must stand as one of the most decisive military encounters west of the Missouri, the Indians—with French arms and encouragement—had thwarted the Spanish drive to the northeast.[11]

Although the Pawnees were probably most responsible for the attack, the Kansas and other Missouri River tribes may have been involved. For example, Boisbriant, the French military commander in Illinois, was later advised of possible Otoe and Missouri involvement when some of their representatives brought in booty seized from the Spaniards.[12] A Spanish declaration of 1720 recorded that the attack had been carried out by "the Pawnees [probably the Skidis] and their allies," which could have included the Kansas.[13] The place where the attack probably took place was at least on the periphery of the Kansa hunting domain, and on March 5, 1750,

[11] The precise site of the Villasur defeat is the subject of considerable disagreement. Alfred Barnaby Thomas, citing the somewhat less than reliable "Villasur Diary," placed it about eight leagues below the confluence of the North and South Platte rivers between the present towns of Maxwell and Brady, Nebraska. Others argue for a site about twenty-five leagues up the Platte from its junction with the Missouri. The most exhaustive study is that of Gottfried Hotz, who catagorically challenges Thomas and makes a firm case for a site about four or five leagues upstream from the mouth of the Loup in the area between present-day Columbus and Genoa, Nebraska. See Alfred Barnaby Thomas (trans. and ed.), *After Coronado: Spanish Exploration Northeast of New Mexico, 1696–1727*, 36–37; Folmer, *Franco-Spanish Rivalry*, 280–83; George E. Hyde, *Pawnee Indians*, 38–41; Addison E. Sheldon (trans.), "New Chapter in Nebraska History—The Battle at the Forks of the Loup and the Platte, August 11, 1720," *Nebraska History and Record of Pioneer Days*, VI (1923), 1–29; Gottfried Hotz, *Indian Skin Paintings from the American Southwest*, 178–200.
[12] Hyde, *Pawnee Indians*, 41; Folmer, *Franco-Spanish Rivalry*, 283–84.
[13] Folmer, *Franco-Spanish Rivalry*, 283.

Don Tómas Vélez Cachupin, civil and military governor of New Mexico, provided more concrete evidence of possible Kansa action against Villasur. Pedro Satren, spokesman for a small party of French traders who had recently arrived in Santa Fe, told Cachupin that

the Canes (or Kances) nation are white Indians, very proficient in the use of firearms, and . . . are the ones who routed the Spaniards who, in the year 1720, to the number of fifty, penetrated to this region under the command of Don Pedro de Villasur, Don Antonio Valverde y Cosío being governor of this kingdom of New Mexico.[14]

Satren's exaggeration of the exclusive role played by the Kansas and his concomitant failure to mention the Pawnees probably resulted from his eagerness to refute the Spanish charge that the French had been personally involved in the attack. Absolute proof of this is not available, but circumstantial evidence of indirect French involvement is overwhelming.[15] Considering the commercial pattern then developing in the Lower Missouri and Kansas valleys, it is difficult to believe the profit-minded French traders would not have encouraged the Kansas (and other tribes of the Lower Platte-Missouri Valley) to help stand off a Spanish advance from the southwest. Like the Pawnees, Otoes, and Missouris, the Kansas by then had come to expect regular visits by the *coureurs de bois* and thus had every reason to react as they did against Villasur. Perhaps the Kansas were beginning to understand that they had a vital role in the imperial struggle between France and Spain.

The Spaniards were understandably concerned over the Villasur disaster. Fearful that the French-sponsored Indian attack in the Platte Valley was the beginning of a more general French drive toward New Mexico, Valverde, on October 8, 1720, requested immediate military assistance to counteract the threatened invasion. In Mexico City the viceroy requested that the Santa Fe garrison be restored to its full strength; he also demanded the establishment of

[14] Hackett, *Pichardo's Treatise*, 315. A Paloma warrior told Governor Valverde that the Kansas were allied with some "white people," Valverde to Valero, November 30, 1719, cited in Thomas, *After Coronado*, 143.

[15] Valverde to Valero, November 30, 1719, cited in Thomas, *After Coronado*, 143; Hotz, *Indian Skin Paintings*, 219–20.

an additional presidio at La Jacarilla, northeast of Taos. Subsequent intelligence which came to the attention of Governor Bienville, but which eventually proved to be false, reported that the Spaniards also had plans to erect a fortification somewhere on the Kansas River. But the French were unable to take advantage of Villasur's defeat. There were some reports that the Spaniards intended to return to avenge their loss and Bienville therefore ordered Boisbriant to build a fort on the Kansas River; however, the order was not carried out. On an international scale, a military confrontation was increasingly less tenable, primarily because of a developing Franco-Spanish *rapprochement* that was ultimately to culminate in the signing of the Treaty of Madrid on March 27, 1821. After this settlement, relations between the two powers improved, and while the Spanish interest in the Great Plains diminished greatly, the French busied themselves with what they considered the more practical questions of Indian policy and the troublesome details of the fur trade.[16]

With the fur trade in French North America in a state of chronic disorder following the War of the Spanish Succession, the Crown in 1717 patented the Company of the Indies to bring a semblance of stability to this important enterprise. The action was part of the more general financial scheme of John Law, royal financier, who now issued circulars depicting the prairie-plains of Upper Louisiana as abounding with bison; this commodity, through the cooperative efforts of the Indians and traders, would help pay France's debts. More specifically, the granting of a royal monopoly to the Company of the Indies involved an attempt to halt the troublesome activity of the Canadian *coureurs de bois* and *voyageurs*, who traded with the Missouri River tribes under vague licenses granted by French authorities in Montreal and Quebec or in many cases with no license at all. To divert the fur traffic toward New Orleans, and thus more directly to the Continent, fortifications were to be erected on the Mississippi and Missouri where traders licensed at New Orleans would dispose of their skins and

---

[16] William E. Dunn, "Spanish Reaction Against French Advance Toward New Mexico, 1717-1727," *Mississippi Valley Historical Review*, II, (1915), 357-59; Folmer, *Franco-Spanish Rivalry*, 284-85.

pelts, aid in containing the Spanish threat from the southwest, and in the process bring profits to both the company and the Crown.[17]

The plan required, of course, the establishment of regular commercial relationships with the Kansas and their allies. It was complicated by the fact that the Canadians had encouraged these tribes to raid for captives among the Padoucas,[18] a nomadic group of people who ranged the High Plains northeast of New Mexico and whose presence there constituted a buffer between the French and Spanish frontiers. Understandably, the seizure of slaves for sale to French planters in the Lower Mississippi Valley was, in the opinion of the Company of the Indies, "not only contrary to the ordinances of the King, but also very prejudicial to the good commerce of the Company and the settlements which it . . . proposed to make in the said country."[19]

Other possible complications suggested that French colonial policy relative to the Kansas and their Indian allies must be formulated with caution. A premature Franco-Padouca understanding might anger the Missouri River tribes to such an extent that they might refuse to exercise their crucial role in the fur trade; but if the nefarious traffic in slaves continued, France might not succeed in opening an overland route to the mineral wealth of New Mexico. On the other hand, if the French stopped buying slaves, there was the danger they would be sold to the Foxes, traditional enemies of the French; in turn, this might result in a formidable Kansa-Fox alliance and an end to the fur trade. All things considered, the future of French commercial influence in the Lower Missouri and Kansas valleys appeared to hinge on the control of the slave trade; the encouragement of a more cordial relationship between the Kansas, their allies, and the Padoucas; and the enforcement of more stringent regulations for the fur traders.[20]

[17] Phillips, *The Fur Trade*, I, 448–51.

[18] Traditionally, the Padoucas were thought to have been Comanche Indians, but more recent archaeological investigation suggests they were the Plains Apaches. See James H. Gunnerson, "An Introduction to Plains Apache Archeology: The Dismal River Aspect," BAE *Bulletin 173*.

[19] Gregg, "The Missouri Reader," 516.

[20] Henri Folmer, "Étienne Veniard de Bourgmont in the Missouri Coun-

When the French learned that the Spaniards were planning to build a presidio somewhere on the Kansas River,[21] the Company of the Indies asked Governor Bienville to erect on the Missouri a fortification that would serve a variety of purposes. It would be a center for opening an overland route to New Mexico and a point of defense against a possible Spanish attack; it would serve as a base from which the Padoucas might be induced to join the French alliance of tribes; its garrisons would halt the slave traffic, lessen the Canadian influence among the Kansas and other Missouri River tribes, and establish a more orderly (and profitable) commerce with them. For the Kansas, the execution of this policy probably led to their first direct encounter with French officialdom, as opposed to their earlier contacts with *voyageurs, coureurs de bois*, and other itinerant traders from the north.[22]

Selected to carry out the French design was Étienne Veniard de Bourgmont, former commandant at Detroit, who had deserted his post sometime after 1705 to marry an Indian girl and take up the life of a *coureur de bois* and unofficial explorer. His travels in the Missouri River country led to the publication in 1717 of his *Description de La Louisiana*, in which he told of his experiences among the Kansas, Osages, and other tribes of that region. Eventually his exploits came to the attention of the Company of the Indies (before 1719, the Company of the West), and on July 26, 1720, Bourgmont was appointed commandant of the Missouri River, with orders to implement the French plan of expansion.[23]

Following the usual political bickering with company officials and a relatively uneventful journey up the Mississippi and Missouri rivers, Bourgmont and his poorly provisioned infantry company arrived at the principal Missouri village opposite the entrance of the Grand River on November 9, 1723. Here his Indian friends assisted

try," *Missouri Historical Review*, XXXVI (1941–42), 209; Mathews, *The Osages*, 138; Mari Sandoz, *The Beaver Men: Spearheads of Empire*, 95.

[21] Hoffhaus, "Fort de Cavagnial," 428–29; Phillips, *The Fur Trade*, I, 478.

[22] Hoffhaus, "Fort de Cavagnial," 428–29; Gregg, "The Missouri Reader," 516–21.

[23] Gregg, "The Missouri Reader," 513–14; Archives du Service Hydrographique de la Marine (Paris), Vol. 67, No. 18, cited in Nasatir, *Before Lewis and Clark*, I, 12; Folmer, Étienne Veniard de Bourgmont," 282.

him in erecting the crude structures known as Fort Orleans, while Bourgmont nursed a chronic fever and busied himself with plans for the journey to the Kansa village and the country of the Padoucas. An advance party commanded by M. de Saint Ange left by water on June 25, 1724, their pirogues laden with goods to be traded for slaves, pelts, and horses; Bourgmont, with a small detachment of troops, one hundred Missouris, and sixty-four Osages, departed by a more direct overland route on July 3. After three difficult days of marching in the summer heat, this overland group was intercepted by two Kansa messengers, who informed Bourgmont that "the chiefs were awaiting him at the head of the prairies." On the morning of July 8 the Missouri River was crossed at a point about thirty leagues above the mouth of the Kansas River. Here, on the banks of a small tributary of the Missouri at the site of the "Grand village de Quans," the Kansas probably experienced their first diplomatic and commercial confrontation with an official representative of a European nation.[24]

Happily anticipating the arrival of M. de Saint Ange's flotilla of pirogues, the Kansas gave Bourgmont's party a warm welcome. After assuring the French commander that they would accompany him on his peace mission to the Padoucas, one of the chiefs stepped forward to voice his people's feelings toward the French:

Thus you may depend upon us. . . . We have watched you during the years that you have passed among us; you have never deceived us; you crossed the Great Lake; you promised us to return, you have kept your word. Thus we love you, we are listening to you, and we shall follow you wherever you wish; we have no other will than yours.[25]

Bourgmont was then wrapped in a great buffalo robe and carried to the lodge of the principal chief. Here more speeches of welcome and friendship were delivered; gifts of pelts and provisions were distributed among Bourgmont's men, who were feasted in a generous manner. Everything pointed to the establishment of a peaceful and profitable relationship between the two groups.

[24] Gregg, "The Missouri Reader," 515-16, 521-23; Villiers Du Terrage, *La Découverte du Missouri*, 88, 94, cited in Nasatir, *Before Lewis and Clark*, I, 20-21.
[25] Gregg, "The Missouri Reader," 523.

From the French point of view, the Kansas represented a valuable ally in their plan to deal with the Padouca question and the Indian slave trade. At the time of Bourgmont's visit there were a number of Padouca slaves at the Kansa village;[26] if these could be returned to their own people and traded for promises of a dependable and more regulated Franco-Kansa commercial relationship, a major objective of the French plan of expansion toward New Mexico would have been accomplished.

From the Kansa point of view, Bourgmont's diplomacy and commercial proposals represented an attractive means of getting more guns, powder, knives, cloth, utensils, and other goods, perhaps at better terms than could be had from the Canadians. Experiences with the latter group had introduced the Kansas to European ways of barter and commercial competition, and they were determined to make the most of Bourgmont's visit.

Before the gifts delivered by Saint Ange were distributed, Bourgmont sent for the Kansa chiefs and told them how essential it was to maintain peaceful relationships with the Missouris and Osages. But, he warned, "if you quarrel with the other nations who have come with me, you will also always quarrel with me." As for the Padoucas, those nations who opposed making peace with them would, on the order of "the Great Chief across the Great Ocean," be completely destroyed by Bourgmont and his men. Bourgmont then turned to the fur trade:

And for myself, I announce to you, when you and your people come to the French settlements, you can trade with our people, and they will furnish you with all the goods you need for your nation. To this end, you will only have to bring a quantity of peltries; you will have to make a talk presently to all in your village, and say to the people, men, women, and even the children that they have only to come trade their peltries to the French who are with me and I have promised to them trade with you.[27]

If the French hoped to obtain horses and supplies primarily on their own terms, they were destined to be disappointed, for by now

[26] *Ibid.*, 524.
[27] *Ibid.*, 525–28; Margry, *Explorations of the Tributaries of the Mississippi*, 28.

the Kansas were not inexperienced in such matters. While negotiating for several horses, Bourgmont quickly realized that he would have to pay more than he expected. He added two measures of powder, thirty balls, six strings of beads, and four knives to the original price of one horse, but the Kansas were still not satisfied. They told him that a year earlier some Frenchmen had offered them double the quantity of merchandise Bourgmont was prepared to pay, "but nevertheless they did not trade with them, knowing that M. de Bourgmont needed horses for his journey to the [Padoucas]."

At this point Bourgmont voiced his anger by threatening to continue his journey without the horses. After a lengthy council, the Kansa chiefs returned and, in the words of Bourgmont, "threw themselves at him crying, caressing him, asking him if he were angry." Bourgmont said he was not and explained that each was master of his merchandise. According to Bourgmont the chiefs were so impressed with his strong stand that the commercial impasse was easily resolved in his favor. However, it is apparent that the Kansas were primarily fearful of obstructing a new avenue of trade even before it had been formally opened, and this concern probably explains why they hastened to tell Bourgmont:

But we beg you to let us serve you. We are 500 warriors at the least, who are all ready to march with you and bear your munitions and merchandise which you will have to take for your needs [to the Padoucas]. And we promise not to abandon you. Whether you make peace or war, we will not quit you. You may count upon us as on the Frenchmen who accompany you. Here are five slaves, of which we make you a present with two horses and some packs of furs. We pray you receive them on behalf of our tribe and believe that we are your children.[28]

Illness prevented Bourgmont from an immediate resumption of his journey to the Padoucas. Instead, he instructed a trader named Gaillard to accompany the Kansas, who were on their way to the buffalo country; Gaillard was to escort the principal Padouca

[28] Villiers Du Terrage, *La Découverte du Missouri*, 88, 94, cited in Nasatir, *Before Lewis and Clark*, I, 20–21; Hyde, *Pawnee Indians*, 42–44; Folmer, *Franco-Spanish Rivalry*, 287–88; Phillips, *The Fur Trade*, I, 478.

chiefs to the Kansa village on the Missouri for a peace council. In August, 1724, at some point on the Upper Saline or Smoky Hill rivers, the Padoucas were encountered and persuaded, by a liberal distribution of presents, to smoke the pipe with the Kansas and with the other Missouri River tribes later that fall. By October, with his health restored and with the close cooperation of the Kansas, Bourgmont was able to preside at a peace council held at a point some ten days' march west of the Missouri. The resulting "treaty" was at best indecisive, for it was primarily based on the amount of gifts Bourgmont could distribute at that time. The Padoucas readily accepted a French flag; they promised to deal with French traders and assist in the preservation of peace on the Great Plains. But the Kansas and the other Missouri River tribes still considered the slave trade too lucrative to be abandoned overnight, and it remained to be seen whether the French would actually provide regular commercial contacts so far west. Although it was "only a distance of twelve days" to Taos, Bourgmont decided it was too late in the season to continue toward New Mexico, so he returned to Fort Orleans. He was recalled in 1726, and in 1729 the fortification and trade center he had constructed at the mouth of the Grand River was abandoned.[29]

Meanwhile, the Kansas continued to trade with the Canadians. In fact, so abortive was the French plan to regulate the trade that in 1728 the Company of the Indies sold its trade monopoly to two Canadians, Marain and Outlas, who agreed by written contract to ship their pelts and skins to New Orleans. Whether they lived up to this agreement is doubtful, for in 1736 their contract was revoked and the trade of the Missouri and Kansas River country was simply thrown open to all traders. The result was cutthroat competition, violence, and cheating on all sides. For France, Bienville's Upper Louisiana policy was an unhappy failure; for the Kansas, it was the occasion for considerable confusion and, more important, a chance to observe and understand the cynical character of the European invader.[30]

[29] Phillips, *The Fur Trade*, I, 479.
[30] *Ibid.*, 480.

The chaotic state of affairs might have continued had not two Canadian traders, Pierre and Paul Mallet, revived Governor Bienville's dream of opening a commercial route to New Mexico and permanent trade with the Indians. Traveling across the Great Plains from the north in the summer of 1739, the Mallet party reached Santa Fe, where, to their surprise, they were welcomed by the Spaniards. After noting the commercial opportunities there, the Mallets returned to Illinois in 1740 by way of the Canadian and Arkansas River country; by March, 1741, four of the party were in New Orleans with a glowing description of the profits awaiting the French in New Mexico. Accordingly, Bienville authorized Fabry de La Bruyère, a naval officer at New Orleans, to "perfect" the discovery of the Mallets. While traveling up the Arkansas and Canadian rivers, he was to look for new mines, establish commercial relations with New Mexico, and cultivate the loyalty of the Indians, including the Kansas, so that the English would not be able "to arm and corrupt them." But Fabry failed to reach Santa Fe, and with Bienville's expenses for westward expansion amounting to more than seventeen thousand livres, the latter was relieved by authorities in Paris in 1741 and replaced by François-Pierre Rigaud, Baron de Cavagnial, the Marquis de Vaudreuil.[31]

Commensurate with Vaudreuil's desire to succeed where Bienville had failed, the new governor gave more immediate attention to the Kansas and their role in the fur trade. On the basis of a report received from M. Bertet, a military commander sent to the Illinois country in 1724, Vaudreuil, through an official ordinance of 1744, decided to counteract the "disturbances and dissensions" of the *voyageurs* by granting a five-year trade monopoly to Joseph Deruisseau, who was given control of all trade on the Missouri and its tributaries from January 1, 1745, to May 20, 1750. He was to establish himself at a new fort erected near the principal Kansa village, which by this time had been moved south to the mouth of Salt Creek, just north of the present Fort Leavenworth boundary. The site of Fort de Cavagnial, as the stout stockade was named,

[31] Folmer, *Franco-Spanish Rivalry*, 297-300; Hoffhaus, "Fort de Cavagnial," 430.

was selected primarily because the "friendly Kansa[s] were a dependable source of high grade furs" and the location was strategic in terms of both the fur trade in general and the much discussed overland route to Santa Fe. According to the French military engineer La Gautris, the fort also had a good topographical location on the western bluffs of the Missouri River. Deruisseau was authorized to issue licenses to the other traders; he was also to preserve peace among the other tribes of the region, control the unruly Canadians, and "penetrate from that place" to New Mexico.[32]

During the four- or five-year period before 1750 when Deruisseau commanded the fur trade and Chevalier François Coulon de Villiers served as first commandant at Fort de Cavagnial, the Kansas apparently enjoyed a relatively profitable and orderly relationship with the French. In 1747 Governor Vaudreuil advised the ministry that the various "abuses and disorders" had been checked and that the Canadians were well under control. However, conditions soon changed. Villiers was succeeded as commandant at Cavagnial in 1750 by Augustin-Antoine de La Barre (Seigneur de Jardin), and the latter was tragically murdered by one of his own soldiers, who had gotten drunk on brandy illegally obtained from two Canadians. La Barre was replaced by Louis Robineau de Portneuf, an "energetic and versatile" officer, who was no more successful in policing the Kansa fur trade than La Barre. So susceptible were the Kansas to the cheap trinkets, price slashing, and brandy of the Canadians that by 1752, under the influence of a *voyageur* named Avion, they moved from their main village at Cavagnial to a new location on the Kansas River not far from its confluence with the Missouri. Their regular supply of furs and their quieting influence over the "turbulent Missouris" were considered so important that Portneuf soon requested Major Mactigue Macarty, commandant of Illinois, to move the fort to the area where Avion had recently enticed the Kansas.[33]

---

[32] Hoffhaus, "Fort de Cavagnial," 425–31; Archives Nationales (Paris), Colonies, C13A, Vol. XXVIII, folios 224–32, cited in Nasatir, *Before Lewis and Clark*, I, 35–36.

[33] Archives Nationales (Paris), Colonies, C13A, Vol. XXVIII, folios 224–32, cited in Nasatir, *Before Lewis and Clark*, I, 41; Hoffhaus, "Fort de Cavagnial,"

Fort de Cavagnial was not rebuilt at the mouth of the river, nor was Portneuf able to provide the Kansas with a regular, profitable market for the average one hundred bundles of pelts and skins they wanted to trade each year. Several factors were responsible for the demise of official French influence among the Kansas. For one thing, the granting of a monopoly to Deruisseau was not financially successful, nor had the garrisons at Fort de Cavagnial been able to control the *voyageurs*. The fur trade of the Lower Missouri Valley simply was not bringing to Upper Louisiana the prosperity that the French had anticipated, so the government was understandably reluctant to assume the main burden of colonial expansion in that region. Moreover, the profits demanded by private investors were too high to attract much interest. The renewal of war with Britain in the 1740's interfered with the export trade, and the few French boats loaded with Kansa and Osage pelts that did get to New Orleans—and eventually past the British raiders—had to pay prices that were, from the standpoint of the risk and expenses involved, generally prohibitive.[34] Furthermore, New Mexico Governor Cachupin's shoddy treatment of such French traders as Pierre Mallet, Jean Chaupuis, and Louis Feuilli indicated that the French plan to discover mineral wealth and establish the long-awaited commercial route between the Missouri River and Santa Fe was doomed to failure.[35]

The continuing decline of French economic influence west of the Mississippi was matched by a marked increase in English activity there. During the troubled years between King George's War and the outbreak of the French and Indian War, the English made serious efforts to extend their commercial enterprise to the Kansas and other tribes of the Lower Missouri Valley. By supplying and unofficially encouraging at least some of the *voyageurs* or by sending their own agents to the Kansas with superior merchandise at

423–31; Calvin T. Pease and Ernestine Jension (eds.), "Illinois on the Eve of the Seven Years' War, 1747–1755," *Collections of the Illinois State Historical Library,* XXIX (1940), 548–50.

[34] Phillips, *The Fur Trade,* I, 480.

[35] Folmer, *Franco-Spanish Rivalry,* 300–303; Dunn, "Spanish Reaction," 361–62.

lower prices, the English hoped, of course, to turn them against the French.

In January and again in March, 1752, Commandant Macarty from Fort de Chartres complained to French authorities of the substantial inroads being made by the English: all the Missouris, two villages of the Great Osages, and at least some of the Kansas had been "won over" by either the British or their Indian allies in the Illinois country. If the French were allowed to sell their merchandise at cheaper, more competitive rates, complained Macarty, "this contagion would not spread."[36] With the expenses accompanying the increased hostility between France and England, it is extremely doubtful that any serious consideration was given to Macarty's suggestion. Rather, the French commandant was probably left largely to his own resources, which in terms of the English threat to the Ohio Valley required that he do everything in his power to maintain the loose French alliance with the Kansas and their tribal allies.

Indicative of Macarty's diplomatic prowess, as well as the traditional French influence with the Kansas, was his rather surprising success in recruiting a sizable body of Kansa warriors for the defense of Fort Duquesne on the Ohio. Perhaps Macarty was able to convince at least some of the tribal leaders that it was a question of defending the land where their forefathers had once resided. Or it may have been accomplished through the liberal distribution of brandy. In any event, the French officer provided them with arms and ammunition and extracted from them a promise to rendezvous with the main Franco-Indian force at or near Fort Niagara. However, the Kansas arrived too late in the spring of 1755 to participate in the campaign against General Edward Braddock. Disillusioned with the confusing character of the white man's conflict and cut off from the line of French supply, they were forced to make the long, difficult journey back to the Missouri Valley unassisted. Sick and starved to the point of eating their own

36 D'Orgon to Vaudreuil, Natchez, October 7, 1752, cited in Nasatir, *Before Lewis and Clark*, I, 43–44, 48; Pease and Jension, "Illinois on the Eve of the Seven Years' War," 447–48.

horses, remnants of the Kansa expeditionary force arrived at their main village in the heart of winter, nearly seven months after they had left the scene of the Anglo-French conflict and part of the same Ohio Valley once claimed by their ancestors.[37]

In the years immediately preceding the end of the French and Indian War and the French evacuation of Fort de Cavagnial in 1764, the Kansas continued to gather skins and pelts for disposal with those traders who offered them the highest-quality merchandise. Economically, these were good years for the Kansas. They learned well the advantage resulting from competition developing between the French and British, who came to realize that this tribe, from its strategic position at the mouth of the Kansas River, could encourage, hinder, or even block further commercial penetration into the vast fur reserves of the Middle Missouri and Arkansas valleys.

At the same time, the Kansas were plagued with problems having profound and long-range consequences. During the military conflict between France and Britain, smallpox broke out at a number of military posts in the Great Lakes region. It is possible that the epidemic reported at the Kansa villages by Louisiana Governor Kerlerec in 1758 was a result of personal contact with the few infected warriors who were able to make the return journey from Fort Niagara. Or the dread disease may have been introduced by traders from the north. In either case, the resulting fatality rate was exceedingly high, especially among the warrior ranks. Moreover, a further reduction in the number of young Kansa males in the 1750's—perhaps as much as 50 per cent—resulted from costly military encounters with the Black Pawnees west of the Missouri River. For many years this Caddoan tribe had resided in the Middle Arkansas Valley, but a disruption of the regular French traffic in arms and ammunition (because of British competition) and the transfer of Louisiana to Spain in the mid-1760's forced them north to the Platte Valley to compete for animals in the general area where the Kansas (and the other Missouri River tribes)

[37] Hoffhaus, "Fort de Cavagnial," 448–49; Coues, *The Expeditions of Zebulon Montgomery Pike*, II, 531.

had gone virtually unchallenged for many years. Since the situation arose at a time when the demand for furs was increasing substantially, the efficiency of many Kansa hunting parties was hampered by the necessity of remaining alert to the constant possibility of a Pawnee attack; soon the tribe, especially the younger warriors, determined that the best defense was a quick and decisive counter-attack. The Pawnees were equally reluctant to accommodate the Kansas. Thus was inaugurated a century of Kansa-Pawnee warfare, a conflict that severely taxed their resources and, like the recurrence of smallpox and cholera, greatly reduced the population of both tribes.[38]

Rapidly changing conditions at the international level also had a significant impact on the Kansas. On November 3, 1762, by the secret Treaty of Fontainebleau, the ownership of Louisiana was transferred to Spain, and less than four months later, by the Peace of Paris of February 10, 1763, France ceded the Illinois country east of the Mississippi to Britain. However, not until 1766 did Spain take formal control of Louisiana; meanwhile, the commerce of the interior was left in the hands of French traders, such as Pierre Laclede, the active partner in the firm known as Maxent, Laclede, and Dee. In 1763 French authorities in New Orleans granted the company an eight-year monopoly on all of the Missouri River fur trade, including that of the Kansas. Together with Auguste Chouteau and a group of French Creoles—for example, the Sarpys, the Papins, and the Vásquez family, who eventually became associated with the Kansa trade—Laclede, by adopting French commercial practices and a liberal interpretation of restrictions handed down by Spain in 1770, made St. Louis the political and economic center of Upper Louisiana (Spanish Illinois).[39]

In general, the Spanish decision to allow French economic

[38] Archives Nationales (Paris), Colonies, C13A, Vol. XL, folios 135–40, cited in Nasatir, *Before Lewis and Clark*, I, 52; Stearn and Stearn, *The Effect of Smallpox*, 43; Hyde, *Pawnee Indians*, 70–71.

[39] Hyde, *Pawnee Indians*, 71; Abraham P. Nasatir, "Ducharme's Invasion of Missouri: An Incident in the Anglo-American Rivalry for the Indian Trade of Upper Louisiana," *Missouri Historical Review*, XXIV (1929), 3–4; Jack M. Sosin, *The Revolutionary Frontier, 1763–1783*, 11–13.

authority to continue uninterrupted in much of Upper Louisiana was a qualified success, but in the Missouri country—especially among the Kansas and Osages—it was otherwise, largely because of actions by French-Canadian traders. Now under nominal British authority, they had openly defied the Proclamation of 1763 and had complained bitterly about the Imperial Plan of 1764, which required rigid regulation of the interior fur trade by commissaries stationed at the various military posts in Illinois. For example, when Sir William Johnson, superintendent of the Northern District, attempted to implement the rule requiring the Indians to trade only at designated posts, Scottish merchants at Montreal and the *coureurs de bois* protested with good cause against the corruption and profiteering of the post commanders. In this they were soon supported by Sir Guy Carleton, governor of Canada. Carleton and his associates convinced Johnson and the Board of Trade that the stringent license system would lead to a loss of affection among the Indians and perhaps the end of British authority in Illinois; ultimately, Carleton asserted, the imperial regulation of the fur trade could be of benefit only to French and Spanish operations beyond the Mississippi.[40]

By 1768 the mounting expense of supplying the posts and the increasing competition of itinerant Franco-Spanish traders were enough to convince the Board of Trade that the time to abandon the Imperial Plan of 1764 had arrived. Regulation was now left to the colonies, which in practice meant virtually no regulation at all; most of the interior posts were abandoned, troops were withdrawn, and the French-Canadians were once again free to bargain at the Indian villages as they saw fit. Together with the withdrawal of French troops from Fort de Cavagnial in 1764 and the formal assumption of Spanish authority at St. Louis in 1770, these developments caused the Kansa trade to be characterized by confusion, violence, and excessive international competition in the years immediately following the French and Indian War. From their strategic location near the confluence of the Kansas and Missouri rivers, which by this time was recognized as one of the most vital geo-

[40] Phillips, *The Fur Trade*, I, 575–83.

graphical keys to the vast fur kingdom of the Trans-Missouri West, the Kansas were (with the help of the increasingly recalcitrant Osages) in the enviable but difficult position of being able to play the British against the Spaniards and vice versa.[41]

The inability of Spanish officials to control the powerful Osages, who provided a lucrative market for British arms and ammunition after French supply lines were cut during the war, was an instructive experience for the Kansas: it tended to turn them away from the St. Louis merchants. This was especially exasperating to Spain, since the change came at a time when the Kansas contributed, in the words of Francisco Rui, "the most to [the] Misuri fur trade."[42] Like the Osages, the Kansas evidently were able to obtain better terms from the roving Canadians than from Laclede, Chouteau, and other St. Louis traders, who found it necessary to operate under the more rigid Spanish regulations. Of particular concern were the exploits of Jean Marie Ducharme, an adventuresome resident of Cahokia (now in British Illinois) who in 1772 was encouraged by Canadian Governor Carleton to take fifteen hundred pounds of merchandise to trade with the Missouri River tribes.[43] Certainly his consignment was more attractive than the annual sixteen hundred pesos authorized for distribution among all the Missouri River tribes, including the Kansas, by Don Alexandro O'Reilly, Spanish governor of Louisiana. Ducharme spent the winter of 1772–73 among the Osages and Missouris and may have visited the Kansa villages. Although his boats, loaded with pelts, were eventually captured by the Spaniards, the immediate reaction among the Indians was one of insolence toward the more poorly provisioned St. Louis traders.[44]

There is ample evidence of pronounced concern over what the Spaniards considered dangerous and unwarranted British tampering with the Missouri River tribes. In a stinging note to Hugh

[41] Nasatir, "Ducharme's Invasion," 4–5.

[42] Houck, *The Spanish Regime in Missouri*, I, 64.

[43] Lawrence Kinnard (ed.), *Spain in the Mississippi Valley, 1765–1794*, Pt. 1, xxi–xxxiii.

[44] *Ibid.*, 154–55, 235.

Lord, British commander in Illinois, Lieutenant Governor Pedro · Piernas of Upper Louisiana charged:

Such conduct [Ducharme's] is conducive to the renewal of discord, and all the evil does not end here; those violators of the most reserved rights, having to be distrustful of everything after such an action, have spread defamatory speeches against us, and consequently they have added renewed strength to the hatred by the Indians. In order to gain the good will of those tribes they have sacrificed even their own interests selling their merchandise at lower prices than the traders of this side could sell them (another reason for encouraging the real enmity in the spirit of those Barbarians), they have begun by invading the Commerce of the inhabitants of this shore, they have multiplied our anxieties and put our lives in greater perils. Such is the wrong that concerns me and of which I ask satisfaction of you in the name of my Sovereign.[45]

Within a month the British commander had sent Piernas a formal apology, together with a reminder that certain Spanish traders were operating illegally in British Illinois,[46] but it is doubtful that the exchange of notes brought about any appreciable change in conditions among the Kansas and the other Missouri River tribes. The temporary decline of British commercial influence resulted from two things: Governor Carleton's closing, in 1777, of the Great Lakes to all boats except those in the royal service and the outbreak of the American Revolution.[47]

Meanwhile, Franco-Spanish trade with the Kansas showed little improvement. Caught between contending groups of traders who stole, cheated, or often made promises that remained unfulfilled, the Kansas reacted accordingly. They armed themselves, divided into tribal factions based on the most profitable terms that could be had from individual traders, became increasingly more hostile to all traders, and attempted to challenge the assumption that they were to trade only in accordance with rules dictated by Spanish authorities in St. Louis.

[45] Pedro Piernas to Hugh Lord, February 21, 1773, cited in Nasatir, "Ducharme's Invasion," 17.

[46] Lord to Piernas, March 20, 1773, *ibid.*, 19.

[47] Phillips, *The Fur Trade*, I, 627–35.

On April 12, 1773, Piernas informed Louisiana Governor Don Luis de Unzaga that he had seized two Kansa hostages for horses stolen from several Spaniards authorized to trade at the Kansa villages. By May, 1775, conditions had deteriorated to such an extent that the St. Louis traders were afraid to enter the "Cance country," even though about seventy-five hundred pounds of furs were available at the Kansa villages. Conditions improved the following year, but some reports warned that the "speeches" of the Kansas were causing "delay" and in some cases the return of traders with very little peltry. Unzaga was informed on March 18, 1776, that "a great chief of the Kansas" would shortly arrive in St. Louis to attempt a reconciliation; whether this meeting took place is not known, but relationships improved so much by late fall that "soldiers and traders" were "well received." However, the *rapprochement* ended rather abruptly four years later when Spanish authorities in New Orleans received news that seven hunters had been killed by the Kansas. Resorting to the very kind of arbitrary strategy that had been practiced by other colonial powers with commercial and political interests in the Indian country, Spanish agents took advantage of their economic influence with certain bands of Osages by encouraging them to "punish" the troublesome Kansas and thus force the latter to submit to terms dictated by the traders.[48]

For a limited time the Spanish-Osage combination made the Kansas more receptive to the commercial overtures of the Chouteaus and Manuel Pérez, who as partners enjoyed a virtual monopoly of the Kansa trade by 1790.[49] But the arrangement could not last, especially among the powerful Osages; nor was it the only long-range threat to the economic security of the Kansas. After the American Revolution, the British embarked on an ambitious plan to dominate the fur trade of the Trans-Missouri West, soon enjoying considerable success. On April 5, 1791, Pérez reported to Louisiana Governor Esteban Miró that certain "Mississippi sav-

[48] Kinnard, *Spain in the Mississippi Valley*, Pt. 1, 217–18, 228, 235, 394–95.
[49] *Ibid.*, Pt. 2, 253; Archivo General de Indias, Sección Papeles du Cuba, legajos 16, cited in Nasatir, *Before Lewis and Clark*, I, 134–35.

ages," sent as British agents, had seized from the Kansas furs that should have gone to Auguste Chouteau; moreover, the Osages were raiding Spanish pirogues on the Missouri, probably at the instigation of the British. Chouteau also complained that while he was wintering among the Kansas, several Sacs and Foxes had come in with British goods and boasts of receiving more competitive prices. With profits dropping from 300 per cent in the late 1780's to about 25 per cent in 1792 and with rumors spreading that the English were encouraging all tribes of the Lower Missouri Valley to pass war beads and block both Spanish and American expansion, Spanish authorities concluded that it was time to abrogate the monopoly of a few in favor of stricter regulations for those with the means and power to trade with the Kansas on a regular basis.[50]

So it was that on July 20, 1793, Louisiana Governor François Luis Hector Carondelet ordered the creation of a "Syndic of Commerce" and immediate implementation of regulations that would fairly distribute the Kansa trade by lot to licensed traders each July 1. Minimum requirements included at least one year's residence in Louisiana, a promise not to use intoxicating beverages as a medium of exchange, regular business connections with merchants in New Orleans, and rigid price controls. Jacques Clamorgan, a Portuguese trader with powerful political connections in St. Louis and New Orleans, was selected as the first syndic and shortly thereafter was instrumental in organizing the "Company of the Discoverers and Explorers of the Missouri," which, in addition to conducting the Indian trade, was to promote Spanish national interest in Louisiana.[51]

The new Spanish policy met with little success. For the Kansas, whose annual trade was valued at twenty-four thousand livres, it was disastrous. It did nothing to bring peace to the Kansas and

[50] See Minuta del Acta del Consejo de Estado, May 27, 1796, Archivo Histórico Nacional (Madrid), Sección Papeles de Estado, cited in Nasatir, *Before Lewis and Clark,* I, 76–83; Archivo General de Indias, Sección Papeles du Cuba, legajos 17, 122A, 1441–42, 2362, cited in *ibid.,* 143–50; Mathews, *The Osages,* 241–42; Kinnard, *Spain in the Mississippi Valley,* Pt. 3, 22–23.

[51] Zenon Trudeau to Carondelet, St. Louis, May 31, 1794, No. 185, Archivo General de Indias, Sección Papeles du Cuba, legajos 2363, 2364, cited in Nasatir, *Before Lewis and Clark,* I, 86, 186–91.

Osages, who by 1794 were involved in such open warfare that the company was unable to send a single trader to the Kansas. Clamorgan was an arbitrary figure who played favorites and was thus incapable of contending with the British, the Pawnees, and the various unlicensed traders. For too long the Kansas had been the object of unregulated competition, and now they were unimpressed by the inferior Spanish merchandise. The handful of traders licensed by Clamorgan—Benito Vásquez, Gregorio and Juan Bautista Sarpy, J. P. Cabanné, Laurent Durocher, and Zenon Trudeau (then lieutenant governor of Spanish Illinois)—simply could not bring order to the Kansa villages. Nor were they able to make a profit. Clamorgan's personal enemies, including Manuel Lisa and Joseph Robidou, demanded a share of the chaotic trade, and although they did not succeed, their complaints contributed to suspicion and general lack of support among Spanish colonial officials.[52]

British foreign policy further complicated matters. Following the tenuous Treaty of Basel between Revolutionary France and Spain (July 22, 1795), conditions between Spain and Britain deteriorated until war finally broke out between them in October, 1796, a principal factor being renewed British intrusion in Spanish Louisiana. Rather than confront Spain directly in Louisiana, the British resorted to their traditional practice of working through various Indian tribes, including the Kansas. On April 30, 1795, Trudeau informed Governor Carondelet that the British were doubling the price of all pelts and skins the Iowas could seize from the Kansas. Two years later it was reported that a large band of Sioux had distributed 150 rifles and six kegs of brandy among the Omahas in order to give them "more courage" in a military campaign they were planning against the Kansas. The source of supply for the Sioux obviously was the British. That same year, two of

[52] Archivo General de Indias, Sección Papeles du Cuba, legajos 22, 26, 28, 207B, cited in Nasatir, *Before Lewis and Clark*, I, 174, 209, 215, 256–57, 315–16; Carondelet to Carlos Howard, New Orleans, July 28, 1797, enclosing Benito Vásquez to Carondelet, St. Louis, May 28, 1797, Archivo General de Indias, Sección Papeles du Cuba, legajos 24, and Joseph H. Robidou to Gayoso De Lemos, St. Louis, March 7, 1798, Bancroft Library, cited in *ibid.*, II, 530–31, 548; Kinnard, *Spain in the Mississippi Valley*, Pt. 3, 278–79, 363; Richard E. Oglesby, *Manuel Lisa and the Opening of the Missouri Fur Trade*, 18–19.

Clamorgan's men brought to St. Louis the unwelcome news that the Kansas were badly divided in their loyalties and increasingly more difficult to bargain with. According to Frederico Auteman and Josef Gegoutin of the Missouri Company, a group within the tribe would threaten to kill the traders and a contending faction would then offer protection in exchange for merchandise at a price they themselves would dictate. Variations of this scheme were used throughout the trading season and in some instances became so violent that several Kansas were killed. Spanish authorities in St. Louis were understandably concerned. When the occasion presented itself, they jumped at a chance to discuss matters with a prominent but apparently powerless Kansa chief who in effect admitted he was unable to contend with tribal factionalism and external pressures from various traders. In spite of the shoddy treatment his people had received from the Spaniards, Kansa Chief Cour de Brule nevertheless remained firm in his naïve belief that Clamorgan and Missouri Company traders were actually interested in the welfare of his people. "Consent, my father, to my request," he told the governor, "and be persuaded that I will always continue to defend your children from the brutality of my young men, and that I pray to the Master of life for you."[53]

There is no evidence of a formal meeting between Cour de Brule and the Spaniards, but British trade pressure had a telling effect on Spanish commerce with the Kansas. With reports that the British had captured the Ponca and Omaha trade and were continuing to pillage Clamorgan's men, the practice of awarding the Kansa trade by lot to several favorites under Clamorgan's jurisdiction was abandoned in favor of outright monopoly. Gregorio Sarpy and J. P. Cabanné were the temporary victors in 1800, probably because they promised to negotiate a peace treaty between the warring Kansas and Pawnees. When after two years they failed to achieve this, Governor Casa Calvo awarded the Kansa monopoly to Clamorgan with instructions to "offset" the British demand to

[53] Archivo General de Indias, Sección Papeles du Cuba, legajos 29, cited in Nasatir, *Before Lewis and Clark*, I, 323; Zenon Trudeau, Examination of Francisco Derouin, St. Louis, May 14, 1797, Bancroft Library, cited in *ibid.*, II, 516–17.

Portrait of Chief White Plume (ca. 1821), by Charles Bird King, reproduced from Thomas L. McKenney and James Hall, *The Indian Tribes of North America*, Vol. III. Mon-Chonsia, or The White Plume, was recognized by Indian Superintendent William Clark and the Office of Indian Affairs as the principal chief of the Kansa nation in the St. Louis Treaty of 1825.

COURTESY KANSAS STATE HISTORICAL SOCIETY

Meach-o-shin-gaw (Little White Bear), one of the seven principal Kansa chiefs in the 1820's and 1830's. The original drawing was made by George Catlin in 1841 and copied by I. Harris, Sr., in 1843 as an illustration for James Cowles Prichard's *Histoire naturelle de l'homme* (Paris, 1843).

COURTESY KANSAS STATE HISTORICAL SOCIETY

Man of Good Sense, a young Kansa warrior, by George Catlin. This
1831 oil painting was based on a sketch Catlin made at either the Blue
Earth or the Mission Creek villages.

COURTESY SMITHSONIAN INSTITUTION

The wife of Bear Catcher, by George Catlin. This 1831 oil painting was based on a sketch Catlin made at either the Blue Earth or the Mission Creek villages.

COURTESY SMITHSONIAN INSTITUTION

A war dance in a Kansa lodge as seen by Samuel Seymour in 1819. The sketch is believed to be the first one printed (1822) in what is now Kansas.

COURTESY KANSAS STATE HISTORICAL SOCIETY

A delegation of Kansa leaders conferring in Washington with Commissioner of Indian Affairs James W. Denver in 1857. Three members of the delegation were Hard Hart, White Hair, and The Wolf; the other two were not identified.

COURTESY KANSAS STATE HISTORICAL SOCIETY

A Kansa war bundle, about 24 inches long.

COURTESY MUSEUM OF THE AMERICAN INDIAN,
HEYE FOUNDATION

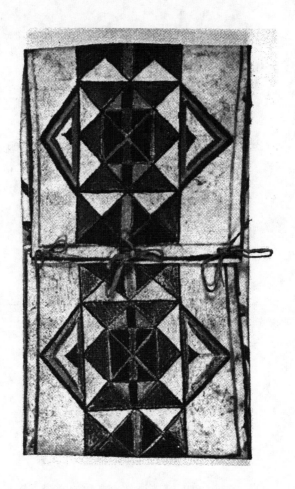

A parfleche painted by an unidentified Kansa
artist. Its dimensions are about 26 by 52 inches.

COURTESY MUSEUM OF THE AMERICAN INDIAN,
HEYE FOUNDATION

The Kansa subagency on the Kansas River south of Williamstown, first operated by Daniel Morgan Boone and Dunning McNair. Cyprian and Frederick Chouteau had a trading post there (*inset*), and Chief White Plume's village was nearby.

COURTESY KANSAS STATE HISTORICAL SOCIETY

The Kansa mission and school on the banks of the Neosho River in Council Grove. The native stone building was erected in 1850–51 and abandoned in 1854. It has been restored and is now a state museum.

COURTESY KANSAS STATE HISTORICAL SOCIETY

One of the stone houses constructed for the Kansas by the federal government in the mid-1860's on the Neosho Valley Reservation a few miles south of Council Grove.

COURTESY KANSAS STATE HISTORICAL SOCIETY

The main street of Council Grove as it appeared in the 1870's, about the time the Kansas were forced to abandon their nearby reservation and villages.

COURTESY KANSAS STATE HISTORICAL SOCIETY

Pi-sing (Game), a Kansa warrior, photographed in Washington in 1868 by A. Zeno Shindler.

COURTESY SMITHSONIAN INSTITUTION

An unidentified Kansa woman, probably photographed in the 1870's or early 1880's.

COURTESY KANSAS STATE HISTORICAL SOCIETY

Chief Al-le-ga-wa-ho, who by tribal election became one of the three principal Kansa chiefs in 1867 after Kah-he-gah-wah-ti-an-gah was deposed for killing a Kansa warrior without cause.

COURTESY KANSAS STATE HISTORICAL SOCIETY

Wah-shun-gah, principal chief of the Kansas in the 1880's after the tribe was forced to move to Indian Territory in 1873. The photograph may have been made by C. M. Bell in Washington about 1880.

COURTESY SMITHSONIAN INSTITUTION

Kansa Indian boys posing with traditional weapons at the Washungah Agency, ca. 1905, in the Indian Territory to which the tribe was forced to remove in 1873. In 1901, Indian Commissioner William A. Jones ordered all Indian males to cut their braids and style their hair according to white standards. Notice also the white men's garb, especially the hats so closely associated with the cowboy culture of the time.

COURTESY KANSAS STATE HISTORICAL SOCIETY

"open up" Spanish passage to the extensive fur country west of the Missouri. This was in 1802, two years after the secret Treaty of San Ildefonso set the guidelines for the transfer of Louisiana back to France and one year before the acquisition of that vast domain by the United States.[54]

Meanwhile, the Kansas had abandoned their villages on the Missouri in favor of new locations in the Kansas River Valley. By 1800 their principal village had been reestablished on the north bank of the Kansas near the mouth of Blue Earth (Big Blue) River, well away from the better-armed Omahas, Sacs, and Iowas.[55] While this move provided the Kansas with a greater measure of natural protection from the east, as well as more convenient access to untapped hunting grounds to the west, it placed them in closer proximity to the Pawnees; and they were closer to the Arkansas Valley, which was still claimed by the powerful Osages. Profit-seeking Franco-Spanish traders, who after 1803 experienced little difficulty in shifting their nominal allegiance to the United States, followed the Kansas, thereby accelerating the economic revolution that was threatening the very existence of traditional Kansa society. Behind them came the even more aggressive Anglo-American agrarians, whose main interest was land and who would ultimately complete the alteration of Kansa society begun by European traders more than a century earlier.

[54] Juan Manuel de Salcedo to Charles Delassus, New Orleans, February 3, 1802, and Delassus to Salcedo, St. Louis, May 13, 1892, Sección Papeles du Cuba, legajos 77, 2367, cited in Nasatir, *Before Lewis and Clark*, I, 112; Summary by Delassus of Trade Licenses Issued at St. Louis, 1799–1804, and Sarpy and Cabanné to Casa Calvo, New Orleans, April 26, 1800, Indian Trade and Fur Companies, MHS, cited in *ibid.*, II, 592, 614–15; Delassus to Casa Calvo, St. Louis, November 29, 1800, Bancroft Library, and Clamorgan to Casa Calvo, New Orleans, April 27, 1801, Clamorgan Collection in Pierre Chouteau Collection, MHS, cited in *ibid.*, 622–23, 635.

[55] Perrin Du Lac, *Travels through the Two Louisianas*, 51; Nicholas Biddle (ed.), *The Journals of the Expedition Under the Command of Capts. Lewis and Clark*, II; Osgood, *The Field Notes of Captain William Clark*, 71.

CHAPTER 4 THE INDIAN POLICY
OF A NEW NATION

THE moral tone of U.S. Indian policy was a fundamental characteristic of federalism under the Constitution of 1789. Although it provided no great obstacle to the forces of western expansion, the policy involved Indian proprietary rights to the lands they occupied and protection of these rights until they were legally abrogated by treaty with the federal government. In contrast to the more punitive policy of the Confederation, Secretary of War Henry Knox emphasized in a major position paper dated June 15, 1789, "that a liberal system of justice should be adopted for the various tribes within the limits of the United States." But he also stressed the possibility of conquest "in case of a just war," a development which was to produce disturbing consequences for the Indians in the near future. With the cooperation of President Washington, Knox succeeded in having Congress pass laws agreeable to his philosophy of nominal Indian rights.[1]

The law of July 22, 1790, dealt with trade and intercourse, including stipulations for securing commercial licenses, rules for punishing whites guilty of crimes committed in Indian country, and the prohibition of private land purchases. It was strengthened on March 1, 1793, when Congress passed a bill authorizing the expenditure of funds to promote "civilization" among the tribes and the

[1] Reginald Horsman, *Expansion and American Indian Policy, 1783–1812*, 54–55.

appointment of federal agents to help accomplish this noble objective. The boundaries of the Indian country were formally established by the law of May 19, 1796. Of crucial importance to the Kansas and other western tribes then occupying lands in Spanish Louisiana, it empowered the President to expel persons who might settle in areas where the Indian title had not been extinguished. Of more immediate importance to the Kansas was the law of April 18, 1796, which created the government factory system for the conduct and regulation of the fur trade. In spite of later complaints that it was primarily designed to eliminate the influence of private traders, the factory system envisaged a much broader purpose. Diplomatically, it sought to counteract the actions of foreign powers among the Indians; economically, it hoped to drive the aggressive British traders out of business; militarily, it was intended to serve as a preventative to frontier warfare. From a humanitarian point of view, the objective was to provide the Indians with a regular supply of goods at fair and honest prices; for the Kansas, however, it was nearly a decade before the government factory at Fort Osage, located on the Lower Missouri River, was operative. Meanwhile, private traders dominated the scene and the system in general suffered considerable economic disruption during the War of 1812.[2]

The acquisition of Louisiana Territory by the United States in 1803 meant, of course, that national Indian policy was at least theoretically applicable to the tribes of the Lower Missouri Valley. Distance, the absence of reliable information, and the tradition of foreign intrigue in the area militated against immediate implementation of Indian policy in the Trans-Missouri West. Until these problems could be solved, the government took the path of least resistance and for the most part trusted the Franco-Spanish commercial group in St. Louis to look after the national interest on the Missouri frontier. Pierre Chouteau, scion of the powerful Laclede-Chouteau family, was appointed Indian agent for the District of

[2] *Ibid.*, 62–63; Prucha, *American Indian Policy*, 86–88; Katherine Coman, "Government Factories: An Attempt to Control Competition in the Fur Trade," *Bulletin of the American Economic Association*, Fourth Series (1911), 374–75; Kate L. Gregg, "The History of Fort Osage," *Missouri Historical Review*, XXXIV (1939–40), 445.

Upper Louisiana by Secretary of War Henry Dearborn on July 17, 1804, and was given the difficult assignment of providing protection for explorers, cultivating "peaceful conditions" among the various tribes, and introducing the Indians to the "arts of civilization," both agrarian and domestic. Had the Kansas then received (as they did not) the plows, hoes, axes, and spinning wheels recommended by Dearborn, they surely would have been as surprised (and recalcitrant) as the veteran traders in their midst.[3]

There was, in fact, some evidence that President Jefferson himself was skeptical about any immediate adoption of a sedentary life by the Indians of the Far West.[4] Meriwether Lewis wrote him on November 16, 1803, that the Kansas were roving trappers who furnished the various traders with about eight thousand "fine deer skins" each year. That most of these traders were less than sympathetic to the interests of the United States in Louisiana was quite apparent to Lieutenant General James Wilkinson, who told Secretary Dearborn on September 22, 1805, he needed no less than six companies of troops and at least six pieces of artillery to keep the British from opening additional commercial avenues west of the Mississippi. A month later, Wilkinson advised Dearborn that while en route to establish a post at the Otoe villages near the mouth of the Platte, he and his men were intercepted by a party of "Canzès," who, after a "rude and unfriendly interview," killed one of the hunters and forced Wilkinson to retreat to St. Louis. The general feared the Kansas had been "excited by [Spanish] agents from St. Afee," but he assured his superior that matters were under control, since "a word to [his] friends the Osages would destroy them [the Kansas]."[5] Later reports from Wilkinson emphasized his belief that Spain was serious in her purpose to oppose the United States by "erect[ing] a strong Barrier of hostile Savages, to oppose us in time of War and to harass our frontier in time of peace."[6]

[3] Clarence Edwin Carter (comp. and ed.), *The Territorial Papers of the United States*, XIII, 31–33.
[4] Horsman, *Expansion and American Indian Policy*, 114.
[5] Donald Jackson (ed.), *Letters of the Lewis and Clark Expedition With Related Documents, 1783–1854*, 139; Carter, *Territorial Papers*, XIII, 230, 297–98.
[6] Carter, *Territorial Papers*, XIII, 357.

Thus it was the real and/or rumored machinations of Britain and Spain, not an immediate desire to "civilize" the Missouri River tribes, which in late 1805 prompted Jefferson and the War Department to have Captain Amos Stoddard of St. Louis conduct a number of western Indian leaders to Washington, where they might be counseled on the merits of a more cordial relationship with the United States. In the nation's capital, where they remained until April 11, 1806, chiefs representing the Kansas, Osages, and Pawnees were encouraged by the President to engage in commerce and a "useful intercourse" with the new nation. But the persuasive character of this advice was at best marginal. Rather, it was the liberal distribution of presents at St. Louis and the display of a small but determined military force led by Lieutenant Zebulon Montgomery Pike in the Indian country which marked the beginning of a peaceful understanding between the Osages and Kansas, as well as the inauguration of American authority over the latter tribe.[7]

Coming hard on the heels of an abortive Spanish diplomatic mission, led by Lieutenant Don Fecundo Malgares from Santa Fe to the Pawnee village on the Republican River, Lieutenant Pike's brusque display of military power and his candid meeting at the same remote village in September, 1806, constituted a rather remarkable achievement in terms of Kansa-Osage relationships. In contrast to the continuation of Kansa-Pawnee hostility, a feeling of mutual understanding between the Kansas and Osages developed to such a degree that in 1819 Thomas Say could report more than a decade of "uninterrupted" peace between the two tribes. Other factors, such as the establishment of a government factory at Fort Osage in 1808, contributed to the Kansa-Osage *rapprochement*, but Pike's expedition was singularly significant, especially when it is recalled that during the long march to the Republican Valley, his Osage guides led him nearly one hundred miles off course because they were "more afraid of the Kaws [Kansas] than . . . could possibly have [been] imagined." Moreover, the Pawnee council came at a time when the Little Osages were reported planning to attack the Kansas and a struggle for control of the Lower Missouri

7 *Ibid.*, 243–44; Jackson, *Letters of Lewis and Clark*, 265–66, 282–83.

River fur trade was being joined between Manuel Lisa, the "Black Spaniard," and the powerful Chouteau family of St. Louis.[8]

Establishing good relations between the Kansas and Osages contrasted sharply with the turbulent nature of the fur trade. What the Kansas wanted, of course, was a cheap supply of firearms, ammunition, blankets, vermilion, hardware, flour, whiskey, and trinkets for the peltry they had to offer. They also demanded that the traders—regardless of whether they were American, British, French, or Spanish—visit their villages on a regular basis. But conditions in Upper Louisiana at the turn of the century dictated that such requests were difficult, if not impossible, to fulfill. On a national scale the "enterprising and ambitious Americans," as Regis Loisel, a Spanish trader in St. Louis, described them, were determined "to avail themselves of any means in their power to win the mind of the savage nations." Unlike General Wilkinson, who in somewhat less than reliable terms made a point of the Spanish threat in his reports to Secretary Dearborn, Meriwether Lewis considered the British the source of "all pending evils on the frontier." Meanwhile, the Franco-Spanish merchants in St. Louis continued to fight among themselves for a share of the trade, including that of the Kansas.[9]

After 1800 at least four groups working out of St. Louis sought to monopolize the Kansa trade. The first may be described as the independent traders, an undetermined number of individual operators or small partnerships (like that of Gregorio Sarpy and J. P. Cabanné) who took the Kansa trade from Jacques Clamorgan in 1800 by promising the Spanish governor they would reconcile the differences between the Kansas and Pawnees. The second group

[8] Coues, *The Expeditions of Zebulon Montgomery Pike*, II, 562, 576, 585; William E. Connelley (ed.), "Indian Treaties and Councils Affecting Kansas: Dates and Places, Where Held, Names of Tribes, Commissioners and Indians Concluding Same," *CKSHS*, XVI (1925), 746–47; *James' Account of S. H. Long's Expedition*, I, 272; Oglesby, *Manuel Lisa*, 36–37.

[9] Carter, *Territorial Papers*, XIII, 229; *ibid.*, XIV, 200; Regis Loisel to Charles Delassus, St. Louis, May 28, 1804, Archivo General de Indias, Sección Papeles du Cuba, legajos 2368, cited in Nasatir, *Before Lewis and Clark*, II, 739; Annie Heloise Abel (ed.), *Tabeau's Narrative of Loisel's Expedition to the Upper Missouri*, 170–71.

included those more affluent merchants who were members of Clamorgan's Discoverers and Explorers of the Missouri, a powerful company with plans to monopolize the trade of the entire Lower and Middle Missouri Valley. When Sarpy and Cabanné failed to establish an understanding between the Pawnees and Kansas, Clamorgan's group—at least from the standpoint of Spanish commercial regulations—was awarded the Kansa trade. However, his position was everything but secure. In the eyes of most traders he symbolized the dangerous force of monopoly, and in this his principal opponent was Manuel Lisa, a fiery but brilliant Spaniard whose objective was not unlike that of Clamorgan. While Lisa and his agents (comprising the third group) made some inroads against Clamorgan's attempted monopoly, a fourth group, the powerful Laclede-Chouteau clan, was busy fighting Lisa. At the same time, Auguste and Pierre Chouteau were hopeful of dominating the Kansa trade, a plan which appeared reasonable from the vantage point of the Osage monopoly they had enjoyed for a number of years. The four groups fought intensely among themselves, with little regard for the welfare of the Indians. Yet they often found a common meeting ground in the threat of better-supplied British traders and in their concern over what implementation of official U.S. Indian policy in Louisiana after 1803 might mean.[10]

Perhaps in anticipation of Pike's mission to the Pawnee village, General Wilkinson formed a loose alliance with the Chouteaus. On

[10] Zenon Trudeau to François Carondelet, St. Louis, May 31, 1794, No. 185, Carondelet to Trudeau, New Orleans, July 12, 1794, Juan Manuel de Salcedo to Charles Delassus, New Orleans, February 3, 1802, Delassus to Salcedo, No. 142, St. Louis, May 13, 1802, Archivo General de Indias, Sección Papeles du Cuba, legajos 77, 2363, 2364, 2367, Regulations for the Illinois Trade, St. Louis, October 15, 1793, Bancroft Library, cited in Nasatir, *Before Lewis and Clark*, I, 86, 112, 186–91; Summary by Delassus of Trade Licenses Issued at St. Louis, 1799–1804, and Sarpy and Cabanné to Caso Calvo, New Orleans, April 26, 1800, Bundle, Indian Trade and Fur Companies, MHS; Delassus to Caso Calvo, St. Louis, November 29, 1800, Bancroft Library; Clamorgan to Casa Calvo, New Orleans, April 27, 1801, Clamorgan Collection, MHS; Salcedo to Delassus, New Orleans, February 3, 1802, Archivo General de Indias, Sección Papeles du Cuba, legajos 2367, cited in *ibid.*, II, 592, 614–15, 622–23, 635, 672; Phillips, *The Fur Trade*, II, 230, 237–41; Oglesby, *Manuel Lisa*, 15–19; Milo M. Quaife (ed.), "The Journals of Captain Meriwether Lewis and Sergeant John Ordway Kept on the Expedition of Western Exploration, 1803–1806," *Wisconsin Historical Publications Collections*, XXII (1916), 400.

July 17, 1804, acting on Wilkinson's recommendation, Secretary of War Henry Dearborn appointed Pierre Chouteau Indian agent for the District of Upper Louisiana. Even though Lisa's economic power was then in ascendance, Wilkinson, as the first U.S. governor of Louisiana, was probably aware of the Chouteaus' considerable influence with the powerful Osages and how it might be expanded to include other tribes. With Pierre's appointment, then, the Chouteaus secured an important advantage with the Osages, and with little difficulty it was enlarged to include the Kansas after Pike's mission of 1806. Pierre served Wilkinson and the government until March 7, 1807, at which time William Clark was named to succeed him. Like his predecessor, Clark was no novice in frontier politics; he understood well the importance of working through established traders, so, in spite of the rigorous requirements of the federal licensing system, the Chouteaus' economic privilege among the Kansas remained virtually intact.[11]

After the meeting with Pike at the Pawnees' Republican River village, the Kansas joined the Osages to spend the winter of 1806–1807 hunting and trapping on the tributaries of the Arkansas and Lower Smoky Hill rivers. When they returned to their main village at Blue Earth River and their old trading camps near the mouth of the Kansas, they found few traders awaiting them and little demand for their peltry. Although this condition was partly a result of the struggle between the various trading interests, it was also a consequence of the War Department's determination—on the basis of Clark's advice—to establish the factory system and enforce the federal Indian statutes in that region.

With Jefferson and Dearborn receiving unfavorable reports about the activity of private traders, plus additional evidence of continued Spanish influence among the Kansas and Osages, the decision to build the Fort Osage factory on the Missouri was made. Construction of the triangle-shaped fort, located about forty miles below the mouth of the Kansas River and "handsomely situated . . . [to provide] an extensive view up and down the river," probably began in early September, 1808. George C. Sibley, late assistant

11 Carter, *Territorial Papers*, XIII, 31–32; *ibid.*, XIV, 109.

factor at Fort Bellefontaine, was appointed head factor, and on October 2 troops to garrison the post began to arrive. Sibley quickly took the position that only licensed traders should be allowed to deal with the Indians, a philosophy which was in agreement with the government's general plan to encourage the various tribes to conduct their commercial transactions under the watchful eye (and military protection) of the factor.[12]

Theoretically, the new system was an obvious improvement over previous conditions; in practice, the Fort Osage experiment was plagued with problems. As early as June, 1808, Governor Lewis decided to issue no more commercial permits until a military force was stationed in Indian country. The private traders objected almost immediately because of what Lewis called "their blind infatuation for the possession of peltry and fur." The Kansas were no less disturbed. Unaccustomed to traveling so far to reach the traders, they became insolent and resorted to robbing and abusing the few traders who dared to enter Indian country in defiance of the government's embargo.

In desperation, the poorly provisioned Kansas finally realized the necessity of making the long and dangerous trip to Fort Osage. Some arrived on September 27, 1808, hungry and understandably anxious to smoke the peace pipe. More came each day, so that by October 10 nearly one thousand were camped in the vicinity of the factory. According to Sibley, they asked his forgiveness for having mistreated the traders and requested permission to "settle" near the post, something which they obviously had no intention of doing.

After much bickering, trading finally commenced on the twelfth; by the sixteenth Sibley "was induced to shut the store against them on account of their insolent and violent conduct." Later he explained to Secretary Dearborn that the Kansas had "evinced a disposition to persue a line of conduct toward the Factor, which they had been accustomed to shew towards their

[12] *Ibid.*, XIV, 198–99, 220; Bolton, "Papers of Zebulon M. Pike," 817; Brooks, "George C. Sibley's Journal," 169–70; Robert W. Frazer, *Forts of the West*, 75–76.

traders." A complete halt to all commercial intercourse made the Kansas "very humble" and, in Sibley's opinion, "brought [them] to a true sense of their situation."

However humble and sensible they may have appeared to Sibley, the Kansas clearly were not pleased with the new arrangement. Despite Sibley's assertion that Fort Osage was easily accessible, it was well over one hundred miles from the main Kansa village and at least two hundred miles from the principal area where they did most of their hunting and trapping. Moreover, while traveling in families and large groups, the Kansas were vulnerable to the lightning-like attacks of small Iowa, Sac, and Pawnee raiding parties. It is hardly surprising, then, that Kansa spokesmen repeatedly complained to Chouteau about the traders' failure to visit their villages, as had been the custom in the past.[13]

Renewed conflict between the Kansas and Pawnees in 1809 further hampered the successful operation of the Fort Osage factory, and it became apparent to Sibley that until he could personally confer with leaders of both tribes, the government's authority in the region would remain marginal. Increasing animosity between the Kansas and the Republican River Pawnees over hunting grounds in the Lower Republican and Middle Kansas valleys, a factional struggle for leadership among the Pawnees—involving an irresponsible and abortive attempt by Chief Sharitarish to establish his authority over all the Republican, Kitkehahkis, and Grand Pawnees—and the repeated stealing of horses and other property by both groups of antagonists brought on the conflict. Perhaps it was Sharitarish's desire to impress his fellow tribesmen that encouraged him to pick unnecessary quarrels with the Kansas, who took the initiative and attacked the Pawnee's main village on the Republican. The surprise attack by about one hundred warriors was no contest. A high-ranking Pawnee chief and his family of fifteen were swiftly killed, and forty others died trying to escape. As a result,

[13] Brooks, "George C. Sibley's Journal," 178; Carter, *Territorial Papers*, XIV, 199–242, 344; Gregg, "Fort Osage," 445; Jackson, *Letters of Lewis and Clark*, 480.

the Pawnees were forced to abandon the Republican site in favor of a new location on the Platte.[14]

News of the Kansa attack was a source of great concern among the traders, especially those associated with Manuel Lisa's newly organized St. Louis Missouri Fur Company, and the Chouteaus, who had substantial investments in the operation. One member of a company expedition to the Mandan and Gros Ventre villages which left St. Louis in the late spring of 1809 wrote:

The Cansas have long been the terror of the neighboring Indians, their temerity is hardly credible; a few weeks since a band of 100 warriors entered the Paunie village, or what is more generally called the Paunies Republic, and killed the principal chief and his family of 15 souls; they were immediately pursued and upwards of 40 of them cut to pieces; these people cannot be at peace with the white or red people; they rob, murder and destroy when opportunity offers; fortunately for their neighbors, they are few in number, and their daily outrages serve to lessen their numbers still more . . . .[15]

Adding, perhaps, to the company's fear that the Kansas and/or Pawnees might obstruct the movement of large (and expensive) expeditions to the Upper Missouri, this information probably came to Sibley's attention at Fort Osage not long after William Clark in St. Louis had informed Secretary Dearborn that a large party of Sacs was "out at War on the Missouri against the Kanzas and Osages." Collectively, such reports convinced Sibley that in order to protect the St. Louis merchants and the national interest as stipulated by official factory regulations, he must visit the Kansa and Pawnee villages and seek a formal reconciliation. Even though he was "seriously and earnestly cautioned not to trust [them]," the Kansas held no particular brief against the United States at that time; in fact they welcomed the visit of a prominent white spokesman—and possibly some traders—to their Blue Earth village. Cer-

[14] Jackson, "Journey to the Mandans," 184; Coues, *The Expeditions of Zebulon Montgomery Pike*, II, 407; Hyde, *Pawnee Indians*, 102–105.
[15] Jackson, "Journey to the Mandans," 184.

tainly this kind of arrangement was preferable to traveling the long and possibly dangerous route to Fort Osage.[16]

Peaceful conditions prevailed in the Kansas and Republican valleys in the months following the Kansa victory over the Pawnees. As a result, Sibley postponed his peace and fact-finding mission until the spring of 1811. Finally, on May 11, accompanied by two interpreters, eleven Osage scouts, and a prominent Osage war chief, Sans Oreille, Sibley left Fort Osage. Following the Osage hunting trace to the Missouri and then "North 70 [degrees] West" to the Kansas River, the government factor was cordially greeted some distance from the main village by Chief Shone-gee-ne-gare and about one hundred Kansa warriors. At the village he was received "with all the courtly etiquette and ceremony used by these people on what they consider[ed] a great and very important occasion." Indeed, the almost continuous feasting and kind attention provided were, in Sibley's words, "much more than had [been] expected."[17]

In contrast to the barbarous characterization of the Kansas by spokesmen for the Missouri Fur Company, Sibley was favorably impressed with what he observed at Blue Earth. The 128 lodges, located on the north bank of the Kansas River, were "rather neat and cleanly" in appearance, and the Kansas "certainly [were] by no means insensible to the virtue and importance of cleanliness." Near the village were about a hundred acres of corn, beans, and pumpkins recently planted by the women, and in sight of the town was a beautiful prairie where hundreds of children were herding a large number of fine-quality horses and mules. All was "bustle busy hum and merriment," for the tribe was planning the summer buffalo hunt, which Sibley described as "the greatest enjoyment of their life." Particularly gratifying were the "several flags with the Stars and Stripes, flying in different parts of the town, besides the large and handsome one that gracefully waved over the lodge of the great chief." In the past they had been "the terror of the lower

[16] Carter, *Territorial Papers*, XIV, 271; Brooks, "George C. Sibley's Journal," 173–74.

[17] Brooks, "George C. Sibley's Journal," 170–73.

Missouri," but the Kansas now convinced Sibley they were under-going a truly significant reformation. Upon his return to Fort Osage later that summer, he wrote Clark in St. Louis: "I assure you that I have great hopes of the Kansas becoming one of the best tribes in your agency."[18]

Yet Sibley's rather idyllic description of conditions at the Blue Earth village was somewhat exaggerated. Henry Marie Bracken-ridge, who visited Fort Osage about the time Sibley returned from his western journey, reported that a party of Osage and Kansa warriors had just arrived from an apparently successful "scalping party" against the Iowas. In their elation they abused the traders and caused such repeated disturbances that the guards were ordered to whip one warrior into submission with a cat-o'-nine-tails. An event of this sort, involving a small party of warriors far removed from the main body of their respective tribes, was hardly unique at a remote government post like Fort Osage, but from a broader perspective it was perhaps symptomatic of a deep-seated division developing within the Kansa political realm. Even Sibley recog-nized such a possibility in a note of pessimism he included in his otherwise glowing account of conditions at Blue Earth.

It was during his visit to Blue Earth that the Fort Osage factor first observed the patriarchal character of Kansa society, an arrange-ment whereby the tribe was governed by a head chief and a council composed of the oldest and most distinguished warriors. Apparent-ly this traditional political system was then undergoing significant modification because of what Sibley referred to as "the jealousies arising from the ambitions, and turbulent dispositions of some of the [younger] and minor chiefs." However, his appraisal of the situation was at best an oversimplification. It involved no realistic consideration of the war-game patterns common to most tribes of the prairie-plains, nor did it recognize increasing Kansa friction with the Pawnees and other tribes to the northeast. It also ignored the significant adjustments which the Kansas were forced to make in accordance with the government's factory system. Nevertheless, Sibley, who may have been anxious to impress his superiors in St.

[18] *Ibid.*, 174–77; Sibley to William Clark, July 22, 1811, Sibley Papers.

Louis and Washington, concluded that the head chief, "a man of sense and firmness, as well as a great warrior," would soon reestablish his authority.[19]

Sibley's primary objective was to effect a peaceful understanding between the Kansas and Pawnees. Accompanied by representatives of the Kansas and Osages, he left the Blue Earth village on May 22; six days later his party reached the new Pawnee village near the confluence of the Loup and Platte rivers. After informing his hosts that he had come to fulfill the promises made by Pike in 1806, Sibley distributed U.S. flags and medals among chiefs representing the Kansas, the Osages, and three additional bands of Pawnees and told them that in the future they would be allowed to enjoy "free and uninterrupted" trade with the government factory at Fort Osage. Vague as it was, this promise—and a liberal distribution of gifts—impressed the various headmen, who in return pledged to keep the peace. "How long it will remain so," wrote Sibley, "remains to be proved."[20]

The events of the next few years demonstrated that Sibley's caution in the matter was justified. Unable to forget their defeat and forced evacuation of the Republican Valley at the hands of the Kansas in 1809, Sharitarish and the Pawnees attacked the Blue Earth village in 1812. Under the brilliant leadership of Burning Hart, the outnumbered Kansas again defeated the Pawnees, who this time lost eighty of their best warriors and nearly all of their horses.

With a second major victory in less than five years, the Kansas might have been satisfied to respect the promises made on the Platte in the spring of 1811; yet from their point of view, nothing could have been less logical. A visitor to their village at the time reported that it was a maxim to raise to the ranks of chief only those "who [had] most distinguished themselves in the stratagems of the field." Before the 1812 encounter, Burning Hart had been a relatively obscure figure; now he enjoyed considerable status, and other

[19] Henry Marie Brackenridge, *Views of Louisiana Together With a Journal of a Voyage Up the Missouri River in 1811*, 217–18; Brooks, "George C. Sibley's Journal,"176–77.
[20] Brooks, "George C. Sibley's Journal," 178–79, 188–89.

92

minor warriors—fully aware of the head chief's inability to contend with a young, popular war chief—were probably more than anxious to pick up where Burning Hart had left off. There was also the attraction of obtaining plunder, as well as a more secure foothold in the Platte Valley. In any case, there followed a poorly planned Kansa attack on the Loup River Pawnees (probably in late 1812), a stinging defeat, and the death of thirty of the Kansas' most prized warriors.

Among many other Indians of the Trans-Missouri West, the loss of 30 warriors would not have greatly diminished the tribe's ability to wage war, but the Kansas were limited in number. Never having more than 500 warriors in historical times, they had been reduced to about 450 fighting men by the beginning of the nineteenth century. With the loss of 30 more in 1812, their position—in terms of competition for a fair share of the natural fur and skin supply, as well as a capacity to contend with the white man's advance—was not at all enviable.[21]

Following their defeat by the Pawnees, one observer, who considered the Kansas the "greatest scoundrels of the Missouri," described them as virtually "humbled."[22] Had it been known to them, this evaluation would no doubt have been challenged by some factions then contending for a leadership position within the tribe. In 1812 the Osages (who dominated the area generally south and east of Kansa country) and the Otoes (whose lands were mainly to the north) were at war, for reasons similar to those underlying the Kansa-Pawnee conflict. The Kansas, by now at least nominal allies of the Osages, were soon drawn into the struggle. Not long after the Pawnee's victory, an Otoe war party, returning from an "irruption" into Osage country, passed near the Kansa village. One member dropped behind and stole several horses that had been left unguarded. Within a short time he was intercepted by a party of Kansas, who beat him, discharged a gun loaded only with powder into his face, and recovered the horses; however, the Otoe recov-

[21] Hyde, *Pawnee Indians*, 105–106; *James' Account of S. H. Long's Expedition*, XV, 91–92; Amos Stoddard, *Sketches, Historical and Descriptive, of Louisiana*, 462; Perrin Du Lac, *Travels through the Two Louisianas*, 56.
[22] Brackenridge, *Views of Louisiana*, 75.

ered and was able to reach his own village. In the spring of 1813 a war party from this village returned to avenge the insult and in a surprise raid killed five Kansa women and children. In this manner the Kansa-Otoe war, which continued intermittently until the fall of 1816, was precipitated.[23]

The Kansa fur trade remained in a state of disorder. The continued threat of Indian attacks on their main village prevented the Kansas from taking advantage of Sibley's offer to trade "free and uninterrupted" at Fort Osage. At the same time, certain private traders complained to Secretary of War William Eustis that the government's factory system was dividing the various tribes into factions, thus making their villages vulnerable to their enemies. Such complaints, of course, must be understood within the context of the traders' concern over too much government competition, but they contained at least a grain of truth. At times the Kansas clearly were victims of conditions that prevented them from taking full advantage of the government's regulatory machinery at Fort Osage; as a consequence, they were encouraged to continue the old practice of waiting for the traders to come to them. By this time, however, many merchants, including Lisa's group, were more interested in the fur resources of the Upper Missouri. Not many bothered to venture into the Kansas and Arkansas valleys, and those who did faced the risk of becoming involved in the various intertribal disputes. Some, in fact, were badly treated and robbed of their merchandise.

There is no doubt that the Kansas, plagued with internal dissensions, were increasingly contemptuous of the white man's promises and his bargaining techniques. Ezekiel Williams, for example, who may have been one of Lisa's hunters, was robbed and held captive for a time by a Kansa hunting party on the Arkansas in June, 1813. Although some of his merchandise was eventually recovered by Sibley, Williams' experience is a good example of what Brackenridge had warned of as early as 1811. The Kansas, he said, "have rarely, if ever, been known to spill blood of a white man . . . [but] when a white hunter is found on their lands, they take his furs & his arms; he is then beaten with ramrods and driven off."[24]

[23] "Notes on the Missouri River," 348–49.

Under these distressing conditions the Fort Osage factory and the government's policies were of little benefit to the Kansas. On the basis of licenses granted in 1816 and 1817, Gabriel and Francis Chouteau were legally entitled to trade with the Kansas, probably near the mouth of the Kansas River.[25] In 1818 Colonel John O'Fallon, nephew of William Clark and sutler at recently established Cantonment Martin on Cow Island, located in the Missouri River channel just below present-day Atchison, reported he would make "4 or 500 dollars by the [Kansa] Indian trade" that season; that he was officially licensed is exceedingly doubtful.[26]

Widespread evidence that the government was unable to make the licensing system effective through its factory at Fort Osage was encouragement for a host of unlicensed traders to provide the Chouteaus with what amounted to unrestrained competition, especially following the burst of economic activity that characterized the Missouri frontier after the Panic of 1819. While some of Chouteau's men were robbed of horses and merchandise by roving Kansa war parties, other unlicensed traders went after the Kansa trade with a vengeance. Writing to Secretary of War John C. Calhoun in November, 1819, Indian Agent Benjamin O'Fallon (the younger brother of John O'Fallon) complained: "During the season of Trade, the poor creatures [the Indians] are kept in a State of Confusion, by dozens [of traders] at the same time, pulling them in as many opposite directions to accomplish their necessary interests."[27] What can only be described as a vicious struggle for an exceedingly limited supply of pelts on the Lower Missouri was taking place. For

[24] Carter, *Territorial Papers*, XIV, 587–89; John C. Luttig, *Journal of a Fur-Trading Expedition on the Upper Missouri, 1812–1813*, 35; "Ezekiel Williams' Adventures in Colorado," Missouri Historical Society *Collections*, IV (1913), 199–205; Frederic E. Voelker, "Ezekiel Williams of Boon's Lick," Missouri Historical Society, *Bulletin*, VIII (1951), 19–24; Brackenridge, *Views of Louisiana*, 218.

[25] Carter, *Territorial Papers*, XV, 191, 378.

[26] John O'Fallon to T. A. Smith, November 5, 1818, manuscript copy of "The Pioneer Soldiers of Missouri, Kansas and Iowa," William Barclay Napton Papers, Manuscript Division, KSHS.

[27] Deposition taken for George C. Sibley, Representing Demur and Chouteau, by Basil and Brusierre of Howard County, Missouri, n.d., 1817, Indian Papers, MHS; John W. Steiger, "Benjamin O'Fallon," in LeRoy R. Hafen (ed.), *The Mountain Men and the Fur Trade of the Far West*, V, 263.

the Kansa trade alone there were, according to one recent calculation, at least "four groups and an unknown number of legal and illegal independents contend[ing] for a business which could support only one."[28]

From all sides pressure was mounting in support of change, even to the point of abandoning the factory system. On the basis of some less than objective evidence provided by the Chouteau interests, Ninian Edwards, first governor of Illinois Territory, asserted that the factor often evaded his official responsibilities and thus was "not prone to a zealous performance of a business in which he [had] no personal interest." It was a telling kind of argument, similar to that of Senator Thomas H. Benton of Missouri, outspoken advocate of unbridled frontier expansion, and Ramsay Crooks, John Jacob Astor's "right hand in the extension of the business of the American Fur Company." Secretary Calhoun charged that the private traders often supported their favorite chief, thus producing "intestine commotions and division in the tribe." Another dimension was added to the debate by John R. Bell, a scientist attached to the Long Expedition. Bell told the Senate Committee on Indian Affairs that the tribes in the vicinity of the mouth of the Kansas River preferred to deal with private traders "because [they] offered better goods at lower prices." To this Benton added that the yearly commerce at Fort Osage—like that of most government factories—was less than the factor's annual salary alone. Crooks complained, without supporting evidence, that reports of private traders cheating and encouraging violence in Indian country were greatly exaggerated, while Sibley asserted perceptively that his position as an official factor was not unlike that of "a wretch under sentence of death."

As expected, the factory system was officially abandoned in 1822. After this date the government, through statutes passed in 1822 and 1824, simply increased the bonds required of licensed traders, extended the time limit of the licenses, and authorized the various Indian agents to designate the legal places where trade could be conducted. On the basis of their close relationship with

[28] Richard E. Oglesby, "The Fur Trade as Business," in John Francis McDermott (ed.), *The Frontier Re-examined*, 118.

the powerful American Fur Company, their influence with Indian Bureau officials on the frontier, their experience with the government's licensing system, and their good standing with the powerful Osages, the Chouteaus were now able virtually to dominate the Kansa trade from their government-designated posts at Kawsmouth and in the Lower Kansa Valley.[29]

While the factor's authority in the fur trade was thus obliterated, the Kansas found it desirable either to improve or clarify their relationships with the federal government and the recalcitrant Otoes. During the War of 1812 William Clark reported to Secretary of War John Armstrong that the British were making "great exertions" to win the allegiance of the Kansas and the other Missouri River tribes and use them as one means of driving the American population from the Trans-Mississippi West. Whether the British actually carried on negotiations with the Kansa leadership is not known; after the Treaty of Ghent, however, the War Department lost little time in arranging "friendship treaties" with a number of tribes, including one negotiated with the Kansas at St. Louis by Ninian Edwards and Auguste Chouteau on October 28, 1815. Following the usual distribution of an undisclosed quantity of presents, the three principal headmen—Cayegettsazesheegaw (Old Chief), Cayezettanzaw (Big Chief), and Cayebasneenzaw (Little Chief)—and sixteen prominent warriors agreed, in the tradition of earlier talks with Pike and Sibley, to live in perpetual peace under the protection of the United States.[30]

It was one thing to negotiate such a treaty, but quite another to convince either the British or the Kansas that the government had the power and determination to establish its authority in Indian country. Not until 1817 was an official friendship treaty negotiated with the Otoes.[31] Meanwhile, their animosity toward the Kansas

---

[29] Coman, "Government Factories," 374–84; Royal B. Way, "The United States Factory System for Trading with the Indians, 1796–1822," *Mississippi Valley Historical Review*, VI (1919), 234; Steiger, "Benjamin O'Fallon," 270; Adams, "Reminiscences of Frederick Chouteau," 433; Gilbert J. Garraghan, *Catholic Beginnings in Kansas City, Missouri*, 48; W. H. Miller, *The History of Kansas City*, 12.

[30] Carter, *Territorial Papers*, XIV, 787–88; Charles J. Kappler (comp. and ed.), *Indian Affairs: Laws and Treaties*, II, 123–24.

[31] Kappler, *Indian Affairs*, II, 139.

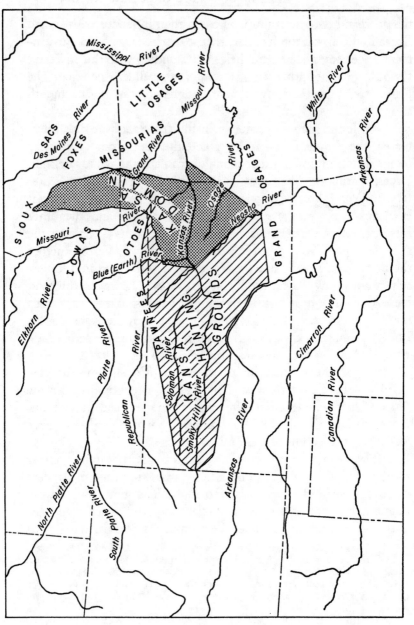

The Kansa domain, 1816–18, based on the notes of Auguste Chouteau
and George C. Sibley

was matched by occasional attacks by both tribes on the strategic Missouri River fur traffic. According to a map based on notes prepared by Auguste Chouteau in February, 1816, the Otoes, like their Pawnee allies in the Upper Kansas, Republican, and Platte valleys, represented a formidable obstacle to Kansa penetration of the lucrative fur country of the Upper Missouri.[32] Under such circumstances, then, it is understandable that the Kansas were anxious to talk peace with the Otoes, even in spite of the surprise Otoe assault of 1813. Finally, in the fall of 1816, the Otoes sent word by a trader indicating that if the Kansas desired to smoke the pipe, they would make some of their headmen available for that purpose at their village near Council Bluffs. After considerable delay, apparently caused by the Otoes' absence on a hunting expedition, eight Kansa spokesmen arrived at the Otoe village in the spring of 1817, only to discover that the Otoes had recently fled in the face of an alleged approach by hostile Sioux from the north. Two of the Kansa party proceeded on to the temporary Otoe camp to announce their arrival; in their absence, an Otoe war party, motivated by what one white traveler called "their diabolical passions," surprised and killed the six Kansas who remained behind.[33]

Such disturbances, coupled with claims by some western newspaper editors that Indian attacks were mainly sponsored by the British, prompted the War Department to sponsor the Yellowstone Expedition of 1818–19, a major objective of which was to erect a fort at the mouth of the Yellowstone River. Secretary Calhoun later revised his initial plan to include several expeditions, among them Major Stephen H. Long's scientific survey and a strategic display of military power among the Indian tribes of the Missouri Valley. Zoologist Thomas Say was attached to the Long Expedition; it was he who was so cordially welcomed at the Kansas' Blue Earth village in August, 1819. The military mission, first commanded by Colonel Thomas A. Smith and then by Captain Wyly

[32] Map Exhibiting the Territorial limits of Several Nations and Tribes of Indians agreeable to the Notes of A. Chouteau reduced & laid down on a Scale of 80 miles to the inch by R. Paul, February, 1816, Map No. 884, Tube 702, Cartographic Branch, National Archives (cited hereafter as NA).
[33] "Notes on the Missouri River," 349.

Martin, erected Cantonment Martin in 1818, primarily to emphasize the government's authority. The cantonment provided personnel for an attempted reconciliation between the Kansas and the Otoes in 1819.[34]

At the Blue Earth village, which Say reached on August 20, the Kansas sought advice and protection for a peace delegation they wished to send to the Otoes and their Missouri-Iowa allies on the Lower Platte. However, John Dougherty, subagent and interpreter for the recently established Indian agency for the Upper Missouri, denied them immediate assistance; rather, he suggested they send a delegation to meet Agent Benjamin O'Fallon and Captain Martin's troops at Cow Island. Anxious to pursue virtually any course of action that might contribute to an understanding with the Otoes, the Kansas readily agreed.[35]

En route to the Missouri River, the party of about 150 Kansas was joined by an Osage war party returning from an unsuccessful expedition to the Otoe village. The combined group finally arrived at Cantonment Martin on August 24. Here it quickly became apparent that the government's primary objectives were to reprimand the Kansas for past errors, impress them with a display of military technology, and warn them of the futility of abusing traders. These accomplished, Subagent Dougherty was to accompany the Kansas to the Platte and help them compromise their differences with the Otoes. By the time the Kansas reached Cow Island, Major Long's force had arrived aboard the *Western Engineer*, a shallow-draft steamboat designed to make an indelible impression on the unsuspecting Kansas.

The vessel's bow, styled in the form of "a huge serpent, black and scaly, rising out of the water . . . [and] vomiting smoke," caused great concern among the Kansas, who concluded that the Great Spirit's fire had been chained by the white man and somehow made

[34] Roger L. Nichols, *General Henry Atkinson: A Western Military Career*, 47–50.

[35] William Clark to the Secretary of War, November 15, 1829, copy from Manuscript Books, Office of Superintendent of Indian Affairs, No. 4, p. 6, Dougherty Papers, KSHS; *James' Account of S. H. Long's Expedition*, XIV, 99, 187.

to move the craft. Using this spectacular display to great advantage, Agent O'Fallon experienced little difficulty in securing quick and sweeping promises from the Kansas that they would stop abusing the traders, especially after he had informed them that the government would, if necessary, take decisive military action to enforce its policies. The grand finale to the affair was the firing of shells and rockets into the night sky, which, in O'Fallon's words, "appeared to increase much the exaulted opinion they have entertained of our means of war." He proudly reported to Sibley at Fort Osage: "I have just finished counciling with them [the Kansas]. They promise to conduct themselves better for the future. From some cause or other, a great revolution has taken place in the nation. Their deportment [is] less offensive than formerly [and] since among us [they have] conducted themselves with a good deal of circumspection."[36]

Confident that the Kansas had been properly impressed with the authority of the United States, Dougherty accompanied them to the Otoe village, then located on the left bank of the Platte about forty miles above its confluence with the Missouri.[37] According to one account, their arrival in September "threw the [Otoe] village into a ferment, in which the women evinced their indignations, and wishes for the war to continue, by loud reproaches, and threats to the messengers."[38] Another report told of great confusion. While the Kansas "lamented aloud," an Otoe woman ridiculed the visitors as "wrinkled-faced old men, with hairy chins, etc., ugly faces and flat noses." Another, whose husband had only recently been killed by a Kansa warrior, tried unsuccessfully to kill He-roch-che (Real War Eagle) while he was addressing his enemies in the council lodge.[39] Yet the Otoe leaders were receptive to tentative peace overtures, perhaps because they realized that government troops were in the area. They presented horses to He-roch-che and his

[36] *James' Account of S. H. Long's Expedition*, XIV, 175–78; Carter, *Territorial Papers*, XV, 562; George J. Remsburg, "Isle Au Vache," *TKSHS*, VIII (1903–1904), 439–40; B. O'Fallon to G. C. Sibley, August 25, 1819, Sibley Papers.
[37] Berlin Basil Chapman, *The Otoes and Missourias*, xvii; *James' Account of S. H. Long's Expedition*, XV, 102, 103.
[38] "Notes on the Missouri River," 349–50.
[39] *James' Account of S. H. Long's Expedition*, XV, 101–102.

messengers, engaged in friendly conversation, smoked the calumet, and appeared genuinely interested in at least a temporary understanding. However, nothing precise was agreed upon relative to the future, nor was any action taken with regard to the Kansa proposal that "a large level road . . . connecting our villages . . . near which no one can conceal himself" be established. He-roch-che's rather succinct statement that "our nations have made peace frequently, but a peace has not hitherto been of long duration" seems to have been a perceptive summary of the proceedings on the Lower Platte. There was, in fact, a notable lack of evidence that Dougherty was concerned over the inconclusive character of the talks. From his point of view the government had honored its promise to act as a nominal intercessor between two troublesome tribes, and this was, at least for the time being, adequate.[40]

The government's noncommittal position at the Kansa-Otoe council of 1819 was, perhaps, mainly a consequence of other negotiations already under way—negotiations which prepared the way for several land-cession treaties that would force the Kansas to abandon the Lower Missouri and Kansas valleys and clear the way for traders, land jobbers, and farmers. In the years immediately following the creation of Missouri Territory in 1812, there prevailed widespread skepticism concerning the establishment of farms and towns on the edge of the "Great American Desert," but it was not long before this attitude changed in favor of one claiming that lands in western Missouri increased in fertility as one traveled westward. Strategically situated at the mouth of the Kansas River and the Missouri Valley hinterland northwest of Fort Osage, the obstinate Kansas represented a troublesome bottleneck, indeed an obstruction, to frontier expansion. This situation, plus the repeated complaints of the traders and the apparent inability of the Kansas to live peacefully with their Indian neighbors, seemed to require decisive action on the part of the federal government.[41]

On March 16, 1818, Missouri Territorial Delegate John Scott presented to Congress a petition asking for statehood. Although

[40] Ibid., 103–105.
[41] A. Theodore Brown, Frontier Community: Kansas City to 1870, 16–17.

this request was not granted until 1821, Indian Bureau officials in the Territory reacted to the statehood movement almost immediately.[42] In St. Louis William Clark instructed Sibley at Fort Osage to "enter into a provisional arrangement with the Chiefs and principal persons of [the] Kanzas Nation, for the purchase of a portion of the Territory they claim on the waters of the Missouri and Arkansas Rivers." Sibley received his instructions sometime during the summer of 1818; on November 5 the Fort Osage factor sent Clark a memorandum concerning a preliminary land-cession treaty which had been negotiated on September 25.

Having heard Sibley's proposal and having discussed the matter "without the least persuasion or compulsion in the presence of nearly the whole of their Nation," the three principal chiefs and eight warriors had agreed to "sell" that portion of their lands lying south of the Missouri between the mouth of Tabo Creek (about eight miles east of present Lexington, Missouri) and the mouth of the Nodaway River and extending southwest in a triangular pattern to the Neosho River by way of the mouth of the Delaware, then back to the Missouri by way of the Tabo watershed.

For this vast domain the Kansas were promised $2,000 worth of cloth, vermilion, guns, ammunition, kettles, hoes, axes, knives, flints, awls, and tobacco, to be issued each September for an indefinite period; a blacksmith was also promised—to keep their guns and implements in good repair. Accompanying Sibley's claim that the immediate distribution of goods "had no sort of connection with the purchase of lands," the preliminary bargain was nevertheless sealed with a gift of goods valued at $460, "given by the Government purely as a proof of good will and motives of benevolence." And lest he be reprimanded for having gone beyond his instructions, Sibley was quick to point out: "I am certain that I can point out a tract of 20 miles square, in the Territory offered for sale . . . which will in two years . . . [be] equal to ten years of the annual payment to be made to the Kansas."[43]

[42] Edwin C. McReynolds, *Missouri: A History of the Crossroads State*, 72.
[43] Sibley to Clark, November 5, 1818, manuscript copy, Indian Papers; Memorandum of a Preliminary Treaty, September 30, 1818, Sibley Papers.

Political turmoil precipitated at the national level by the Missouri statehood movement, plus the temporary dislocation of the fur trade brought on by the Panic of 1819, influenced Congress to take no action on Sibley's preliminary treaty. On February 3, 1819, Sibley wrote Clark that the Kansas would be at Fort Osage in May and would want to know what the government had decided with regard to the purchase of their lands.[44] This brought no response, for there was apparently developing a consensus that Sibley should have negotiated for an even larger cession. While the statehood issue was being debated in Congress, Clark advised Calhoun that the Sacs and Foxes (then colliding with the powerful northern Sioux confederacy) were about to move against the tribes of the Missouri, including the Kansas.[45] Clearly, pressure for a more comprehensive Indian settlement was mounting in spite of a few temporary obstacles.

Cognizant of what was termed "the irregular form of the frontier, deeply indented by tracts of Indian territory," the Senate Committee on the Public Lands had considered, as early as January, 1817, the desirability of removing all Indians from any "intimate intercourse with the whites."[46] The committee's deliberations were well in line with what was happening on the Missouri frontier. Survey problems, private land claims, and the adjustment of pre-emption rights in the Territory had prevented widespread public-land disposal before 1818; but President Monroe authorized the public sales to begin in that year, and by early 1819 the Franklin (Howard County) land office alone was able to dispose of up to nearly a quarter of a million acres per month at an average price of $3.85 per acre.[47]

From his vantage point at Fort Osage in 1819, Agent O'Fallon complained of a brisk whiskey traffic developing with the Indians; later, in Washington, his damning testimony contributed sub-

44 Carter, *Territorial Papers*, XV, 516.

45 Chapman, *The Otoes and Missourias*, 2; William T. Hagan, *The Sac and Fox Indians*, 86.

46 Report of Senate Committee on Public Lands, January 9, 1817, cited in Prucha, *American Indian Policy*, 226.

47 Malcolm J. Rohrbough, *The Land Office Business*, 133–34.

stantially to the official end of the factory trading system.[48] To Clark he wrote that the Kansa trade should be confined to an area no farther east than the mouth of the Kansas.[49] By 1825 his complaints were buttressed by those of military officials in St. Louis, who reported that "several persons [had] moved over the Indian boundary upon the Kansas lands, and [were] erecting houses."[50]

Meanwhile, Missouri had achieved statehood and such enterprising merchants as William Becknell and Thomas James had demonstrated the economic potential of a commercial highway between the Missouri frontier and Santa Fe. In short, by the early 1820's the Indian Bureau and Congress could provide a number of very convincing reasons for pushing the Kansas farther west, beyond the boundaries Sibley had negotiated in 1818.

More than anyone else, it was Sibley who assumed a leadership role in the unfolding plan to extinguish all Kansa land claims in the new state of Missouri. On January 10, 1824, he sent a long letter to Missouri Senator David Barton in which he extolled the virtues of western Missouri and the priority of removing the Kansas from that region. Under the general appellation of "The Garden of Missouri," Sibley wrote:

Besides the uncommon excellence of the soils and beautiful aspects of the Country, it possesses other great natural advantages that would render it a garden indeed, if once settled and owned by our enterprising Citizens—This fine tract of Country [claimed by the Kansas in Missouri] now lies on unproductive Wilderness, utterly useless to the Savages who claim it; and interdicted to our People, thousands of whom are now anxiously waiting for our Govt. to purchase it, that they may enter upon it and reap from it those great advantages which it is presumable the God of nature designed to the use of Civilized Man. Were this section purchased by [the] Govt. and immediately placed in Market, the rapidity of its settlement and improvements would undoubtedly surpass that of any other part of the State or Union. Its rich and exuberant soils would quickly yield a copious overflow of valuable commodities to enrich the State. The water

48 Steiger, "Benjamin O'Fallon," 263.
49 O'Fallon to Clark, December 15, 1824, LR, OIA, St. Louis Superintendency.
50 H. T. Ruidan (?) to Sibley, March 8, 1825, Sibley Papers.

falls which are numerous . . . would soon give life to manufacturing establishments, and our State would be strengthened by the speedy accession of another community of hardy freemen. . . . I believe there are more than an Hundred instances within my own knowledge of Men with families, who are now squatters on the Public Land, who are able to purchase, but who will not 'till they can purchase in the tract I am speaking of.[51]

In sharp contrast to this laudatory view of the "Garden," Sibley emphasized the negative consequences of keeping it outside the public domain. Without the prospect of obtaining farms for their exclusive use, the settlers could not be expected to improve themselves; indeed, the real danger was the adoption of customs contrary to Sibley's concept of progress:

Meanwhile they are utterly useless to themselves or the States, living chiefly upon the bounties of wild Nature, the Venison and Honey and wild fruits of the Land. They necessarily contract habits of violence & a sort of semi-savage barbarism of manners that in some degree unfits them for the duties of civilised life. They are in short homeless wanderers, and such is the stubbornness of their Nature that they will rather remain as they are than to forego the great privilege of occupying the home of their own free choice. For my own part I could never approve that policy which seems to have been too often adopted by the General Government of refusing access to any very desirable sections of the Public Domain 'till some other sections less desirable by far are sold and settled. This sort of "Bible and Cheese" policy will never be submitted to by Emigrants.[52]

Apparently Sibley was equally persuasive with the Kansas. His counsel, taken in conjunction with the Sac and Fox threat from the north, the continued intrusions of white settlers on the Kansas' Missouri lands, and, especially, the prospect of a generous annuity settlement, convinced the Kansas that the time had come to negotiate a major land-cession treaty. Accordingly, the chiefs and principal warriors met with Clark, Sibley, and other government commissioners in St. Louis in early June, 1825, and agreed to "cede to the United States all the lands lying within the State of Missouri,

51 Sibley to Barton, January 10, 1824, Sibley Papers.
52 *Ibid.*

to which the said nation [had] title or claim."[53] In addition, the Kansas agreed to relinquish title to their lands west of Missouri,

> beginning at the entrance of the Kansas river into the Missouri river; from thence North to the North-West corner of the State of Missouri; from thence Westwardly to the Nodewa river, thirty miles from its entrance of the big Nemahaw river into the Missouri, and with that river to its source; from thence to the source of the Kansas river, leaving the old village of the Pania Republic to the West, from thence, on the ridge dividing the waters of the Kansas river from those of the Arkansas, to the Western boundary of the State line of Missouri, and with that line, thirty miles, to the place of beginning.[54]

For this generous cession the tribe was granted a $3,500 annuity for a period of twenty years and a reservation thirty miles wide, beginning twenty leagues west of the mouth of the Kansas River and extending west to a point to be determined by the President upon the completion of an official survey.[55]

Other stipulations of the treaty clearly established the government's intention of forcing an economic revolution upon the Kansas. To discourage trapping and the chase, the commissioners included an article authorizing the government to provide agricultural implements, 300 cattle, 300 hogs, and 500 domestic fowl, all to be delivered at the Kansa village. To guide them in their transition to agriculture, a blacksmith and agriculturist were also provided. The education of their children was to be funded from the sale of thirty-six choice sections of their land in the Lower Big Blue Valley just southeast of the mouth of the Kansas River. And to assist them in starting a new way of life unhampered by claims against their annuities, it was provided that the government would

[53] Kappler, *Indian Affairs*, 222.
[54] *Ibid.*
[55] *Ibid.* According to Charles C. Royce, the western limit of the Kansa lands, probably based on the government survey of Isaac McCoy, was about thirty-five miles east of the present western boundary of Kansas; see Charles C. Royce (comp.), *Indian Land Cessions in the United States*, Plate 26. In a map prepared for "Kansas or Kaw Tribe of Indians vs. United States," the line was extended some thirty miles west of the Kansas state boundary; see Map Showing the Kansas lands in the case of the Kansas or Kaw tribe of Indians vs. the United States, Court of Claims F64, June 1, 1932, Map 11321, Tube 1387, Cartographic Branch, NA.

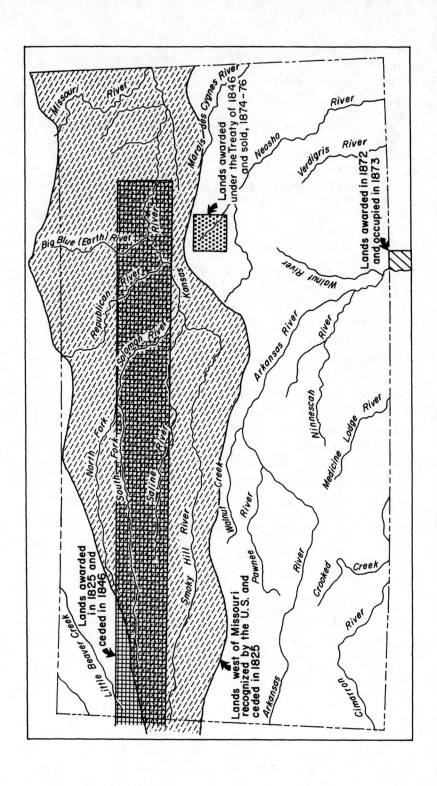

assume a $500 debt owed to Francis Chouteau, as well as other debts and/or claims to a maximum of $3,000. As an apparent inducement to a quick conclusion of the negotiations, another $2,000 worth of general merchandise was authorized for immediate distribution. Finally, of signal importance to the tribe's social and economic destiny was the promise to issue fee-simple titles for 640-acre plots to each of the twenty-three "half breeds of the Kanzas nation . . . commencing at the [eastern] line of the . . . reservation, and extending down [the northern bank of] the Kanzas river for quantity." The St. Louis negotiations were concluded on June 3 and proclaimed law on December 30, 1825.[56]

Article 11 of the treaty provided that the United States should forever enjoy the right to navigate freely the rivers and streams in the new Kansa reservation, but nothing was said about such privileges on the overland trails. The commercial value of the Santa Fe Trail had by now increased substantially, and there lurked the danger that the Kansas might obstruct this vital traffic, especially in the vast expanses of the Middle and Upper Arkansas valleys. Reacting to political pressure from Missouri and an increasing national interest in the New Mexico trade, President Monroe in 1825 approved a law providing for an official survey of the Santa Fe Trail and the maintenance of cordial relationships with the several tribes along the route. Accordingly, on August 16 of that year, Sibley, Benjamin H. Reeves, and Thomas Mathers, members of the government survey team, met several Kansa dignitaries at the Sora Kansas Creek crossing of the Santa Fe Trail (Dry Turkey Creek crossing in present McPherson County), about 240 miles southwest of Fort Osage. Here the Kansa chiefs and headmen agreed to allow the survey party to continue its work unmolested; for the negligible sum of $800 in cash or merchandise paid directly to tribal leaders, the trail was to be "forever free for the use of the citizens of the United States and of the Mexican Republic."[57] Thus were the Kansas brought under the jurisdiction of U.S. Indian policy.

From the government's point of view, solutions to a number

[56] Kappler, *Indian Affairs*, 222–25.
[57] *Ibid.*, 248–51.

of vexing problems had been found. The Kansas had been removed from the state of Missouri and close proximity to at least some of their tribal enemies. No longer would they be able to obstruct the vital commercial routes to New Mexico and the northwestern fur country. Government assistance in the form of annuities would minimize their dependence on the fur trade, and with proper guidance and instruction they would gradually shift to a more sedentary culture. Traders, agents, and half-bloods living near the eastern boundary of their lands would set the standards for a model American existence as their children learned the virtues of a settled, orderly life. At the same time, they would be allowed to make use of a sizable hunting domain to the west in the vast watershed of the Kansas River, a place where they could still practice the old way of life while adjusting to the new.

In spite of these seemingly attractive features, the government's plan was overoptimistic. Nothing had been done to arrange an acceptable understanding with the Pawnees and other wide-ranging tribes who by tradition claimed a share of the hunting grounds assigned to the Kansas in 1825. There was no guarantee that the annuities promised would satisfy the tribe's minimum needs, nor was there evidence that a competitive trading system would benefit the Kansas, not just the traders. At that time there was talk at the national level of making the entire region west of Missouri a permanent Indian territory, but no specific assurances were made that the Kansa reservation boundaries would not be redrawn to accommodate other tribes. Moreover, the persistent activity of squatters and land speculators in American settlement history pointed to the obvious difficulty of containing even a few enterprising white men at the eastern boundary of the Kansas River Valley. Finally, there were the obvious difficulties accompanying a prescribed cultural revolution. Would the traditional Kansa political leaders be able to adjust to the new dispensation, or would they find it easier to serve as middlemen for outside interests? How would the tribe as a whole react? What role would the half-bloods be expected to play? These were some of the more difficult problems facing the Kansas in the years immediately following the treaties of 1825. A cultural crisis of major proportions was developing, but there is little evidence that government officials perceived its basic dimensions. Rather, they took the course of least resistance by assuming that the general problem had been solved, that there remained only a few minor details which would somehow be worked out, perhaps with the material and spiritual assistance of Christian missionaries.

CHAPTER 5 THE FAILURE
OF THE MISSIONARIES

An important aspect of Kansa history in the period following the treaties of 1825 was the careless, indeed illusive, manner in which the government's promises were fulfilled. Articles 3 and 4 of the negotiations concluded at St. Louis clearly stated the government's intention to provide the Kansas with the means and guidance for adjusting to a sedentary existence. Under the watchful eye of Indian Bureau agents, agriculturalists, and blacksmiths and with the aid of a financial subsidy to satisfy their basic needs during the transitional stage, the Kansas were to abandon hunting, trapping, and intertribal warfare in favor of the aspirations and mundane tasks of white frontier farmers. Though excessively optimistic, it was, perhaps, a reasonable plan. Given the circumstances of prompt and enlightened administration, as well as protection from various outside interests, the government's strategy might have succeeded in time; but these conditions did not prevail, and the Kansas—like so many other tribes—ultimately fell victim to the government's best intentions.

With the treaties of 1825 the Kansas came under the jurisdiction of the St. Louis Indian Superintendency, then headed by William Clark. Earlier, in the spring of 1824, the Upper Missouri Agency at Council Bluffs had been placed under Clark's authority, and it was to this agency, then headed by Benjamin O'Fallon, that the Kansas were assigned. In 1826 O'Fallon resigned his post, effective the following year; he was replaced by John Dougherty, an aggressive subagent at Council Bluffs who enjoyed close relationships with the Missouri Fur Company and a variety of interests besides the tribes under his jurisdiction. When federal troops withdrew from Council Bluffs in 1827 and upon the recommendation of Colonel Henry Leavenworth, Dougherty was authorized to move the Upper Missouri Agency to the recently established installation known as Cantonment Leavenworth (renamed Fort Leavenworth in 1832). The new location placed Dougherty closer to the Lower Kansas Valley, but his station was still too far from the Kansa villages to provide the tribe with regular, effective guidance. On the other hand, this change may have encouraged a few individuals, especially the half-bloods and at least one prominent chief, to abandon the Blue Earth village location, retrace their earlier route of migration, and establish a temporary settlement on the banks of the Kansas River a few miles above present-day Lawrence. Shortly thereafter and continuing for the next three years, Pawnee pressure and anticipated government benevolence encouraged a major withdrawal from the Blue Earth site, so that by 1831 there were at least three new and distinct Kansa villages, all located near the confluence of Mission Creek and the Kansas River just west of what is now Topeka.[1]

Joshua Pilcher, prominent American Fur Company official and personal enemy of Dougherty, accused Dougherty of neglecting the tribes under his immediate jurisdiction. There were sound reasons for the charge, but the subagent managed to visit the Kansas on at least two different occasions, once when they needed medical aid and again when they were in need of assistance in settling their differences with the Republican Pawnees.[2] Of greater significance

[1] William Clark to Secretary of War, November 15, 1829, typed copy, Dougherty Papers; Field Survey Notes of Major A. L. Langham, October, n.d., 1827, LR, OIA, St. Louis Superintendency; Isaac McCoy to John H. Eaton, April 20, 1831, LR, OIA, Fort Leavenworth Agency; Sketch of Kansas River and Vicinity Relating to Indian Lands, Map No. 88, Tube 55, Cartographic Branch, NA; Map of [West]ern Country by Isaac McCoy . . . 1832, Map No. 227, Tube 444, Cartographic Branch, NA; Morehouse, "History of the Kansa," 346; Edgeley W. Todd (ed.), *The Adventures of Captain Bonneville*, 21.

[2] John Dougherty to Lewis Cass, March 9, 1828, Dougherty Papers, KSHS.

in the disintegration of traditional Kansa culture, however, were the roles played by Baronet Vásquez and the Chouteau commercial clan of St. Louis. As early as December 15, 1824, O'Fallon advised Clark that the center of the Kansa trade should be shifted from Fort Osage to the area around the mouth of the Kansas River.[3] This recommendation, plus Article 2 of the St. Louis treaty of 1825, provided the justification for Clark's appointment that same year of Vásquez as subagent for the Kansas. While Dougherty probably remained in the dark concerning this administrative change, Vásquez, who held an army commission and had gained some fame as one of Zebulon Pike's interpreters, was aware of the rewards his new position might command. He confided to his brother: "I should deceive myself greatly if a great deal of money is not to be made in this place." The residence he established at Kawsmouth (near the mouth of the Kansas River) served as both a temporary Kansa subagency and the nucleus of a small settlement where the Chouteaus (with the apparent cooperation of Vásquez) continued to dominate the Kansa trade. It was also the place where Daniel Morgan Boone, Clement Lessert, and Gabriel Philebert enjoyed the financial returns from their recent appointments as Kansa agriculturalist (farmer), interpreter, and blacksmith, respectively, while displaying only the most casual interest in their official responsibilities.[4]

The untimely death of Vásquez on August 5, 1827, provided Superintendent Clark the opportunity to move the subagency farther west, to a point near the temporary Kansa settlement west of present Lawrence (just south of Williamstown). The site was believed to be on one of the allotments awarded to the Kansa half-bloods in 1825, but it was actually situated on the western edge of the Delaware Reservation as determined by the supplementary Delaware treaty of 1829, a situation which precipitated chronic difficulties between the two tribes. Here, some twenty to thirty

[3] O'Fallon to Clark, December 15, 1824, LR, OIA, St. Louis Superintendency.
[4] Garraghan, *Catholic Beginnings*, 29–30; *The History of Jackson County, Missouri, Containing a History of the County, Its Cities, Towns, Etc.*, 380; "Kansas Agencies," CKSHS, XVI (1923–25), 773.

miles east of the main Mission Creek villages, Dunning McNair and Boone acted as special agents until February, 1829, when Marston G. Clark, William Clark's cousin, was appointed Kansa subagent.[5]

As expected, Cyprian and Frederick Chouteau soon established trading posts at Mission Creek and, in spite of Clark's protests, in the immediate vicinity of the subagency headquarters. Obviously the Chouteaus were more interested in getting their hands on the Kansa annuity fund than the few skins and pelts the tribe might wish to dispose of, for with bacon at forty cents a pound, salt at twenty cents a cup, and trinkets which cost ten cents at St. Louis bringing six dollars each at Mission Creek, they were in an excellent position to profit handsomely. Subagent Clark complained bitterly of such profiteering to his cousin in St. Louis. Among other things the Chouteaus were undermining his influence with the Kansas; their sharp commercial practices were encouraging the tribe to break up into contending political factions, and the young warriors were becoming increasingly restive. Superintendent Clark may have been disturbed by these developments, but there is no evidence to indicate that he took steps to correct the situation. Petty differences between competing clans remained unsettled and in fact were soon aggravated by the arrival of Christian missionaries at the Kansa villages.[6]

Missionary activity among the North American Indians has been the subject of considerable investigation, but judging by the nature of the evidence generally used, most of the literature is excessively polemical. This is especially true of studies designed to document God's absolute and necessary role in human history. Nor

[5] Louise Barry (comp.), "Kansas Before 1854; A Revised Annals," *KHQ*, XXVIII (Spring, 1962), 41; Rothensteiner, "Early Missionary Efforts Among the Indians," 78–81; Isaac McCoy to John Eaton, January 31, 1831, Isaac McCoy Papers; William Hendricks to Francis Noble, February 17, 1829, LR, OIA, St. Louis Superintendency; Irving, *Indian Sketches*, 238–39; J. S. Chick to Thomas S. Huffaker, April 19, 1906, Joseph S. Chick Papers, Manuscript Division, KSHS; J. C. McCoy to W. W. Cone, August, n.d., 1879, John C. McCoy Papers, Manuscript Division, KSHS; Isaac McCoy to John H. Eaton, April 20, 1831, LR, OIA, Fort Leavenworth Agency.

[6] Adams, "Reminiscences of Frederick Chouteau," 433; Miller, *History of Kansas City*, 31; Marston Clark to William Clark, July 28, 1830, and Clark to F. Chouteau, December 20, 1831, LR, OIA, St. Louis Superintendency.

are some secular studies much more significant, since they often disguise a pointless antiquarianism under the cloak of alleged objectivity. Recently, anthropologists and historians have clarified at least some of the problems underlying cultural conflict and have tried to place them in a more balanced historical perspective.

In closely argued analyses of Christian Indian missions, it should be emphasized that to sympathize or denounce detracts from the more important fact that the contending groups "behaved according to their own cultural systems." While the several denominations argued whether it was proper to civilize or Christianize first (but never to the exclusion of the other), "so most Indians did not unravel the two" when the missionary arrived in their midst. Thus "each culture opposed the other as a totality," and mutual accommodation was impossible. Applied to the Kansas, however, this kind of self-defeating confrontation was not really possible, for cultural erosion at the hands of the white man preceded the arrival of the Christian missionary by at least a century.[7] In fact it is possible that the failure of early missionary efforts among the Kansas was largely a result of the Wind People's having had considerable experience with so-called white civilization before the missionary's arrival and that they were in the process of adopting certain behavioral patterns not unlike those contributing to the secularization of the missionary's own ideals.

From its frontier outpost on the Illinois side of Missouri, it was the Roman Catholic church that first attempted to take the Gospel to the "pagan" Kansas. As early as May, 1702, Father Marc Bergier, leader of a society at Cahokia known as the Seminary Priests of Quebec, advised his superiors of the opportunities the Kansas afforded for the missionary enterprise. Unlike the Osages, who were "too numerous," or the Missouris, who were "too reduced" for any immediate accomplishment, Father Bergier considered the Kansas an ideal compromise between the two.[8]

Though they may have agreed with this candid appraisal of

[7] Robert F. Berkhofer, Jr., *Salvation and the Savage*, ix, 5–6, 107.

[8] Nasatir, *Before Lewis and Clark*, I, 6; Hoffhaus, "Fort de Cavagnial," 427–28; Gilbert J. Garraghan, *Chapters in Frontier History*, 62.

the situation, there is no evidence that the Catholic hierarchy acted on Bergier's suggestion. Certainly the early years of the eighteenth century were troubled times in the Trans-Missouri West, and when viewed in the larger context of the international rivalry for the fur trade, such factors as time, distance, and a shortage of funds discouraged any immediate implementation of the priest's plan. Nevertheless, it should be noted that a majority of the trappers and traders who dealt with the Kansas before formal missionary activity was initiated were at least nominal Roman Catholics and therefore in a position to exemplify the more secular and mundane aspects of Christian behavior.

According to a record dated 1727, the French Catholic leadership in North America budgeted six hundred livres that year "for the support of a missionary at [the] Kanzas [village]," perhaps at the village visited by Bourgmont in 1724.[9] What, if anything, was done with the sum is uncertain. There is no corroborative evidence of organized mission activity until renewed Catholic interest led to an abortive attempt to convert some of the Kansas, notably the half-bloods and their children, shortly after the land cession-treaty of 1825 had been negotiated. In 1818, not long after his arrival in St. Louis, Bishop Du Bourg wrote a friend:

Turn your eyes on hundreds of Indian tribes that seem but to wait for instruction in order to embrace the faith. How touched you would be if you could be witness of the frequent deputations which I receive from them, the religious respect which they testify to me, and the urgent prayers which they address to me, to be their father, to visit them, and to give them men of God.[10]

Du Bourg's concern for the Indians was partly the result of information and encouragement from Superintendent William Clark and Catholic fur traders at St. Louis. Pointing out that several Protestant groups, particularly the Baptists, were interested in extending their influence to check what Lewis Cass called the Catholic propensity to emphasize "speculative creeds and unmeaning ceremonies," Clark in 1825 urged Father Charles Felix Van

9 Morehouse, "History of the Kansa," 338.
10 Rothensteiner, "Early Missionary Efforts Among the Indians," 62.

Quickenbourne of the St. Louis Diocese to establish a mission at the Kansas' agency.[11]

Several years passed before the Baptists and other Protestant denominations entered the field, but the Catholics took no chances. Among other things, Article 5 of the 1825 treaty provided "that thirty-six sections of good lands on the Big Blue river [just south of the mouth of the Kansas], shall be laid out . . . and sold for the purpose of raising a fund, to be applied, under the direction of the President, to the support of schools for the education of the Kanzas children."[12] Totaling 23,040 acres and worth nearly $30,000 at the minimum government price, these heavily timbered and strategically located sections represented an attractive means for Christian leaders to finance at least part of their missionary work. The federal government was not then opposed to supporting organized religion, especially since the various denominations took the position that "civilization [that is, education in the broadest sense] and Christianity were inextricably combined."[13]

Initially, the Catholics enjoyed certain advantages beyond a financial commitment from the government and the cooperation of the St. Louis traders. By authorizing the half-bloods to receive the twenty-three prize sections of land immediately east of the newly created Kansa Reservation, the government—perhaps unknowingly —encouraged the spread of political dissent within the tribe; those chiefs who received no land grants were understandably disturbed, while others with half-blood connections claimed a superior status. At the same time, the latter group appreciated the importance, indeed the necessity, of cultivating closer relationships with the government and the missionaries. As the tribe moved east after 1825, Fool Chief, Hard Chief, and American Chief, with no apparent half-blood relations, located their villages well within the boundaries of the new reservation. Chief White Plume, on the other hand, established his much smaller village near the government agency, probably because of his daughter's marriage to Louis

---

[11] Lewis Cass, "Indians of North America," *North American Review*, XIII (1826), 115; Garraghan, *Catholic Beginnings*, 27–28.

[12] Kappler, *Indian Affairs*, 223.

[13] Berkhofer, *Salvation and the Savage*, 6, 25.

Gonville (a French trader) and the awarding of four half-blood grants to his grandchildren. With pressure exerted on him by pro-Catholic government officials, White Plume soon found himself alienated, at least in part, from the more influential members of his tribe; and it was he, not the three chiefs at Mission Creek, whom the Catholic fathers exploited as a means of gaining a foothold with the Kansas.[14]

In an apparent effort to make the government's agency more responsive to the Kansas' needs, Superintendent Clark invited Chief White Plume to confer with him at St. Louis in the spring of 1827. Here the surprisingly articulate Kansa leader, an Osage by birth, who enjoyed his position by acts of bravery and tribal election, had an opportunity to describe some of the problems his people faced. He told Clark of increasing competition between contending villages and factions and the danger of having too many chiefs, which by implication he attributed to the repeated interference of government officials and unprincipled agents. He feared that by his association with the white man he might lose certain lands near the main Kansa villages that rightfully belonged to his children, and he complained bitterly of the corrupt and unpredictable manner in which the annuities were distributed. To establish cordial relations, he demanded a restatement of the government's good faith and intentions, a substantial stone house for himself near the agency headquarters, and an unmarried or "single Catholic priest" to minister to himself and his people.[15]

Aware of the official plan to sell the tribe's education lands and thus make it possible for some organized group to "civilize" the Kansas, Bishop Rosati of the St. Louis Diocese was understandably interested in White Plume's request, as was Joseph Anthony Lutz, an ambitious young priest who only recently had been assigned to

[14] Cone, *Historical Sketch of Shawnee County*, 6–7; McCoy, *History of Baptist Indian Missions*, 393; Barry, "Kansas Before 1854," XXVIII (Spring, 1962), 59; Connected plat of the survey of the half breed Kansas Indians, A. L. Langham, Surv., 1827, Map No. 94, Tube 60, Cartographic Branch, NA.

[15] White Plume's speech to Clark, May 17, 1827, LR, OIA, St. Louis Superintendency; Marshall, "Journals of Jules De Munn," 325–26; Thomas S. Huffaker to John Martin, May 28, 1910, Thomas Sears Huffaker Papers, Manuscript Division, KSHS.

St. Patrick's Parish in St. Louis. At Lutz's request, Rosati appointed him "Missionary Priest With the Kanzas" with orders to use Vásquez' subagency home at Kawsmouth as a temporary mission station. However, the subagent's untimely death from cholera as he was escorting Lutz to the Indian country in the summer of 1828 necessitated a change in plans. Rather than return to St. Louis, the young priest decided to make a "preliminary" trip to the new subagency some sixty-five miles farther west, where the government had only recently relocated it and where also had been erected the stone mansion requested by White Plume.[16]

Lutz's efforts among the Kansas were anything but successful, even though he made some temporary inroads among the half-bloods. He arrived at the subagency on August 19, 1828, and established his residence with Dunning McNair, who after Vásquez' death served for a short time as a government annuity commissioner. White Plume, who was ill at the time, was elated to have a Tabasco (Black Robe) visit him in person. Through an interpreter he announced:

O, my Father, you are welcome. At last you are here whom I have so long desired. I am happy; but I would rejoice still more if I could celebrate you coming in perfect health. May the Great Healer (Washkanta), I pray, restore my health. It is my intention to assist you in all things that you wish to do among the Kansas.[17]

Knowing that White Plume's recovery was prerequisite to his being able to carry on God's work with the tribe as a whole, Lutz determined "to leave no stone unmoved in order to restore his health." Taking a cue from his French interpreters, he "superseded the medicine with a goblet of rich wine," which had such a pleasing (and apparently therapeutic) effect that the Indian leader readily agreed to use his influence to bring the inhabitants of the other villages to Lutz when they returned from the buffalo country. Meanwhile, the missionary priest busied himself with erecting a

16 Garraghan, *Catholic Beginnings*, 27–29, 33–34; John C. McCoy to W. W. Cone, August ?, 1879, John C. McCoy Papers; Todd, *Captain Bonneville*, 21.

17 Garraghan, *Catholic Beginnings*, 31–33; Lutz to Bishop of St. Louis, September 28, 1828, cited in Rothensteiner, "Early Missionary Efforts Among the Indians," 78–80.

crude chapel and making plans to bring all of the chiefs under White Plume's political authority.[18]

By 1828, however, political unification of the Kansa villages had become only a very remote possibility. The influence of various commercial interests for more than a century had been too pervasive to be compromised in a few days, and the special consideration given the half-bloods (and White Plume's followers) by the treaty of 1825 only served to encourage intratribal factionalism. Not even the delightful prospect of an annuity payment, which was soon to be made at Fort Leavenworth, could temper incipient animosity among the several chiefs. Lutz complained: "The barbarians agreed with almost everything except the plan of permanently locating in one village, and abandoning their hunting life."[19]

There remained, of course, the alternative of taking the Gospel directly to the interior villages as the Protestant circuit riders had done so successfully in the isolated white settlements of the Trans-Appalachian West. Apparently the young priest gave serious consideration to this strategy, but without seriously modifying his long-range objective. He hired an interpreter and selected the day for his departure, but the arrival of a large number of Kansas from the buffalo country and the wild celebration that followed were a source of great discouragement. Writing to Bishop Rosati about his plan to take the Gospel to "the country of the barbarians," Lutz explained that

the contrary seemed to be more advisable on account of the celebration of certain feasts, which occupy the barbarians for the space of two weeks, and which are the occasion of great tumult, drunkenness and strife. I preferred to postpone the visit rather than expose my dignity to insult, [since] I take great care to preserve the authority of my person, never tolerating even the least thing contrary to the respect due me. In the beginning some loose women of the barbarians began to uncover their bodies immodestly in my presence, to whom I said indignantly that they should cover themselves or go away. On another occasion, when I happened to see some immodest women lying on the floor of our house, surpassing the former ones in loose-

---

[18] Rothensteiner, "Early Missionary Efforts Among the Indians," 78–80.
[19] Ibid., 81.

ness, I took flight and requested the interpreter to report the matter to White Plume, which, having been done, I never had another similar experience.[20]

Lutz's unpleasant experience occurred on September 17; the following day he left for Fort Leavenworth, where he remained another six days. To Bishop Rosati he wrote: "The superstition of the Kanzas tribe is more gross than any one could believe and in view thereof I am not in the least hurry to offer baptism to the adults."[21] Lutz had not exaggerated his convictions, for he was clearly disillusioned. From Fort Leavenworth he returned to Kawsmouth; by December 13 he was back in St. Louis. Although it was later charged that he had "spent too much time" with the French settlers,"[22] his failure as a missionary was perhaps as much a consequence of the government's procrastination in disposing of the valuable Kansa educational lands as it was of his inability to understand and contend with an alien culture.

Unlike the Catholics, certain Protestant denominations were more aggressive and not so easily discouraged in their plans to bring salvation to the Kansas. "The day for *cold speculations*, and tedious theories, respecting the fate of the aborigines of America, has gone by," asserted the Reverend Isaac McCoy from his surveyor's camp in Indian Territory in 1831. "Are we what we profess to be—THE FRIENDS OF THE INDIANS? Then let us *manifest our faith by our works*."[23] By the time these forceful words had been directed to philanthropists and Christians throughout the nation, McCoy had done much to establish himself as a leader of the Protestant cause among the Indians west of Missouri. As an effective lobbyist for the Baptist Board of Foreign Missions, McCoy was a champion of Indian removal, a capable propagandist who played an important role in the government's adoption of this

20 *Ibid.*, 82.
21 Lutz to Rosati, September 28, 1828, St. Louis Archdiocesan Archives, cited in Garraghan, *Catholic Beginnings*, 31–32.
22 *Ibid.*
23 Isaac McCoy, "Address to Philanthropists in the United States, Generally, and to Christians in Particular, on the Condition and Prospects of the American Indians, Surveyor's Camp, Neosho River, Indian Territory, December 1, 1831," Pamphlet File, Library, KSHS.

policy. He had traveled widely in Indian country during the late 1820's, which led to his appointment as a government surveyor of various reservation boundaries, and his experiences were of signal importance to the Baptist design for a missionary station among the Kansas.

Early in 1829 McCoy conferred with Marston Clark in St. Louis. The Kansa subagent was quite cooperative and promised to use his influence with regard to public support for the Baptists. Later, in October, accompanied by White Plume and Louis Gonville, McCoy and Clark made a two-week journey to the area west of the subagency, ostensibly "to acquire a more definite knowledge of a portion of the Indian territory," but more likely to get the reaction of the other Kansa leaders to Christian missions. The specific results of the trip were not recorded, perhaps because the delegation was too concerned with land claims and boundaries or was not well received by the Mission Creek chiefs. In any case, McCoy's plans were temporarily frustrated, since he was unable to find a Baptist missionary to take the assignment at that time.[24]

Meanwhile, the Methodist Episcopal church had entered the picture. At a meeting in St. Louis on September 16, 1830, the Missouri Conference of this denomination organized its Indian Missionary Society. The Reverend Thomas Johnson, who had served the circuit at Buffalo, New York, was appointed missionary-superintendent of Shawnee Mission, while his brother William, who came to Missouri from Virginia in 1825, was designated missionary to the Kansa Indians. Shawnee Mission experienced some success from the start, but accomplishments at the Kansa subagency were not nearly so promising. William Johnson obtained living quarters and a small "school room" at the home of Daniel Morgan Boone, the Kansa agriculturist. Here he attempted to instruct a few Indian children from White Plume's village, which was near by, as well as some of the white children at the subagency. The other chiefs, whose villages were farther west, remained aloof and refused to cooperate. Thus during the first six months of his assignment,

[24] McCoy, *History of Baptist Indian Missions*, 412; Barry, "Kansas Before 1854," XXVIII (Spring, 1962), 36.

Johnson occupied himself mainly with "building a small school," attempting to learn the Kansa language, and "preaching every Sabbath" at the little settlement. Obviously, conditions were less than ideal for successful mission work, especially since many of the Kansas were absent on hunting excursions to the buffalo plains. Nevertheless, Johnson remained optimistic. "I say the call is loud," he reported, "for I view [the Kansas] on the threshold of destruction. . . . Suffice it is to say, that I have an ardent desire to do what I can by the help of my Master to rescue my unfortunate fellow creatures from present wretchedness and impending ruin."[25]

Two months later the determined Christian servant reported that Boone's family had "turned to the Lord" and others in the white community were finding "Jesus precious to their souls." Yet no Indian conversions were made, even though Johnson was convinced that some were under "religious impressions." In fact, Johnson was able to spend very little time with the Kansas. Their language was an almost insurmountable obstacle; his brother needed assistance at Shawnee Mission, as did the circuit riders charged with spreading the Gospel among the small white communities of central and western Missouri. With William Johnson's appointment to work with the more cooperative Delawares in 1832, the Kansa Methodist Mission was temporarily abandoned.[26]

Additional factors contributed to the Methodist withdrawal. Subagent Marston Clark seems not to have encouraged Johnson. John T. Irving, Jr., who met Clark at Independence in 1832, reported that the subagent considered clergymen the only class of people on earth he really hated. Referring to the Indians' traditional and apparently indiscriminate practice of stealing (and the uncompromising opposition of the missionaries to this custom), Clark told

[25] Rev. J. J. Lutz, "The Methodist Missions among the Indian Tribes in Kansas," *TKSHS*, IX (1905–1906), 160–62, 193–96; William Johnson to Thomas Johnson, August 31, 1831, and William Johnson to Corresponding Secretary of the Missionary Society of the Methodist Church, June 26, 1831, typed copies, Morehouse Papers.

[26] William Johnson to Thomas Johnson, August 31, 1831, William Johnson to Corresponding Secretary of the Missionary Society of the Methodist Church, June 26, 1831, Thomas Johnson to Corresponding Secretary of the Missionary Society of the Methodist Episcopal Church, February 10, 1832, typed copies, Morehouse Papers; Lutz, "Methodist Missions," 196.

Irving that the white man "must not shut the only road left them to honor and promotion."[27] Irving's information was confirmed by William D. Smith in 1833. Smith, a Presbyterian pastor assigned to ascertain the possibility of establishing Presbyterian missions in the Indian country, described Clark as "an open and avowed infidel . . . a foul mouthed . . . man of inordinate self conceit, and (of course) of very little mind. As might be expected of such a man," Smith warned, "he is at heart opposed to all religious instruction and expresses himself as having no confidence in schools or any attempt to civilize the Indians."[28]

In spite of Clark's undisguised opposition, the missionaries were not easily discouraged. The anticipated income from what appeared to be the impending sale of the Kansa education lands in the Big Blue Valley made them a prime target for Christian conversion, and Isaac McCoy was determined not to allow the Methodists (or other denominations) to gain the advantage. To William Bowles, a fellow Baptist pastor, he wrote:

The Kansas lands are now in market. The Catholics formerly tried to get hold of the proceeds [and] the Methodists also have their eye upon them. I have spoken to Clark [and] am informed by him and the Methodists that we had made a formal application to the Indian Department respecting a [Baptist] mission for the Kanzas and the application of their school funds a year and a half ago. Our Methodist brethren cannot supplant us, if we wish to go with our proposition for the Kanzas.[29]

But this was precisely what the Methodists had done, even before funds were available from the federal government. Complaining that the Methodists had already established a school for the Kansas and Shawnees, Baptist Johnston Lykins warned Jotham Meeker on July 19, 1831, that unless the Baptists seized the initiative, they would soon "fall in the background."[30] A direct and perhaps open

[27] Irving, *Indian Sketches*, 240.
[28] William D. Smith to E. P. Swift, July 29 (?), 1833, Rev. W. D. Smith's Letters from the Shawnee Village, 1833 (cited hereafter as Smith Letters), Manuscript Division, Presbyterian Historical Society, Philadelphia.
[29] McCoy to Bowles, December 1, 1830, Isaac McCoy Papers.
[30] Lykins to Meeker, July 18, 1831, Jotham Meeker Papers, Manuscript Division, KSHS.

confrontation between the two denominations may have been averted at that time by the temporary withdrawal of the Methodists from White Plume's village in 1832. But the education lands and the regrettable conditions reported by William Johnson were more than enough to sustain missionary interest in the Kansas. For the time being, however, the Baptists were content to work with the Shawnees at a site about three miles south of the Methodist mission while McCoy continued to conduct survey operations for the government.[31]

In 1821 the Presbyterians established successful Harmony Mission among the Osages in western Missouri,[32] and shortly after Johnson's mission at White Plume's village closed, they displayed an interest in the Kansas. In the summer of 1833 the Presbyterian Missionary Board sent the Reverend William D. Smith on a general tour of the country west of Missouri to determine the most desirable sites for new mission stations. Smith made his temporary headquarters at the Shawnee Reservation with Joseph Barnett, an educated Shawnee mixed-blood who also served as Smith's guide on a tour that took them to the Delawares, Fort Leavenworth, the Kansa villages, and then back to the Shawnees. In addition, Smith visited and interviewed representatives of the Otoes, Omahas, and Kickapoos; later he visited the Iowas and a number of the smaller emigrant tribes. The tour was instructive, and the overview he gained placed him in a strategic, albeit biased, position to evaluate the Protestant missionary potential among the Kansas.[33]

As was the case with most of the Indians he visited, Smith found the Kansas in need of material assistance and what he termed "spiritual guidance." At one of the Kansa villages in the heat of late July, Smith was so shocked with the filth and generally degraded conditions that in one instance he "was under the necessity of leaving the lodge" rather than remaining to observe the sickly condition of its inhabitants. However, he noted that the Kansas

---

[31] Lutz, "Methodist Missions," 160; Barry, "Kansas Before 1854," XXVIII (Spring, 1962), 186–87.

[32] S. W. Brewster, "Reverend Father Paul W. Ponziglione," *TKSHS*, IX (1905–1906), 20.

[33] Barry, "Kansas Before 1854," XXVIII (Autumn, 1962), 328.

lived "in a delightful and healthy country" where there appeared to be sufficient timber and land well adapted to farming. "They are ignorant, degraded and extremely filthy," he reported, "but owing to their distance from the *White Heathen* they have not [yet] contracted their views to as great an extent as those who live nearer [the settlements]." Concerning their spiritual condition, Smith reported they were "docile in their dispositions" and thus easily turned from the error of their ways. An added attraction was their strong expression to have missions and schools located at their villages.[34]

In spite of these obvious inducements, which seemed all the more convincing after Smith described the Kansas' condition as more critical than that of any other tribe he had visited, no recommendation was made for establishing a Presbyterian mission among them. A number of considerations were involved. For one thing, as Smith well knew, the Presbyterian Missionary Board was hampered by a lack of personnel, a condition common to most frontier missionary operations of the day. Moreover, the Kansa villages were among those most distant from the white settlements, and the tribe's semisedentary economy, which included a four- or five-month hunting excursion to the plains each year, was hardly conducive to rapid and lasting cultural alteration. Their villages were rent by internal dissensions, their poverty was extreme, and the possibility of obtaining any immediate government funding through the sale of their lands was not at all certain.[35] Added to this was the problem of securing reliable interpreters, which in the case of the Kansas, with a powerful French influence as part of their tribal tradition, was particularly acute. "The most of them are low French, and half breeds," Smith complained,

some tainted with infidelity and some with Papacy, and not only irreligious but grossly immoral, who so far from taking pains to interpret a religious discourse correctly (which is very difficult) would knowingly misrepresent, and thus be the means of conveying

[34] Smith to Messrs. Kerr & Cloud, Western Theological Seminary, July 22, 1833, and Smith to E. P. Swift, July, n.d., 1833, Smith Letters.

[35] Smith to E. P. Swift, August 5, 1833, Smith Letters.

to those haunted beings the grossest errors in the form of instruction with the sanction of your authority.[36]

Finally, according to Smith, there was the secular outlook and general obstructionism of the government agents. "You will be placed . . . among those with whom the name of a Missionary is associated either with weak minded enthusiasm or low hypocrisy, and in some cases avaricious speculations," he explained. Why was this so? "Simply because they know their conduct will not be approved of," was Smith's conclusion, especially as it applied to the Kansa subagent, Marston Clark. Even though Clark promised to do what he could to "favor" the Presbyterians, he made no effort to disguise his contempt for Smith and Smith's misguided effort to "civilize" the Kansas. But while Smith castigated Clark as an avowed infidel, the subagent was quick to rationalize his position from a much broader perspective.[37] Realizing that his criticism might bring on him "the anathema of the whole order of the Priest-hood," Clark, in an official letter to William Clark in St. Louis, explained that the late Methodist mission at his agency had accomplished nothing for the Kansas; in fact, he said, William Johnson's school had operated mainly for the children of the white settlers. "These theological gentry," he warned, "sap the foundations of our Republican Institutions, [and are] only interested in patronage, power and money."[38]

Smith's unfavorable report was enough to discourage the Presbyterians, who soon abandoned the idea of a Kansa mission. But the zeal of the Johnsons, who were enjoying considerable success at Shawnee Mission, was not so easily destroyed. On May 24, 1834, William Johnson received his second appointment as Methodist Episcopal missionary to the Kansas, although it was nearly two years before he was able to establish a station at the Mission Creek villages.

Meanwhile, a federal law of June 30, 1834, established the

---

36 Smith to E. P. Swift, July, n.d., 1833, Smith Letters.

37 Smith to E. P. Swift, July 29, 1833, Smith Letters.

38 Marston Clark to William Clark, September 1, 1833, LR, OIA, Fort Leavenworth Agency.

Department of Indian Affairs on a more formal basis. For the Kansas, the resulting administrative changes led to the closing of Clark's agency in present Jefferson County and the tribe's assignment to Agent Richard W. Cummins of the Northern Agency of the Western Territory, with headquarters at more distant Fort Leavenworth. Clark soon left, and with him went the handful of federal employees who had served at the agency; only Joseph James, an interpreter, and James McGill, a blacksmith, remained to work with the Kansas.

Fool Chief's people stayed at the village they had inhabited for several years (on the north side of the Kansas River between Mission and Soldier creeks), while all of American Chief's followers and a few of Hard Chief's people continued to occupy their villages near the mouth of Mission Creek. Another result of Clark's departure—and the return of the Methodist missionaries—was the withdrawal of most of Hard Chief's former followers to a new site some thirty-five miles west (on the Kansas River between present-day Wamego and St. George), ostensibly to be nearer the buffalo country, but more likely to escape the "civilizing" influence of the white man. Whatever the reasons for this significant migration, which may have involved nearly one-third of the tribe, the fact remains that at the time of renewed missionary activity, the advent of less government involvement in the affairs of the Kansas was matched by increased dissension within the tribe's ranks.[39]

Clearly, there was no lack of challenge for the struggling Kansa Methodist Mission. Thomas Johnson visited the Indian country in the spring of 1835 and was shocked at the deplorable conditions at Mission Creek. "I never saw before any part of the human family in so wretched a condition," he informed the readers of the *Christian Advocate and Journal.*

They cultivate only a small portion of ground, and this is done chiefly by the women, with hoes. They do not plow; they have no fences. Their only dependence for meat is on the chase. . . . To find the buffalo they are frequently driven back by their enimies. . . . Unless

<hr />

[39] Lutz, "Methodist Missions," 196; Barry, "Kansas Before 1854," XXVIII (Autumn, 1962), 360–62, and XXVIII (Winter, 1962), 497, 499–500.

we can get these people to change their life and habits, they must perish.[40]

The Johnsons went to work almost immediately. William Johnson made two trips to Mission Creek in the fall of 1835, and by the following spring he was busy erecting temporary living quarters. The government, under the leadership of Agent Cummins, was also active. Twenty acres were fenced at Fool Chief's village, and ten acres were immediately plowed for the planting of corn; a garden was planted near American Chief's village; a blacksmith was hired; and a hewed-log house was erected for White Plume, who apparently was still recognized as the principal chief of all the Kansas. By the fall of 1836 the mission near American Chief's village boasted a partially completed one-and-a-half-story, double-log building designed to serve as a combination missionary residence, sanctuary, and school; attached by way of a crude log passage were a kitchen and smokehouse. A blacksmith shop and residence for the government farmer were located about three miles away, while at the mouth of Mission Creek, about a mile below the main mission building, was the trading post operated by Cyprian and Frederick Chouteau.

Although the Kansas remained aloof, especially with regard to allowing their children to attend school, the missionaries refused to be pessimistic. "It is true, we have privations," admitted Thomas Johnson, "but these things do not discourage us. We are determined to do the best we can, and leave the result to God."[41]

Actually, the Kansas displayed several characteristics that encouraged the Methodists. They were exceedingly fond of talking and tried not to conceal their views on any subject, and when compared to many of the other tribes in Indian country, they seemed more serious and better informed. They attended to their

[40] Thomas Johnson to *Christian Advocate and Journal*, July 16, 1835, typed copy, Morehouse Papers.

[41] Thomas Johnson to *Christian Advocate and Journal*, March 9, 1836, and William Johnson to Thomas Johnson, June 7, 1836, typed copies, Morehouse Papers; Barry, "Kansas Before 1854," XXVIII (Winter, 1962), 513; Thomas Johnson to R. W. Cummins, November 15, 1836, LR, OIA, St. Louis Superintendency; J. S. Chick to T. S. Huffaker, April 19, 1906, Chick Papers.

traditional religious ceremonies in a solemn and dedicated manner; nevertheless, "in all their worship there [was] no confession of sin or knowledge of a Saviour. If they only knew Jesus," complained William Johnson, "and would worship in His name with the same promptness that they attend to their own ceremonies, they would doubtless be a happy people."[42]

A nagging problem for the missionaries was the language barrier. Thus in the early months of 1837 it was with some optimism that they reported the "pious" inclination of one young Kansa who had recently returned to his village after spending nine years in white society. Although he spoke English only "tolerably well" and had nearly forgotten his native language, it was assumed that he would play an important role in helping the Johnsons rescue "the poor, filthy, ignorant Kansas from their wretchedness."[43] But in this the missionaries were mistaken. Two years later they still complained of having no reliable interpreter, and "very little [had] been done in the way of preaching."[44] However, there were indications that changes of a different sort were beginning to occur. Some Kansa men were no longer opposed to working with the women; they were interested in horticulture and stock raising and, according to one visitor, were "abandoning their wigwams of earth and beginning to erect dwellings of logs." Although the sentiment for economic change exceeded by far the actual amount of labor being performed by the men, it was William Johnson's considered opinion that a major advance toward the imparting of religious instruction had been made.[45]

Little wonder, then, at the bitterness and despair that characterized reports describing the events of 1838. The government's failure to recover a number of horses stolen by the Pawnees sometime before 1835 encouraged the Kansas to demand the right to

[42] William Johnson to Thomas Johnson, June 7, 1826, typed copy, Morehouse Papers.

[43] Thomas Johnson to Corresponding Secretary, Missionary Society of Methodist Episcopal Church, December 15, 1837, typed copy, Morehouse Papers.

[44] William Johnson to Corresponding Secretary of Missionary Society of Methodist Episcopal Church, February 12, 1839, typed copy, Morehouse Papers.

[45] *Ibid.*; Barry, "Kansas Before 1854," XXIX (Summer, 1963), 168.

redress their grievances.[46] This was quickly denied by Agent Cummins, with the result that the more aggressive warriors took matters into their own hands. In August, 1838, accompanied by a band of Osages, they attacked a Pawnee hunting party on the Arkansas; eleven Pawnee scalps were taken, while their own losses were four killed and two wounded. A few weeks later, White Plume and four braves died while on the annual fall hunt, apparently from the combination of an infectious disease, "excessive" consumption of whiskey, and exposure. Coming at a time when the Methodists were beginning to experience some success in their plan to break down tribal traditionalism, these events played havoc with their work. No matter what William Johnson said or did, most of the Kansas were now convinced that the tribe was in bad favor with the Great Spirit and that satisfaction against the Pawnees was the only way their unfortunate predicament could be alleviated.[47]

Even so, the missionary cause might have maintained a measure of momentum had it not been for the irruption of a major epidemic at the Mission Creek villages in the summer of 1839. Smallpox vaccine had been available for use among the Kansas for some time, but because of their nomadic habits and petulant quarreling between the Chouteaus and government health authorities in 1833, most members of the tribe had not been vaccinated. In turn, chronic malnutrition made them especially susceptible to the ravages of other infectious diseases. Whether cholera or smallpox, but more likely the latter, the "fever" took nearly one hundred lives within a short time. "But few families escaped the disease," reported Johnson, "and the number of deaths was great in proportion to the number of sick. The awful cries of the Indians around the dead sounded in our ears nearly every day."[48]

[46] Statement taken from Kansa Indians by R. W. Cummins, September 11, 1835, LR, OIA, Fort Leavenworth Agency.
[47] Barry, "Kansas Before 1854," XXIX (Summer, 1963), 156; William Johnson to Corresponding Secretary of Missionary Society of Methodist Episcopal Church, February 12, 1839, typed copy, Morehouse Papers.
[48] William Johnson to Corresponding Secretary of Missionary Society of Methodist Episcopal Church, December 30, 1840, typed copy, Morehouse Papers; Deposition of Clement Lessert to Sam C. Owen, February 2, 1833, Frederick

However, the worst was yet to come. Thrown into a frenzy by the tragic turn of events, most of the Kansas fled west to the buffalo plains, hoping that a combination of open air and fresh meat would improve their condition. The few who remained behind occupied themselves mainly with organizing little war parties to gain satisfaction from their enemies when the opportunity presented itself. Not until late December, 1840, did the tribe return en masse to Mission Creek, bringing news of a decisive "victory" over the Republican Pawnees. Best described as a massacre, the event was, in the words of William Johnson, "so destitute of honor or bravery, that I would gladly have it wiped away from the tribe of people with whom I live."

According to statements made by the victorious warriors, which for the most part were soon confirmed by other reports received by government authorities at Fort Leavenworth, the Kansas, after losing additional horses to the Pawnees, sent out a war party of 65 men. Ten days from Mission Creek they discovered a Pawnee camp left defenseless by the recent departure of the men on a hunting excursion. The camp of 19 lodges and about 150 people was immediately attacked, and within a short time more than 60 women and children were killed and scalped; in addition, 11 prisoners, 10 horses, and all the personal articles the Kansas could pack were taken. "Some they knocked down with a tomahawk, and others they thrust through with a spear," reported Johnson. "The object was for all the young men to become braves by striking with a tomahawk the head of an enemy."[49]

The disillusioned missionary was not exaggerating when he

Chouteau to P. Chouteau, Jr., February 5, 1833, M. Clark to William Clark, September 1, 1833, and R. W. Cummins to William Clark, March 24, 1835, LR, OIA, Fort Leavenworth Agency; Dr. Joseph de Trefontaine to Joshua Pilcher, September 6, 1839, LR, OIA, St. Louis Superintendency; Barry, "Kansas Before 1854," XXIX (Summer, 1963), 182. One study suggests the Kansas may have contracted smallpox in 1838 from the Pawnees, who were infected by Sioux captives taken in the Upper Missouri country. See Stearn and Stearn, *The Effect of Smallpox*, 86.

[49] Barry, "Kansas Before 1854," XXIX (Autumn, 1963), 339; William Johnson to Corresponding Secretary of Missionary Society of Methodist Episcopal Church, December 30, 1840, and January 30, 1841, typed copies, Morehouse Papers.

described the situation at Mission Creek as "paralyzing to all our operations." Anticipating that the Pawnees would soon attempt to gain revenge, the Kansas divided most of their time among war songs, the Scalp Dance, and preparations for the counterattack. Families who had started building houses near the mission, indicating some interest in the sedentary life, were "now the subjects of laughter and sport by the new-made braves."[50] A delegation of Methodist dignitaries who visited the Mission Creek villages the following spring were not at all welcome, even though they obtained promises from at least some tribal leaders that corn would be planted that season. Some of the Kansas admitted that the white man's life was "easiest and most comfortable," yet they studiously avoided any comparative discussion of their own religion and Christianity. Rather, they took the position that the Methodists, by previous "interviews" with their people, had in effect violated the sacred tribal taboos and thus were at least indirectly responsible for the premature death of some of their people.[51]

From the Methodist perspective, an alternative tactic at this point was to educate—in the broadest sense—a few Kansa children, perhaps at a distant manual-labor school. Here they would at least have an opportunity to associate with other young people from the more sedentary tribes. In 1838 Thomas Johnson obtained $10,000 from the Methodist Missionary Board in New York for this purpose, to be expended under the direction of the Missouri Conference at the Shawnee Reservation. Government authorities in Washington advanced an additional $5,000 and promised an annual subsidy of $2,500 thereafter. The construction of dormitories and shops and the fencing of about five hundred acres began in early 1839; by fall the school was opened to sixty-seven boys and girls from nine tribes. Cognizant of the potential for cultural assimilation at the Shawnee Mission Manual Labor School, William Johnson was apparently successful in convincing Fool Chief and at least one

[50] William Johnson to Corresponding Secretary of Missionary Society of Methodist Episcopal Church, December 30, 1840, and January 30, 1841, typed copies, Morehouse Papers.

[51] James M. Jameson to editor of *Western Christian Advocate*, May 20, 1841, typed copy, Morehouse Papers.

minor chief that to enroll a few young boys would not offend the Great Spirit.[52]

In the spring of 1841, while escorting eleven Kansa boys to the Shawnee Reservation, Johnson became ill from exposure. In his weakened condition he contracted pneumonia, which led to his death in April, 1842. It was a shattering blow to the Methodist cause among the Kansas, as were Johnson's last words of advice. In candid terms he recommended that formal religious indoctrination at Mission Creek be abandoned. Before they could profit in any way from Christian instruction, the Kansas would have to be "partially civilized and taught in some other language than their own." Teaching by sign language, according to the dying missionary, was wholly unsatisfactory, as was their native tongue, since they simply had no words to explain "moral and religious ideas." While the Methodist leaders pondered these words without changing their minds, the Kansa boys were returned to their own people. Several died soon after their arrival at Mission Creek, and as a result Hard Chief refused to allow any more children to leave his village. He was firmly convinced that this latest tragedy was caused by his children having "smelled the big knife" while at the school.[53]

Disregarding the rather clear attitude of the Kansas, as well as the advice of a dedicated Christian who had worked with them for nearly a decade, Methodist officials refused to abandon their plan to teach Christianity at Mission Creek. A heated controversy with the Baptists over church membership and doctrine in the western Missouri border country at that time, plus the monetary attraction of the Kansa education lands, fortified their determination. Accordingly, the Reverend G. W. Love was appointed in 1843 to pick up where William Johnson had left off. But Love was no more successful than his predecessor. "Why it is so we cannot tell,"

[52] James Anderson, "The Methodist Shawnee Mission in Johnson County, Kansas 1830–1862," *Trail Guide*, I (1956), 9–10; Lutz, "Methodist Missions," 197; Barry, "Kansas Before 1854," XXIX (Autumn, 1963), 348.

[53] Lutz, "Methodist Missions," 197; Barry, "Kansas Before 1854," XXIX (Winter, 1963), 432; George P. Morehouse, "Kaw Indian Mission," manuscript copy, n.d., Morehouse Papers; Adams, "Reminiscences of Frederick Chouteau," 428.

reported yet another delegation of pastors who visited the Kansas in November, 1843. The Indians seemed friendly enough, even willing to discuss the need of some instruction for their children, yet Love's religious labors, in the words of the delegation, "seemed as water spilling upon the ground." Understandably, the inexperienced missionary left his post at Mission Creek before a year had passed.[54]

The final chapter of the Methodist experience at Mission Creek began in 1845 when the Reverend J. T. Perry, who had married William Johnson's widow the previous year, was commissioned to establish a Kansa manual-labor school modeled after the one at the Shawnee Reservation. It was, of course, a much less ambitious plan, and although a few children were instructed at Mission Creek later that year and a few acres of corn were planted, the project was a dismal failure. Looming large in the Kansas' outlook was the fear that a settled, agrarian life constituted an open invitation for the Pawnees to attack them at a central location; for Perry, it amounted to a formidable obstacle, one impossible to overcome. There were other problems, too. The school was poorly supported by both the government and the church, the weather was not conducive to farming that first season, and there were rumors that a new treaty might result in relocating the tribe farther west. Moreover, in 1845 the Methodist Episcopal church was "rent asunder" over the slavery question, and resulting identification with the Southern point of view made it the target of political strife and internal dissension. When Perry went to work for the government as official Kansa farmer in 1846, Mission Creek Manual Labor School was closed and the Methodists retreated.

Nearly fifteen years of work with the Kansas had accomplished very little. No converts could be reported, yet there was

---

[54] Copy of Communication from Methodist Missionaries to Baptists, March 12, 1842, and John G. Pratt to Missionaries of Methodist Episcopal Church, Ind. Territory, April 22, 1842, John G. Pratt Papers, Manuscript Division, KSHS; Lutz, "Methodist Missions," 198; Thomas H. Harvey to T. Hartley Crawford, December 23, 1844, LR, OIA, Fort Leavenworth Agency; Rev. William Patton, "Journal of a Visit to the Indian Missions, Missouri Conference," Missouri Historical Society *Bulletin*, X (1954), 179.

reason to believe that the government could continue to cooperate with the missionaries. It was a cheap way to administer Indian policy, and after all, the Methodists could at least claim some experience, if not success, in bringing "civilization" to the "savage."[55]

[55] Lutz, "Methodist Missions," 179, 198; J. T. Peery to W. W. Cone, December 30, 1880, Kansas Indian Papers, Manuscript Division, KSHS; Anderson, "The Methodist Shawnee Mission," 14.

CHAPTER 6 "WHAT SHALL BE DONE WITH THE KANSAS?"

Reshaping the Kansa way of life along Christian lines was an important part of the government's strategy to force the tribe into cultural revolution. Indeed, an appraisal of the missionary effort within the broad spectrum of Kansa history after 1825 warrants the conclusion that the Methodists' failure at Mission Creek was a staggering blow to the government plan and a primary obstacle to the tribe's entrance into the mainstream of white American civilization. If, however, it is remembered that many white Americans of that time considered civilization and Protestant Christianity as synonymous or at least complementary ideals, the complexity, not the simplicity, of the attempted revolution is apparent.

A number of problems besides the blundering of a few uncompromising missionaries plagued the government's over-all strategy. Certainly not the least was the government's narrow assumption that the Kansas actually desired to alter their way of life. It was anticipated, of course, that a few individuals or clans might be slow to appreciate the virtues of a sedentary existence; but attitudes were expected to change, especially as others, with their hands on the plow and their eyes to the future, began to improve their condition in the orthodox manner of the American yeoman. For example, exemplary tactics clearly can be seen in the government's gift of 640-acre plots to some of the Kansa half-bloods in 1825 and in the

138

special concessions granted Chief White Plume shortly after the treaties negotiated that year were ratified.

Whatever their initial reaction to this apparent generosity, the half-bloods eventually realized that land claims along the major rivers in Indian country appreciated in value and that the fashionable means of getting ahead lay in speculation, not farming. By 1840 Superintendent Joshua Pilcher reported that most of the half-bloods were living in St. Louis, where they were repeatedly besieging his office with requests to sell their lands along the Kansas River.[1] Two years later Indian Commissioner T. Hartley Crawford was informed that the half-bloods were "so destitute of the necessities of life" that their only alternative was to sell their lands so they could "settle down to [the] life of agriculture."[2] In spite of this seemingly noble request and Crawford's apparent desire to cooperate, it was the failure of Congress to authorize the issuance of fee-simple titles and the right of alienation, not the half-bloods' desire to take up the life of the yeoman farmer, which prevented them from becoming frontier land jobbers.[3] White Plume, who announced he was proud to be "an American and not a beggar," was no less interested in certain land claims he believed should be returned to himself and his children in the Stranger Creek area. But it was not long before he reached the painful conclusion that by casting his lot with the white man and accepting special considerations from the government, he was encouraging discord and lessening his own influence with the younger Kansa war chiefs.[4]

That the Kansas had little or no enthusiasm for tilling the soil was apparent. For more than a century they had enjoyed a modified hunting and trapping economy, one in which a combination of

[1] Joshua Pilcher to T. Hartley Crawford, February 27, 1840, LR, OIA, Fort Leavenworth Agency.

[2] D. D. Mitchell to Crawford, April 18, 1842, LR, OIA, St. Louis Superintendency.

[3] In 1860 Congress extended the alienating power of the fullblood Kansas to the half-bloods, but the decision was reversed two years later; see *U.S. Statutes at Large*, XII, 21, 628.

[4] White Plume's speech to William Clark, May 17, 1827, LR, OIA, St. Louis Superintendency; J. C. McCoy to W. W. Cone, August ?, 1879, John C. McCoy Papers.

European and American traders provided a market for skins and furs not needed for day-to-day survival. Horticulture, which was the responsibility of women and children, was exceedingly limited; crops were raised for only two purposes: domestic consumption or distribution among neighboring tribes on a mostly nonprofit basis. For example, it was with considerable confusion and concern that government authorities learned in 1839 that the Kansas were sharing their very limited corn supply with "most any tribe" that asked for it.[5] Since their economic position appeared to be approaching the level of abject poverty, this custom simply made no sense to Indian agents, who viewed it outside the framework of the tribe's traditions and culture.

Other obstacles besides an indigenous aversion to commercial agriculture discouraged the Kansas from altering their economy. Even a casual reading of the St. Louis treaty of 1825 suggests that nearly everything required to implement the desired change was provided. In practice this was not the case. Of crucial importance was the provision that a government agent, farmer, and blacksmith were to reside at or near the principal villages.[6] Yet in the two decades after the treaty was ratified, this provision was loosely enforced or completely ignored. Never did the agent (or subagent) live closer than twenty miles to the main tribal villages, and in some instances the distance was between fifty and seventy-five miles. Moreover, a chronic turnover in official personnel assigned to the Kansas, along with continual reorganization of the Department of Indian Affairs at the agency level, resulted in a confusing array of agents, subagents, assistant agents, special agents, commissioners, blacksmiths, farmers, or simply no one to look after the government's obligations to the Kansas.[7]

Agents, whose salaries were seldom paid on a regular basis, were not particularly dedicated to pursuing their official duties

[5] R. W. Cummins to Pilcher, October ?, 1839, LR, OIA, St. Louis Superintendency.

[6] Kappler, *Indian Affairs*, 222–23.

[7] "Kansas Agencies," 773; Marston G. Clark to Elbert Herring, October 31, 1834, War Department Regulations and Decisions, William B. Marcy, Secretary, Copy of Orders, March 1, 1848, LR, OIA, Fort Leavenworth Agency.

according to the letter of the law. Illness, distance, and time hampered the work of some; others confined their attention to their own interests while remaining on the Indian Department's official payroll. In 1832, for example, when the Kansas were experiencing particularly difficult conditions in the Mission Creek area, Subagent Marston G. Clark was, according to an outside observer, "living like a patriarch, surrounded by laborers and interpreters, all snugly housed, and provided with excellent farms" at the so-called subagency headquarters some twenty-five miles to the east.[8]

It was especially difficult for the government to retain competent and dedicated employees to work with the Kansas for any length of time. Symptomatic of the problem was the rapid turnover and general confusion surrounding the position of Kansa blacksmith (or mechanic). Gabriel Philebert, an occasional public servant with dubious qualifications, served in this capacity as long as the subagency was located near the Missouri border at Kawsmouth, but he resigned his appointment in 1827 when Superintendent William Clark ordered the subagency moved to the eastern edge of the Kansa Reservation as stipulated in the treaty of 1825.[9] For a limited time an unidentified Indian (perhaps a Shawnee), who in Francis Chouteau's words wanted to "learn the Black and Gun Smith business," was employed; however, he was abruptly dismissed in 1830 when Subagent Clark gave the job to Claibourne Calvert, who probably had political connections with White Plume, the half-bloods, and certain private trading interests.[10] Calvert submitted his "resignation" on December 17, 1835, ostensibly because of "bad health," the failure of the government to pay him on a regular basis, and what he called "a great many privations."[11] Some of the Kansas had a more realistic explanation when they

[8] John Dougherty to Lewis Cass, March 9, 1832, Dougherty Papers, KSHS; Cummins to Crawford, July 31, 1830, LR, OIA, Fort Leavenworth Agency; Isaac McCoy to John Eaton, January 31, 1831, Isaac McCoy Papers; Todd, *Captain Bonneville*, 20.

[9] Deposition of Louis Gonville, n.d., 1830 (?), Pierre Chouteau-Maffitt Collection, Chouteau Papers, Manuscript Division, MHS.

[10] Charges of Francis Chouteau against an employee of the Kansas, n.d., 1830, typed copy, Chouteau Papers.

[11] Claibourne Calvert to Cummins, December 17, 1835, LR, OIA, Fort Leavenworth Agency.

complained that Calvert refused to do repair work brought to him and that he whipped them when they requested his help in securing food and supplies.[12]

Earlier, in March, 1835, Richard W. Cummins of Fort Leavenworth Agency had suggested to William Clark that if the blacksmith shop was to be of any service at all, it had to be moved to Mission Creek near the villages of Fool Chief, Hard Chief, and American Chief. This was done in the early months of 1836, probably to coincide with the opening of the second Methodist mission. However, the government provided no additional appropriation for the move, so the one thousand dollars needed to relocate the facility was taken from the already strained Kansa agriculture fund.[13] Meanwhile, in rapid succession, Nelson A. Warren, Elias M. Walker, and Charles Fish served as blacksmiths or assistant smiths during a fifteen-month period immediately after Calvert's resignation. That this diverse array of poorly paid officials functioned in the manner intended by the government is doubtful.[14]

More serious as an obstacle to the government's plan to help the Kansas was the conflict that developed between Subagent Clark and the Chouteaus. Clark, who received his appointment in 1829, was at least nominally identified with the Indian Department's agrarian strategy, even though he personally questioned its practicality. By virtue of the authority accompanying his position, he was responsible for granting annual licenses to private merchants who submitted formal applications to the government, a difficult and thankless task. Clark also had authority to decide whether the Kansas should receive their annuities in money or goods, and he was free to use his influence in determining the places where the traders could establish their headquarters. Permits granted to the various merchants did not, however, preclude the government's prerogative to negotiate directly with commercial jobbers for sup-

[12] Cummins to William Clark, December 12, 1835, LR, OIA, Fort Leavenworth Agency.

[13] Cummins to William Clark, March 20, 1835, Cummins to C. A. Harris, July 30, 1836, LR, OIA, Fort Leavenworth Agency.

[14] Cummins to C. A. Harris, July 30, 1836, and March 15, 1837, LR, OIA, Fort Leavenworth Agency.

plies needed by the tribe. Indeed, the general effect was that the Indian Department, through its designated agency or subagency personnel, was competing with the licensed traders. The situation was further complicated by the fact that the tribe was undergoing a critical economic transition during which its diminishing supply of skins and pelts was still being purchased mainly by traders who had been officially licensed. No explicit guidelines were provided to indicate whether the annuities should be given to individuals, to heads of families, or to tribal leaders; nor was it certain whether agreements (or contracts) entered into by individual Indians for the payment of money, goods, or compensation for alleged depredations were legally binding.[15]

The interplay of these forces further compromised the Indian Department's efforts to deal effectively with the Kansas. In April, 1828, just before Marston Clark's appointment as subagent, word was received by Superintendent William Clark in St. Louis that the government commissioners were experiencing great difficulty in making "an equal distribution" among the Kansas. More trouble was anticipated, and military authorities were advised "to take a few troops along" for the next annuity issue.[16] Factionalism was obviously increasing within the tribe, and the private traders were making their influence felt. In this the Chouteaus, as well as their American Fur Company sponsors, played a significant role.

Since the early years of the nineteenth century the Chouteau family of St. Louis had enjoyed a major share of the Kansa trade. Centered around a rude post near the mouth of the Kansas River, it had been diminishing in value for some time, but now that the tribe was guaranteed an annual income by the government, the interest of these enterprising merchants was understandably renewed. In the autumn of 1829 Frederick Chouteau (the youngest son of Jean Pierre Chouteau, Jr.), with the cooperation and backing

[15] The federal law of 1847 which revised the Trade and Intercourse Act of 1834 held that annuities were to go to individuals or heads of families or, with the consent of the tribe, for purposes "as will best promote the happiness and prosperity of the members." All "executory contracts" were to be null and void and "of no binding whatsoever." See *U.S. Statutes at Large*, IX, 204.

[16] William Clark to John Dougherty, April 13, 1828, Dougherty Papers, KSHS.

of the American Fur Company, established a trading post near Horseshoe Lake about one mile from Marston Clark's Kansa sub-agency but on the opposite (or southern) side of the Kansas River. Two of Frederick's brothers, Francis and Cyprian, were also involved either directly or indirectly in the operation.[17] Apparently their objectives were at least twofold: to dominate the Kansa trade and to provide consumer goods for the white settlement that would naturally grow around the subagency.

Commercially, the dual role was attractive, but it was precisely what Subagent Clark opposed. His position was that the licensed traders should confine their attention exclusively to the Indians and establish themselves in the immediate vicinity of their principal villages. So it was that the annual license obtained on October 31, 1831, by the American Fur Company for the Chouteaus stated specifically that commercial transactions were to be conducted only at a point "between the two upper villages of the Kanzas," which was at least twenty miles west of Clark's station. In two letters to Frederick Chouteau, one dated October 10 and another December 20, 1831, Clark complained that the disposal of Indian goods in the vicinity of the subagency must stop, since it brought "large bodies of Indians to the great annoyance of the few whites at this place by killing stock, crowding their houses and begging for provisions." Yet the Chouteaus refused to move their trading post to the main Kansa villages until it was reasonably certain that William and Thomas Johnson were going ahead with their plans to establish a Methodist mission in that vicinity.[18]

Clark had other complaints against the Chouteaus. The government's laxity in delivering annuity goods on time gave the traders an opportunity to undermine Clark's influence with the more powerful tribal leaders and further their own interests. Aware of incipient factionalism, the Chouteaus made special commercial arrangements with the chiefs at Mission Creek, while Clark did his

17 Barry, "Kansas Before 1854," XXVIII (Spring, 1962), 58; Garraghan, *Catholic Beginnings*, 51–52.
18 Marston G. Clark to Frederick Chouteau, October 10, 1831, cited in Barry, "Kansas Before 1854," XXVIII (Spring, 1962), 58; Marston G. Clark to Frederick Chouteau, December 20, 1831, LR, OIA, St. Louis Superintendency.

best to deal with the tribe as a whole. It was a critical turn of events, and the resulting confrontation between the two groups provided the setting for violence, misunderstanding, and further subversion of the government's long-range plan for the Kansas.

Big Wolfe, an ambitious warrior who enjoyed little or no prestige in the tribe's traditional power structure, tried to cooperate with Clark and the Indian Department. For this he was murdered in the early months of 1830, probably by Ka-he-gah-wah-tanige, one of the tribal leaders at Mission Creek. Clark believed the murder was planned and executed by "the full chief" and certain "outlaw" leaders working "through and with agents of the American Fur Company." But it was impossible to prove guilt beyond any reasonable doubt.

Certainly the headmen and the Chouteaus were determined to have the final word concerning the disposal of the annuities, for they threatened bodily harm to members of the tribe who objected to their machinations. Privately (probably for personal considerations amounting to a disproportionate share of the annuities) they agreed to prices that were from 20 to 40 per cent higher than the government figure Clark obtained from St. Louis. At least indirectly, then, certain influential Kansas were supporting what Clark angrily described as a scheme to discourage progress toward economic self-sufficiency.[19]

Fearful that the traders were getting the upper hand and that the government's responsibilities to the tribe as a whole were being compromised, Clark threatened to bring in as many troops "as the blades of grass to be seen on the prairies." It was a colossal bluff, of course, but it worked. The Mission Creek chiefs begged forgiveness and asked Clark to use his influence to put them back in "good standing with the Nation." For the traders and their sponsors, it was a temporary setback.[20]

The Chouteaus refused to abandon their plan to operate the Kansa trade on their own terms, rightly concluding that Clark was

[19] Marston G. Clark to William Clark, July 28, 1830, William Clark to John Eaton, August 31, 1831, LR, OIA, St. Louis Superintendency.
[20] Marston G. Clark to William Clark, July 28, 1830, LR, OIA, St. Louis Superintendency.

their primary obstacle. Another opportunity to undermine his official influence and personal reputation presented itself when Francis Chouteau learned in 1830 that Clark had given Louis Gonville, White Plume's son-in-law, some money from the annuity fund to testify in Jefferson, Missouri, at the murder trial of two unidentified Kansas. The accusation was at least partly based on fact. Although the relatively small sum ("$40 or $50 in goods," according to Chouteau) paid Gonville was probably intended to cover his subsistence, Clark's rather arbitrary use of the tribe's annuities, even to protect the possible innocence of the accused, was an irregular action. But Chouteau's dispatch to the Indian Department included a variety of additional charges. The Kansa official was accused of distributing treaty funds in an unfair manner; without apparent cause he had dismissed a young Kansa "who was anxious to learn the business of a Black & Gun Smith;" he had made excessive and illegal profits in the livestock and fur trade; he had repeatedly incurred unnecessary expenses in the operation of his subagency; he was "intemperate . . . while at his agency thereby rendering himself unqualified to discharge his duties"; and he had threatened to "break the Indian Chiefs of said nation" who refused to accept annuities in the manner he had ordered.[21]

If they had been substantiated, those charges surely would have required Clark's immediate dismissal. Corroborative evidence to support only the initial charge was actually submitted,[22] however, and since Clark was soon promoted to the position of full agent, the absence of formal dismissal proceedings against him suggested exaggeration (or outright fabrication) in most of Chouteau's complaints and hinted that the Indian Department had confidence in him as a responsible public official. One thing may have closed the door to any objective consideration of the matter: Marston Clark was Superintendent William Clark's cousin. The latter was in a position to exercise considerable discretion, and under

[21] Charges of Francis Chouteau, Chouteau Papers; William Clark to Elbert Herring, December 28, 1831, LR, OIA, Fort Leavenworth Agency; William Clark to Herring, March 31, 1832, LR, OIA, St. Louis Superintendency.

[22] Affidavit of Louis Gonville, witnessed by Clement Lessert and Daniel M. Boone, n.d., 1830 (?), Chouteau Papers.

the circumstances he might have overlooked certain malpractices on grounds that it was virtually impossible to obtain competent individuals to serve in the more remote subagencies. In any case the fact remains that the white man was divided into contending camps and that the Kansas were not the first and most important consideration of those persons who in one way or another were authorized by the government to look after the Indians' welfare.

The complexity of the situation makes it difficult to determine with any precision the amount of suffering experienced by the Kansas in the two decades after 1825. What can be determined are the general trend and some of the seemingly isolated factors which in one way or another worked to their detriment and which ultimately convinced government officials and private interest groups that additional land-cession treaties were the only tenable solution.

Clark's trouble with the traders and the aggressive posture of the Chouteaus made it possible for certain Kansa chiefs to retain more than a fair share of the tribe's annuities. Yet had it not been the practice to allow the tribe, its councils, its leaders, or a combination of all three to decide each year whether they wished to be paid in specie or goods, a more equitable distribution might have been possible. Quarreling between individuals, clans, and villages became increasingly more commonplace, which in turn led to food shortages, disease, and death by starvation. In 1834, for example, only five chiefs decided for the entire tribe that their annuities should be paid exclusively in specie, while in 1839 an assembly of the whole demanded that they be paid in goods.[23] Meanwhile, in the spring of 1835, Richard Cummins of Fort Leavenworth Agency reported that the Kansas were starving. They had less than twenty bushels of corn and were begging at the settlements or trying to trade a few lengths of elk string for food.[24] William Clark's reference to their "destitute" condition the following year was no

[23] William Clark to Herring, March 30, 1835, Report of Cummins, LR, OIA, St. Louis Superintendency; William Clark to C. A. Harris, January 24, 1838, April 26, 1839, LR, OIA, Fort Leavenworth Agency.
[24] Cummins to William Clark, March 24, 1835, LR, OIA, Fort Leavenworth Agency.

exaggeration, nor was it an exception to the Kansa experience during the course of the next decade.[25]

In 1846, after suffering for two decades under what amounted to little more than the nominal wardship of the federal government, the tribe had no choice but to make the long trip to Fort Leavenworth, mostly on foot, to seek relief. Cummins described their situation as "absolutely destitute." Many were racked with "a billious fever," caused by what Thomas Harvey described as a diet of "roots and sap from the trees." The Sacs and Foxes had given them a few blankets and horses, but they had absolutely "nothing at all to eat when they arrived." A little meat and corn was issued from the military commissary by Cummins, whose awareness of the critical situation faced by the Kansas caused him to admit that "it was painful to my feelings that I could not give them enough to do them some good."[26] To make matters worse, Fool Chief reported that the tribe's latest hunting expedition to the buffalo plains between the Smoky Hill and Arkansas rivers had been a complete failure; moreover, they owed Frederick Chouteau at least fifteen hundred dollars, which would have to be paid out of the last annuity payment available under the St. Louis treaty of 1825.[27]

The interplay of these factors did much to undermine the Kansas' self-confidence. An optimistic outlook toward life, based on the traditions of the past and the promise of the future, became all but impossible; some Kansas became cynical or fatalistic, while others grew increasingly critical of the government's promised concern over their welfare. It was a time of general disillusionment for the Kansas, made even more difficult by the incidence of epidemic disease among their ranks. The irruption of smallpox was all the more tragic because of the casual manner in which government officials confronted the problem.

Variolation as a means of protection from smallpox was first practiced with mixed success in America as early as 1721. Vaccina-

[25] Clark to Herring, March 11, 1836, LR, OIA, Fort Leavenworth Agency.
[26] Cummins to Thomas Harvey, February 14, 1846, LR, OIA, Fort Leavenworth Agency.
[27] Letter of Fool Chief and Hard Chief to "My Father," January 23, 1844, LR, OIA, Fort Leavenworth Agency.

tion, an improved technique involving the introduction of cowpox virus, was announced by Dr. Edward Jenner in 1797 and, at the urging of President Jefferson, was effectively used on "a great embassy of [Indian] warriors" gathered at Washington in 1801. At that time a number of tribes in the Columbia and Missouri River basins were experiencing the full force of the disease. The effect was particularly devastating among the Arikaras, Gros Ventres, Mandans, and Sioux; on the Lower Platte the Poncas suffered heavily, while the Omahas lost nearly two-thirds of their people. Another major epidemic broke out in 1815–16, this time among the tribes of the Red and Río Grande valleys. The Comanches, for example, by their own count lost nearly four thousand souls at this time. The disease spread northward during the next two years, infecting the Iowas and later the Assiniboins and Sioux. Congress passed a bill in 1813 "to encourage vaccination" among the Indians, but the measure was repealed in 1822, probably because the initiative to take action was left to private citizens, not the Indian Bureau. Finally, on May 5, 1832, Congress passed a more realistic law which provided that Indian agents and subagents, under the direction of the Secretary of War, were "to convene the Indian tribes ... for the purpose of arresting the progress of smallpox among the several tribes by vaccination." The sum of twelve thousand dollars was appropriated to fund the measure the first year, with a daily compensation of six dollars to be paid to physicians who agreed to perform the service.[28]

It was reported in 1758 that smallpox and wars with the Pawnees had "substantially reduced" the Kansas.[29] There is no evidence of a large-scale infection for the next half-century, and surprisingly the Kansas were spared during the terrible epidemics of 1801–1802 and 1815–16. In the fall of 1827, however, William Clark reported that at least two-thirds of the tribe had been stricken. Though Clark did not specify the precise nature of the "malignant disease" that took about 180 Kansas' lives within a year, it was probably smallpox, then raging among their Osage allies near by. Fur traders and

[28] Stearn and Stearn, *The Effect of Smallpox*, 53–56, 62–63, 73–78.
[29] Nasatir, *Before Lewis and Clark*, I, 52.

whiskey peddlers plying the Missouri River in 1831 accidentally introduced the disease among the Pawnees, who lost nearly half their number within a few months. It was from this source—or perhaps from the Shawnees and Delawares—that the Kansas were again infected, this time in a devastating epidemic that took no fewer than 300 lives in 1831–32.[30]

Since they were among the tribes experiencing the full force of the epidemic when Congress authorized a plan to check the further spread of the disease, the Kansas were one of the first groups selected for treatment. Unfortunately, the animosity between Subagent Clark and the Chouteaus hampered any immediate realization of this objective. By February 1, 1833, the government had vaccinated nearly 7,000 Indians in the Middle and Lower Missouri Valley,[31] but the badly infected Kansas had been excluded. A possible explanation for this scandalous situation is found in a letter from Superintendent William Clark to Secretary of War Lewis Cass in which Clark complained that Frederick Chouteau had "seriously interfered with Dr. [?] Crow's efforts to vaccinate the Kansas." His information came from Subagent Marston Clark, Chouteau's personal enemy, who demanded that the trader's license be revoked, that his bond be forfeited, and that he be expelled from the Indian country.[32] However, before Cass could take action, the War Department received a deposition from Clement Lessert, a Kansa interpreter and occasional employee of Chouteau, who attempted to refute Clark's charges. That same day an identical deposition was received from Pierre Ravalette, whose relationship to Chouteau was similar to that of Lessert.[33]

[30] Report of William Clark to Commissioner of Indian Affairs (?), October 20, 1827, Clark to T. L. McKenney, April 1, 1828, LR, OIA, St. Louis Superintendency; Rothensteiner, "Early Missionary Efforts Among the Indians," 79; Isaac McCoy to War Department, January 31 and October 15, 1832, Isaac McCoy Papers; Marston G. Clark to William Clark, September 1, 1833, LR, OIA, Fort Leavenworth Agency; Stearn and Stearn, *The Effect of Smallpox*, 78–79; Barry, "Kansas Before 1854," XXVIII (Summer, 1962), 188–89.

[31] Barry, "Kansas Before 1854," XXVIII (Summer, 1962), 196.

[32] William Clark to Lewis Cass, January 7, 1833, LR, OIA, Fort Leavenworth Agency.

[33] Depositions of Clement Lessert and Pierre Ravalette, taken by Sam C. Owen, Clerk for Jackson County, Missouri, February 2, 1833, LR, OIA, Fort Leavenworth Agency.

According to the depositions, Subagent Clark had instructed Lessert to go to the upper village (probably Hard Chief's), where he was ordered to detain the Kansas until Dr. Crow arrived. The Indians were starving and anxious to depart on a hunting expedition, but they displayed no fear of the vaccine and in a cooperative spirit agreed to wait at least three days. However, the government physician did not arrive for "5 or 6 days" and by this time the Indians had "mostly departed."[34] Chouteau's version of the affair was not very much different, although he added some important details. He categorically denied influencing the Kansas one way or another; it was he, not Clark, who had dispatched Lessert to the Kansas' village. He admitted that his traders had distributed supplies and ammunition to the Indians during the three-day interval, but he countered the unfortunate generalization that could be drawn from the action by asserting that the tribe's "miserable condition" was the deciding factor in their abrupt departure for the plains.[35]

Faced with conflicting accounts of the affair and mindful of the strife between Subagent Clark and the Chouteaus in 1830, Superintendent William Clark took the easy way out by advising Commissioner Elbert Herring "to suspend the execution of [his] instructions [to revoke Chouteau's license] until further advised by the Department on this subject."[36] There the matter rested. The plan to vaccinate the Kansas was abandoned for the time being. Indeed, it was not until 1838 that Dr. A. Chute finally submitted an official register of 915 Kansas vaccinated during the spring. Even so, there is reason to question whether they were actually treated. An unidentified disease characterized by a "high fever" struck the tribe at Mission Creek in the summer of 1839. Few families were spared, and within a short time at least 100 Kansas had died. Perhaps it was cholera, which struck the tribe as early as the fall of 1833, or it may have been smallpox. In either case, it prompted no concerted effort to provide medical protection for the Kansas. Chronic disease

---

[34] *Ibid.*

[35] Frederick Chouteau to Pierre Chouteau, Jr., February 5, 1833, LR, OIA, Fort Leavenworth Agency.

[36] William Clark to Elbert Herring, February 23, 1833, LR, OIA, Fort Leavenworth Agency.

continued to plague them: a smallpox epidemic in 1855 claimed at least 400 lives, much to the "satisfaction" of their agent and to "all who [had] any acquaintance with [them]."[37]

In addition to the obstructionist behavior of the traders and the shock of epidemic disease, the erratic weather patterns in Indian country worked against the Kansas' agricultural accomplishments. Torrential spring rains were particularly disastrous. For example, Francis Chouteau's "Randolph Bluffs" depot near the mouth of the Kansas River was completely destroyed by a flood in late April and early May, 1826.[38] The following spring, not long after the Kansas had abandoned their Blue Earth village and had planted their first crop of corn at Mission Creek, another flood swept through the Kansas Valley. The tribe's entire crop was lost; many persons became sick and according to William Clark "a number died before relief could be afforded them."[39]

Nevertheless, government agriculturists did not object when white contractors plowed and planted for the tribe in river valleys that were especially susceptible to flooding. With the rainfall more moderate and the contractors doing most of the work, it appeared that some progress was being made. Taking advantage of "special funds . . . not yet made available," Agent Richard Cummins reported in 1836 that 282 acres on four separate farms had been planted;[40] 300 acres were under cultivation by 1838, and "a few [women] were beginning to use the plough."[41] A "considerable amount" of corn was raised the following year, but most of the surplus cured in preparation for the fall hunt was given away to

[37] Marston G. Clark to William Clark, September 1, 1833, Register of Kansas Indians vaccinated by Dr. A. Chute, May and June, 1838, LR, OIA, Fort Leavenworth Agency; William Johnson to Corresponding Secretary of Methodist Episcopal Church, December 30, 1840, typed copy, and typed copy of "Neosho Valley Villages at Council Grove," Morehouse Papers; John Montgomery to Alexander Cumming, April 31, 1855, LR, OIA, Kansas Agency.

[38] Barry, "Kansas Before 1854," XXVIII (Spring, 1962), 25.

[39] Annual report of William Clark, October 20, 1827, LR, OIA, St. Louis Superintendency.

[40] Cummins to William Clark, August 2, 1836, LR, OIA, Fort Leavenworth Agency.

[41] Cummins to C. A. Harris, September 25, 1838, LR, OIA, Fort Leavenworth Agency.

friendly tribes to the east.[42] By this time many of the Kansas were ill, while others were preparing for the anticipated encounter with the Pawnees. Yet Cummins remained optimistic. Like the Methodists, he apparently believed that a few families, with their small plots of corn, pumpkins, and cabbage, were "gaining in agricultural pursuits" and would set an example for others. Then in late 1840 came the surprise victory over the Pawnees. The heady atmosphere surrounding this significant event constituted a powerful deterrent to agrarian enterprise, and whatever the extent of interest in the yeoman's life that may have survived the victory celebrations, it was virtually obliterated by the spectacular flood of 1844.[43]

Following a mild winter and pleasant early spring, rain began to fall in the last week of March, 1844. It continued almost uninterrupted in the Kansas Valley for nearly a month. Father Christian Hoecken of Potawatomie Catholic Mission recorded that it rained "forty days in succession" and that "great floods covered the country." Rain fell "in such torrents as to remind us of Noah's day," reported one traveler; another reported that at Knife River (now Cross Creek), just west of the Kansa villages, water "rose 15 feet in one day." Indian Superintendent Thomas H. Harvey, then on a tour of the various Indian agencies, was unable to visit the Kansas because of "the overwhelming state of the waters." Not until fall was the full extent of the disaster at Mission Creek known. According to Agent Cummins, the bottom land selected for the Kansa farms had been "overflown from Bluff to Bluff, sweeping off all [their] fencing, houses &cc."[44]

Some individuals attempted to replant their fields several times, but the futility of their efforts was increased when army worms destroyed the young shoots of corn almost as soon as they appeared. With winter approaching and less than a gallon of corn per man, woman, and child on hand, Harvey's incredible dispatch to Commissioner Crawford asked for "less annuities and more Christian

---

[42] Cummins to Joshua Pilcher, October n.d., 1839, LR, OIA, St. Louis Superintendency.
[43] Cummins to Pilcher, September 30, 1840, LR, OIA, Fort Leavenworth Agency.
[44] Barry, "Kansas Before 1854," XXX (Spring, 1964), 65, 72–75.

teaching in organized institutions."[45] Later, after a more realistic appraisal of their deplorable condition, he admitted that "an outright *donation* would do much to restore [the tribe's] confidence in the United States government."[46] But the possibility of such action was remote.

Poorly housed, sick, and starving, increasing numbers of Kansas resorted to raiding the Santa Fe caravans or stealing from the settlements near the mouth of the Kansas River, where unscrupulous white men operated "whiskey shops in their place, using every stratagem in their power to get the Indians to drink."[47] The various individuals and groups who reported losses demanded full and immediate compensation from the government, and in the absence of special appropriations, it became the practice to pay claims out of the annuity fund, often without the tribe's knowledge. The crux of the problem and the tribe's faltering faith in the government were sharply stated by Fool Chief in 1836:

If our great father directs that [Mr.] Hicks be paid for his [stolen] horse, why does he say that the payment must come out of our annuity, when our great *father owes us for hogs, cattle and chickens* due us by the Treaty [of 1825] but which we have never received? Of the hogs due us, one hundred and seven were wanting, and seven of the cattle, but I do not know how many chickens. . . . Father, what I have said is the truth. I don't lie. Our great Father has sent us his word. Now I send back our answer which I wish you my father [Agent Cummins] to send to him.[48]

A cursory and much delayed investigation of the matter by Cummins revealed that Fool Chief was well informed on the subject. The contractor authorized to deliver the livestock to the villages

45 Thomas Harvey to T. Hartley Crawford, October 8, 1844, LR, OIA, St. Louis Superintendency.
46 Harvey to Crawford, November 14, 1847, LR, OIA, St. Louis Superintendency.
47 John Dougherty to William Clark, June 24, and 30, 1828, and Official Record of Kansa Thefts on the Santa Fe Trail to 1831, LR, OIA, St. Louis Superintendency; Mrs. E. D. Meeker to Emoline Richardson, June 12, 1834, Meeker Papers.
48 Fool Chief's Speech at the Kansas Village, recorded by P. R. Thompson, September 16, 1836, LR, OIA, Fort Leavenworth Agency. The St. Louis Treaty of 1825 authorized the tribe to receive 300 cattle, 300 hogs, and 500 domestic fowls. Kappler, *Indian Affairs*, 222.

agreed that a substantial number of animals had been lost "due to warm weather." Considering the Kansas' plight, justice seemed to require some form of compensation, but since the Indian office in St. Louis held a legal receipt of delivery, Fool Chief's charge was ignored. The matter was quietly dropped, leaving Cummins' hands tied. In desperation he could think of nothing better than to recommend that the tribe quit the chase, which in his opinion would "help solve a lot of things and make his job easier."[49] Embittered by the outcome, the Kansas tried to retaliate in 1843 by refusing to authorize further depredation payments out of their annuities, but by this time the objectionable practice had been upheld—in fact, made even more stringent by a special letter from the Indian Department in 1842.[50]

In a seemingly deliberate plan to make life intolerable for the Kansas, a variety of additional problems complicated their predicament. For precise reasons unknown, but probably because of squatter pressure, competition between missionary societies, and the usual machinations of speculators, the tribe's "seminary" (or education) lands paralleling the western Missouri boundary remained unsold. The Chouteaus tried to obtain control of the entire block of thirty-six sections, but their proposal was turned down. Superintendent Harvey admitted, in December, 1844, however, that if disposal were delayed much longer, the land would "be of little value because the settlers [were] taking all the timber."[51] The Kansa half-bloods were no less impatient, and with good reason. For years they had requested that their tracts in the Lower Kansas Valley be sold, but an even more formidable combination of squatters, speculators, emigrant Indians, and government ineptitude prevented it. While the government vacillated and then resorted to delaying tactics, it was with increasing animosity that the half-

[49] Cummins to Crawford, May 31, 1841, and Cummins to Thomas Harvey, February 21, 1844, LR, OIA, Fort Leavenworth Agency.

[50] Cummins to D. D. Mitchell, February 5, 1843, LR, OIA, Fort Leavenworth Agency.

[51] Cummins to Harvey, February 21, 1844, Harvey to Crawford, December 28, 1844, and Harvey to William Medill, LR, OIA, Fort Leavenworth Agency; John S. Phillips to Medill, February 7, 1849, LR, OIA, St. Louis Superintendency.

bloods realized they were being denied the "twenty-five . . . to forty dollars per acre" the Indian Department ultimately conceded the lands were worth.[52]

Finally, there was the potentially explosive problem of intertribal relationships. The St. Louis treaty of 1825 was essentially an orthodox land-cession document; nothing was said about the government's role in prompting peace and understanding between the Kansas and several other tribes who were accustomed to hunting in much of the Smoky Hill country awarded to the Kansas in 1825. Indeed, the traditional idea of tribal sovereignty, especially following a declaration on March 3, 1817, that federal law did not extend "to any offense committed by one Indian against another, within any Indian boundary,"[53] amounted to a rigid hands-off policy that encouraged intertribal conflict. Coinciding with the government's unfolding removal policy, the appearance of squatters and land speculators, and the opening of the Santa Fe Trail, it was virtually certain that conflicts over land, reservation boundaries, hunting rights, and freedom of movement in general would become more pronounced.

The prospect of emigrant Indians arriving in large numbers was a disquieting prospect to the Kansas, as well as to certain Indian Department officials who on the basis of experience could see a difficult situation developing. It was apparent that some of the smaller tribes were unable to contend with the larger, more powerful ones; tribal acquiescence to the government's assimilation strategy was not at all uniform, and relationships between tribes with historical claims to the best hunting grounds remained severely strained. With additional reports of widespread suffering being matched by White Plume's demand for protection from the Republican Pawnees, Agent John Dougherty obtained two thousand dollars from William Clark in the spring of 1828 to preside over a

52 Cummins to Joshua Pilcher, January 15, 1840, Isaac McCoy to Joel R. Poinsett, February 2, 1840, and Pilcher to Crawford, February 27, 1840, LR, OIA, Fort Leavenworth Agency; D. D. Mitchell to Crawford, April 18, 1842, LR, OIA, St. Louis Superintendency; John Montgomery to James W. Denver, June 30, 1857, LR, OIA, Kansas Agency.

53 Prucha, *American Indian Policy*, 211–12.

peace conference at Cantonment Leavenworth. The Kansas and Republican Pawnees were invited, as were the Omahas, Otoes, Iowas, Sacs, Missouris, and Shawnees.[54] Dougherty claimed that the meeting was successful; Clark termed it a "highly honorable" affair, especially with regard to "the friendly feeling expressed . . . towards the Emigrating Indians."[55] In reality the proceedings were hasty, informal, and disillusioning. Apart from distributing a few gifts and listening to the usual promises of mutual friendship, the government had committed itself in no way to a workable plan of enforcement.

Additional difficulties were reported almost immediately. In 1829 the Pawnees murdered a Kansa "for poaching" near Council Grove in the Upper Neosho Valley.[56] White Plume suggested that Brevet Major Bennett Riley, whose Sixth Infantry at Cantonment Leavenworth had been assigned to protect the wagon trains headed for Santa Fe, provide the Kansas with protection while they hunted in "Pawnee country." It was a reasonable proposal, but Riley advised against it on grounds that the Kansa annuity subsidy would have to be terminated if government troops were put to this kind of use.[57] Insulted and angered by this kind of soft talk, some of the more aggressive warriors resorted to violence. By April, 1831, they had killed fourteen Pawnees and had stolen twenty to thirty horses.[58] Clearly, Dougherty's gifts and council had accomplished very little.

Fearful that conditions might deteriorate even more, the Indian Department decided to organize additional peace conferences at Fort Leavenworth and at Independence, Missouri. In addition to most of the tribes who had promised to bury the hatchet in 1828, such emigrant groups as the Delawares, Kaskaskias, Kickapoos, Peorias, Potawatomis, Piankeshaws, and Weas were invited. After the distribution of gifts and an exchange of Kansa and Pawnee

[54] White Plume (translated by Daniel M. Boone) to Clark, August 22, 1827, LR, OIA, St. Louis Superintendency; Dougherty to Lewis Cass, typed copy, March 9, 1832, Dougherty Papers, KSHS.

[55] Dougherty to Lewis Cass, typed copy, March 9, 1832, Dougherty Papers, KSHS; Clark to Dougherty, August 2, 1828, John Dougherty Papers, MHS.

[56] Otis E. Young, *The First Military Escort on the Santa Fe Trail*, 77–78.

[57] *Ibid.*, 66–67.

[58] Dougherty to Clark, April 7, 1831, Dougherty Papers, MHS.

threats that very nearly disrupted the parley of November, 1833,[59] Commissioner Henry L. Ellsworth secured the usual promises from all tribes in attendance that hostilities would cease immediately. The practice of taking action for "private revenge" was to be abandoned; offenders were to be delivered to the Indian agents by their own people; government commissioners were to serve as umpires in all difficulties that might arise; and "the laws of the United States were to be used for punishment."[60]

Although Ellsworth explained to Indian Commissioner Elbert Herring that "what he [had] arranged [did] not commit the United States," the fact remains that when compared to Dougherty's vague negotiations in 1828, Ellsworth's efforts theoretically opened the way for a more certain government responsibility to preserve peace in Indian country. Ellsworth emphasized that all tribes involved in the talks were receptive to the idea of an objective "umpire" acting as peacemaker, and he reminded his superiors "that something [had] to be done to protect [the] small tribes from the larger."[61] Nevertheless, the Indian Department refused to submit the treaty for ratification, perhaps because Ellsworth had exceeded his instructions or perhaps because Congress was then involved in hearings that would lead to a fundamental revision of the Indian statutes. Of considerable relevance to the explosive situation in the Kansas Valley, the Trade and Intercourse Act of 1834 contained a provision allowing the President to use military force to apprehend criminal Indians; more important, perhaps, it provided that the chief executive could use federal troops to prevent or terminate hostilities "between any of the Indian tribes."[62]

Theoretically, then, the way was clear for a possible reconciliation between the Kansas and Pawnees, or at least a tempering of their differences. In practice it was quite the opposite. Perhaps the

[59] Irving, *Indian Sketches*, 250–53.

[60] Unratified Treaty of November 12 and 23, 1833, Documents Relating to the Negotiation of Ratified and Unratified Treaties with Various Tribes of Indians, Unratified Treaties, 1821–1865 (T-494, R 8), NA (cited hereafter as Unratified Treaties, 1821–1865).

[61] Ellsworth to Elbert Herring, November 23, 1833, Unratified Treaties, 1821–1865.

[62] *U.S. Statutes at Large*, IV, 732.

government had too much faith in the Methodists, who in 1834 were busy with their second missionary experiment at Mission Creek. Perhaps it was naïvely assumed that Ellsworth's conference had done some good, even though the government took no official action. Perhaps the arena of conflict was too remote—and too expensive—to be effectively policed. Perhaps those commissioners and agents with the most responsibility simply did not care. In any case there is no evidence that the military authority of the United States was used to compromise basic differences between the two tribes. The nagging problem of hunting rights and the questions of honor, revenge, and personal prestige were allowed to smolder until fanned into a roaring blaze by the Kansas' vicious attack on the Pawnees in 1840.

The arrogant attitudes encouraged by this encounter were aggravated by the tribe's illness, as well as the pressure of missionary activity and the flood of 1844. With the Kansa annuity fund virtually exhausted, it was difficult for the government to continue its policy of procrastination much longer. But what was to be done? Nearly twenty years of tutelage had accomplished nothing. The Kansas had accepted neither agriculture nor Christianity; they were sick, starving, plagued by internal dissension, and virtually hemmed in by unfriendly or more aggressive tribes. White civilization had indeed failed to rescue the "savage." Yet in the darkness of the bureaucratic mind there was a ray of hope: the Kansas' land.

In 1825 the United States reserved "for use of the Kansas nation" a strip of land thirty miles wide, beginning twenty leagues west of the Missouri border and extending to an undetermined point beyond the junction of the Republican and Smoky Hill rivers.[63] Perhaps the bulk of this vast domain, amounting to more than two million acres, could be ceded; the proceeds could then be used to alleviate at least some of the tribe's more immediate problems, while the process of forced acculturation—which, of course, had failed up to that point—could be renewed with greater dedication and vigor on a smaller, more concentrated reservation.

The history of this approach can be traced back to 1831,

[63] Kappler, *Indian Affairs*, 222.

when Isaac McCoy advised the War Department that "in view of the condition of the Kansas . . . it might be expedient to locate [them] at and above the Smoky Hill and Republican rivers."[64] In 1842 George W. Ewing, whose primary interest was land speculation, reported that the Kansas were ready to sell so that, among other things, they could move away from the "Missouri whiskey merchants."[65] Others, including Colonel William Morrison, who was seeking land for the Sacs and Foxes of Illinois, were anxious to get their hands on the Kansa domain.[66] Events unfolded rapidly in 1844. In late January, Fool Chief and Hard Chief sent a letter to Washington in which they insisted they were ready to sell all of the tribe's land east of the Blue (Blue Earth) River—nearly one-third of their entire reservation. Since the tract contained some of the most attractive terrain west of the Missouri, it is difficult to believe that the offer was not engineered, at least in part, by outside interests.[67]

While Harvey and Cummins tried to convince Commissioner Crawford that the Kansas had been forced to accept "a bad bargain" from William Clark in 1825 and that "a liberal [government] purchase . . . would be the easiest means of indemnifying them for their former oversight,"[68] the principal chiefs and about forty braves set out for St. Louis "to see Harvey about a big new treaty." Cummins intercepted them and angrily turned them back,[69] but by this time their patience was exhausted. Determined to take their case to their "Great Father" in person, two Kansa spokesmen eluded military authorities in St. Louis and somehow obtained river passage for Washington. Not until they had reached Wheeling, Virginia, in July, 1844, were they apprehended and speedily sent back to the

[64] McCoy to John Eaton, January 31, 1831, Isaac McCoy Papers.

[65] George W. Ewing to James M. Porter, n.d., 1842, LR, OIA, St. Louis Superintendency.

[66] Thomas Harvey to Crawford, April 8, 1844, LR, OIA, Fort Leavenworth Agency.

[67] Fool Chief and Hard Chief to "My Father," January 23, 1844, LR, OIA, Fort Leavenworth Agency.

[68] Cummins to Harvey, March 6, 1844, LR, OIA, Fort Leavenworth Agency.

[69] Harvey to William Medill, June 26, 1846, LR, OIA, Fort Leavenworth Agency.

Indian country.[70] This almost pathetic effort to obtain relief and ominous reports from the frontier that the Sioux were "making it *increasingly* more dangerous for the border Indians to go to the plains for buffalo" and that the Pawnee war was becoming more widespread,[71] were enough to convince the government that a new treaty was mandatory.

With their bargaining power severely compromised by the tribe's suffering, the chiefs and principal men finally ceded two million acres of their most valuable land—roughly the eastern third of the 1825 reservation—for the miserly sum of $202,000. Amounting to just over ten cents per acre, the sum was divided into thirty annual payments of $8,000, plus $2,000 each year for educational and agricultural improvement. The remaining $2,000 was earmarked for treaty expenses, the erection of a mill at the new reservation, some immediate relief, and compensation to the Methodists for their physical improvements at Mission Creek. Since there was some doubt concerning the sufficiency of timber on the unceded land, it was agreed that the President could "cause to be selected and laid off for the Kansas a [more] suitable country, near the western boundary of the land ceded . . . which shall remain for their use forever."[72]

The Mission Creek treaty was ratified on April 13, 1846, and proclaimed on April 15. Less than three months later Harvey reported that the diminished reservation west of the Republican-Smoky Hill junction was indeed lacking in timber; it was also too close to the Pawnees and not nearly as attractive as the Upper Neosho Valley about thirty miles to the southeast.[73] As usual, the wheels of the Indian Department's administrative machinery ground exceeding slow, and not until the following spring did Harvey authorize Cummins and several Kansa chiefs to spy out the Promised Land. When the chiefs saw the bleak Republican and

[70] David Agnew to Crawford, August 2, 1844, and Harvey to Crawford, August 2, 1844, LR, OIA, Fort Leavenworth Agency.

[71] Harvey to Crawford, October 8, 1844, LR, OIA, St. Louis Superintendency.

[72] Kappler, *Indian Affairs*, 552–54.

[73] Harvey to Medill, July 3, 1846, LR, OIA, Fort Leavenworth Agency.

Smoky Hill country and learned that a Comanche war party had recently visited the area, they readily agreed that the Neosho Valley was a more desirable place to live.[74]

In a move calculated to discourage the Kansas' hunting habits, Commissioner William Medill and Superintendent Harvey decided the new reservation should be no larger than twenty miles square. Harvey favored the area around Council Grove, a regular outfitting post for the rough, hard-drinking Santa Fe Trail merchants, and ordered Cummins to locate the new boundaries around the post with an eye to "the future disposition of the unappropriated lands adjacent to the reservation."[75] Hastily completed in the summer of 1847, the survey was based on faulty maps Isaac McCoy had drawn more than a decade earlier. Cummins advised his superiors that it was "impossible to define the location correctly,"[76] but his complaint was ignored. After all, the "degenerate yet docile Kansas," who according to Harvey "could be forced to move in five days," now had a new home largely removed from the corrupting influence of the Missouri frontier. The government had arranged a more generous subsidy than in the past and had provided the missionary-farmers with the means for breathing new life into the cultural revolution inaugurated in 1825. The emigrant Indians destined to inherit the ceded lands were pleased, and the land speculators were greatly encouraged by the ease with which the treaty of 1846 had been negotiated. In short, the future looked bright.[77]

However, a few clouds could be seen on the horizon. Unopposed, the squatters and timber merchants continued to invade

[74] Harvey to Cummins, May 15, 1847, Cummins to Harvey, July 17, 1847, Harvey to Medill, September 5, 8, and August 11, 1847, LR, OIA, Fort Leavenworth Agency.

[75] Harvey to Cummins, May 15, 1847, LR, OIA, Fort Leavenworth Agency.

[76] Cummins to Harvey, July 17, 1847, Harvey to Medill, September 8, 1847, LR, OIA, Fort Leavenworth Agency. Cummins' map and field notes were placed in the War Department files as "Drafting Division Portfolio K." See frame number 703, LR for 1847, OIA, Fort Leavenworth Agency.

[77] Harvey to Medill, April 19, 1847, LR, OIA, St. Louis Superintendency; Harvey to Medill, April 24 and November 30, 1847, LR, OIA, Fort Leavenworth Agency; Harvey to Medill, March 31, 1848, Letters Received by the Office of Indian Affairs, Osage River Agency (M 234, R 643), NA (cited hereafter as LR, OIA, Osage River Agency).

the unceded lands reserved for the half-bloods and the funding of tribal education, thus reducing their market value even before they were legally a part of the public domain.[78] At Mission Creek the precise nature of the recent treaty remained vague, and the tribe as a whole was reluctant to depart for the new reservation. A few of the more venturesome who made the journey encountered trouble almost immediately when a party of Santa Fe traders attacked them near Council Grove and severely injured at least one Kansa. Harvey was furious and ordered the traders "to pay for the attack"; at the same time, he had good cause to wonder whether the new reservation site was a wise choice.[79] With emigrant Indians beginning to take possession of recently ceded lands and most of the Kansas wandering about in an aimless manner, Harvey and Cummins began to panic. In desperation they fired off to Commissioner Medill a letter which said in its entirety: "What shall be done with the Kansas Indians?"[80]

[78] Harvey to Medill, December 29, 1848, LR, OIA, Fort Leavenworth Agency; John S. Phillips to Medill, February 7, 1849, LR, OIA, St. Louis Superintendency.

[79] Harvey to Medill, May 12, 1848, LR, OIA, Osage River Agency.

[80] Unsigned (Harvey and/or Cummins ?) letter to Medill, October 29, 1847, LR, OIA, Fort Leavenworth Agency.

CHAPTER 7 THE NEOSHO
VALLEY EXPERIENCE

THE 256,000-acre reservation selected as the "permanent" home
for the Kansa Indians in 1846 included that part of the Upper
Neosho Valley which for two decades had served as a resting and
outfitting place on the international trail between Independence
and Santa Fe. Traveling west with General Stephen Watts Kearny
in July, 1846, George Rutledge Gibson described Council Grove—
located on the banks of the Neosho River where the Osage treaty
of 1825 was negotiated—as the last place from which a single person
might safely return to the States. Fed by water from the southern
flank of the low divide separating the Missouri and Arkansas river
systems, the valley had an abundance of rich alluvial soil. A "splen-
did choice of timber" was available and in the opinion of a Cincinnati group interested in colonization after Kansas Territory was
organized in 1854, the climate was far superior to that of the Kansas
River country to the northeast. Indeed, if the conclusion of one
traveler is accepted at face value, the area was nothing less than "an
oasis in the wilderness."[1]

Although these descriptions were exaggerated, the valley was
attractive to easterners, especially when compared to the treeless
plains farther west; and it was inevitable, perhaps, that a white

1 Ralph P. Bieber (ed.), *Journal of a Soldier Under Kearny and Doniphan 1846–1847 by George Rutledge Gibson*, 138–39; Boynton and Mason, *A Journey through Kansas*, 43; Ralph P. Bieber (ed.), *Southern Trails to California in 1849*, 368.

settlement would be established in the vicinity of Council Grove. As was so often the case in the expansion of the American frontier, the federal government took the lead. According to one count, the War Department used more than a thousand wagons to transport vital military stores from Missouri River ports to Santa Fe during the Mexican War. Many of these vehicles required repairs en route, and with this in mind, the assistant quartermaster at Fort Leavenworth sent two blacksmiths to establish a government service shop at Council Grove. This was accomplished in July, 1846, and it served to attract others to the area, well in advance of the Kansa Indians. Among them was Seth M. Hays, who arrived in the summer of 1847 armed with a government license to trade with the Indians and instructions from the Westport firm of Boone and Hamilton to establish a supply store for the convenience of overland freighters. Apparently his enterprise was prosperous enough to attract other merchants, for by 1849 there were "three or four shops" and at least six log houses located on part of the land only recently awarded to the Kansas.[2]

The future of Council Grove as a commercial center looked even more promising with the anticipated arrival of the Kansas and rumors that a new Indian agency would be established in the vicinity. Undaunted by its recent failure at Mission Creek and encouraged by the government's interest in awarding an "education" contract for the Kansas' economic and moral improvement,[3] the Methodist Episcopal Church South sent Allen T. Ward to Council Grove in the fall of 1850 to construct a mission building and help Pierre Chouteau break sod for the tribe's farming operations. By late December an impressive eight-room, two-story stone school had been completed. Near by were two new log houses, a well, and about two hundred acres ready for spring planting. To operate the school and instruct the Kansas in the mental arts, the

[2] Ralph P. Bieber (ed.), *Wah-To-Yah and the Taos Trail by Lewis H. Garrard*, 35; Alice S. Smith, "Through the Eyes of My Father," *CKSHS*, XVII (1926–28), 709; Ralph P. Bieber (ed.), *Adventures in the Santa Fé Trade 1844–1847 by James Josiah Webb*, 298; Bieber, *Southern Trails*, 368.

[3] Thomas Harvey to William Medill, November 30, 1847, LR, OIA, Fort Leavenworth Agency; Harvey to Medill, March 31, 1848, LR, OIA, Osage River Agency.

Methodists selected Thomas Sears Huffaker, whose influence with the tribe for the next twenty years probably exceeded that of any other white person. His assistant was H. H. Webster, an "agriculturist" whose instructions were to teach the Kansas to become economically self-sufficient.[4]

The Kansas were reluctant to move, even though the treaty of 1846 stipulated they were to leave the Kansas Valley by May, 1847. They were destitute of provisions, their new reservation had not yet been officially surveyed, and they had been given no opportunity to select new village sites in the Neosho Valley. Thus the difficult winter of 1847–48 was spent begging and stealing from the emigrant tribes, from the none too cooperative military personnel at Fort Leavenworth, or from the wholly unsympathetic whites who had settled along the western Missouri border. Finally, in late January, 1848, Superintendent Thomas H. Harvey persuaded several Kansa leaders to hold a conference at Potawatomie Agency at St. Mark. Here he issued emergency supplies to the amount of "$3 per capita" and instructed the Kansas carefully, so there would be not the "slightest confusion," concerning what was expected of them and where the tribe was to go.[5]

Despite Harvey's promise, the trek to the Upper Neosho Valley in the late spring of 1848 was made with little or no government supervision. Hard Chief's people located their village near Cahola (Kahola) Creek, a small tributary of the Neosho River some ten miles southeast of Council Grove. The village of Fool Chief, then ruled by Speckled Eye, one of Hard Chief's brothers, and later by Fool Chief the Younger, was established on the right bank of the Neosho about seven miles southeast of Council Grove. Directly northwest was a village controlled by Peg-gah-hosh-she (Big John; probably American Chief), another of Hard Chief's brothers. It was located near the mouth of Big John Creek less than two miles

4 Allen T. Ward to Father, Mother and Sister, December 21, 1850, Allen T. Ward Papers, Manuscript Division, KSHS; "Neosho Valley Villages at Council Grove," Morehouse Papers.

5 Harvey to Medill, January 25, 1848, LR, OIA, St. Louis Superintendency; Harvey to Medill, January 26, 1848, LR, OIA, Fort Leavenworth Agency; Harvey to Medill, May 12, 1848, LR, OIA, Osage River Agency.

from Council Grove and the Santa Fe Trail crossing. All things considered, it was a remarkable achievement for the Kansas to establish all three villages anywhere near where the government wanted them. Certainly Superintendent Harvey's statement that the tribe would be directed to its new reservation without the "slightest confusion" was an empty promise, even though it was not challenged until 1856, when the official survey clearly indicated that Peg-gah-hosh-she's village was the only one located within the boundaries authorized at Mission Creek negotiations in 1846.[6]

Additional evidence of a return to the more traditional policy of official neglect was the government's failure to provide the Kansas with a resident agent during the crucial early years on the Upper Neosho. In place of a separate agency more accessible and responsive to the tribe's needs, a policy of indecision and administrative duplicity was substituted. Jurisdiction for the three villages was shifted from the Fort Leavenworth Agency to the Osage River Agency in 1848, to the Sac and Fox Agency in 1851, and to the Potawatomie Agency in 1853, all of which were at least fifty miles from the Neosho villages. To confuse matters even more, nine different agents—including some who served for less than three months—were at least nominally in charge of Kansa affairs between 1848 and 1855. Not until March 3, 1855, when John Montgomery was assigned to the newly created Kansas Agency at Council Grove, did the tribe have any reasonable access to a public authority other than their quasi-official missionary-teacher.[7] Under these circumstances, then, many individuals became accustomed to stealing from the Santa Fe wagon trains on a regular basis, while certain local merchants "openly flaunted" the federal intercourse laws by providing a steady supply of whiskey at the villages and fencing valuable grazing lands belonging to the tribe. With tempers flaring and violence becoming more common by December, 1854, it was with

6 "Neosho Valley Villages at Council Grove," Morehouse Papers; Survey of Kansa Reservation Received by OIA, September 20, 1856, LR, OIA, Kansas Agency.

7 "Kansas Agencies," 773; Secretary of the Interior to Acting Commissioner of Indian Affairs, September 6, 1853, and George W. Clark to Alexander Cumming.

well-founded concern that several Neosho Valley merchants advised federal authorities that "matters look[ed] ugly for the future."[8]

Between 1848 and Montgomery's appointment in 1855, the Kansas made little or no progress in agriculture. Rather, they came under the damaging influence of unscrupulous white men while remaining almost wholly dependent upon the chase and their annuities for livelihood, this in spite of the Methodist mission and farm operated by Thomas Huffaker at Council Grove after 1851. Like the Johnsons at Mission Creek, Huffaker had little influence with the Kansas. Tribal leaders steadfastly refused to allow girls to attend his boarding school; only a few boys, mostly orphans, were given irregular instruction in reading and writing. Gospel preaching and effective agricultural instruction at the villages were out of the question. In fact the gulf that continued to separate the Methodists and the "heathen Kaws," in the words of the Reverend C. B. Boynton, was "enough to stagger one's belief in the unity of the race."[9]

Fearful that the government would terminate its financial support, Huffaker resorted to instructing a few white children from the Council Grove area, but the Indian Department could not be convinced that the operation was fulfilling its intended purpose. As a result the school was closed in 1854 because of what Huffaker claimed was the government's failure to increase appropriations above fifty dollars annually for each student. He also cited the tribe's categorical rejection of Christian principles.[10] Nevertheless, it soon became apparent, at least to certain officials in Washington,

[8] Petition of David Waldo, James Brown, John J. Johns, ? Reid, Jaboz Smith, William McCoy and William Gilpin to the President of the United States, January 10, 1851, LR, OIA, Osage River Agency; Public Notice of George W. Clark, December 25, 1854, LR, OIA, Potawatomie Agency.

[9] Alexander Cumming to Thomas Harvey, December 21, 1847, LR, OIA, Fort Leavenworth Agency; John Montgomery to Cumming, November 1, 1855, and Testimony of Thomas Huffaker before Hiram W. Farnsworth, February 4, 1862, LR, OIA, Kansas Agency; Boynton and Mason, *A Journey through Kansas,* 117–18; "Neosho Valley Villages at Council Grove," Morehouse Papers.

[10] "Neosho Valley Villages at Council Grove," Morehouse Papers; Boynton and Mason, *A Journey through Kansas,* 117; George W. Clark to Cumming, November 13, 1854, LR, OIA, Potawatomie Agency.

that other factors had contributed to Huffaker's abortive performance at Council Grove.

A commitment to bring Christian civilization to the Kansas was not the only reason the Methodist leader came to the Neosho Valley. Indeed, Huffaker probably viewed his position largely within the context of securing a firm foothold as the tribe's principal trader or perhaps trusted adviser for the handling of annuities and the negotiation of additional land-cession treaties.[11] To a pious and profit-minded individual who for a time enjoyed the advantage of public and private support, all things seemed possible, and so it was that the missionary-teacher made the most of opportunities as they came his way.

After his mission school closed in 1854, Huffaker was involved in a number of enterprises, most of which were in one way or another related to his previous associations with the Kansas. He divided his time among farming, land speculation, town promotion, politics, Indian affairs, and the Methodist Episcopal church. He was also employed as the Council Grove agent for Walker, Northrup, and Chick, a Westport mercantile firm which obtained a license to trade with the Kansas in 1854.[12] On the surface it may have appeared that Huffaker's diverse interests were simply the consequence of hard work and an optimistic outlook for the future of Council Grove. A closer look, however, suggests that his rapid rise in the local business establishment was largely based on his earlier activity at the Methodist mission at a time when his work was mainly funded by the government.

On March 12, 1862, before Morris County Justice of the Peace John F. Dodd, Huffaker admitted that, beginning in October, 1851, and continuing through "a part of 1855," he had sold on credit to the Kansas $1,425 worth of corn, potatoes, and cattle.[13] From Huffaker's point of view, perhaps, this investment gave him

[11] It was scarcely a coincidence that talk of another treaty was reported the same year Huffaker's mission school closed. See George W. Clark to Cumming, November 12, 1854, LR, OIA, Potawatomie Agency.

[12] Walker, Northrup, and Chick to J. W. Whitfield, December 29, 1853, and Whitfield to Cumming, January 21, 1854, LR, OIA, Potawatomie Agency.

[13] Testimony of Thomas Huffaker before Justice of the Peace John F. Dodds, Morris County, Kansas, March 12, 1862, LR, OIA, Kansas Agency.

a solid claim to at least part of the Kansa annuity fund and the experience necessary to serve as middleman for Walker, Northrup, and Chick. But his action clearly involved a conflict of interest, as well as a circumvention of a federal statute of 1847 which stated in part that "all executory contracts made and entered into by an Indian for the payment of money or goods [were] null and void, and of no binding whatsoever."[14]

However, the more intricate details of Huffaker's operations at Council Grove were provided by certain Kansa spokesmen. Pressured by speculators into demanding that their lands be granted in severalty, a Kansa delegation led by Hard Hart, White Hair, and The Wolf obtained a personal interview in Washington with Indian Commissioner James W. Denver in late July, 1857. As expected, the Kansas wasted no words. Hard Hart complained bitterly of white settlers invading the reservation, of land jobbers working through the half-bloods, and of unscrupulous white men attempting to undermine the government's influence with the tribe as a whole. Yet it was Huffaker who received the brunt of criticism. Not only was he described as a "bad missionary" and a teacher "who didn't each anything"; he was charged with forcing fifty young Kansa "scholars" to work for him in two fields "the size of Washington" where corn and other crops were raised for sale to the white settlers.[15]

Ironically, Huffaker had played an important role in the delegation's decision to talk with Commissioner Denver. In 1854, the year Huffaker joined forces with Walker, Northrup, and Chick, President Pierce signed the Kansas-Nebraska Act, which opened Kansas Territory to a veritable army of squatters and speculators before a single acre of Indian land was legally available for settlement.[16] Later that same year, Congress extended the provisions of the Preemption Act of 1841 to the Territory, providing the Indian title to a given claim had been extinguished.[17] In late January, 1855,

14 *U.S. Statutes at Large*, IX, 203–204.
15 Talk–July 22, 1857, with Kaw Indians in Washington, D. C., LR, OIA, Kansas Agency.
16 Paul Wallace Gates, *Fifty Million Acres: Conflicts over Kansas Land Policy, 1854–1890*, 19.

Kansas Territorial Governor Andrew H. Reeder—who was subsequently dismissed for conduct (land speculation) not befitting a public servant—announced that squatters could establish claims in advance of the public survey.[18] In short, the rapidly changing situation in 1854 placed the Kansa lands in considerable jeopardy, and it was left to a handful of federal Indian agents to try to contain the assault.

Initially, it was Potawatomi Agent George W. Clark who had the thankless responsibility of attempting to prevent the twenty-three half-blood and four hundred fullblood sections of land from falling into the hands of outsiders. With virtually no assistance, he confronted white intruders with considerable determination. Clark complained to Superintendent Alexander Cumming that timber was being cut and cabins erected on the half-blood tracts directly across the Kansas River from Lecompton. He demanded immediate action against the employees of David Hall, a federal mail contractor, who were taking claims near Council Grove. He submitted detailed accounts of how territorial officials and private combinations—including one led by William G. and George W. Ewing (whose Kansa license had only recently been revoked)—were determined to grab the entire half-blood domain, and he refused to reconsider the case of Christopher Columbia, a Ewing-sponsored trader at Council Grove whose Kansa license had been revoked in 1854.[19]

Despite the legality and justice of his actions, it was apparent that Clark was playing a lone hand. "The settlers in this Territory are losing all respect for the Indian Department," he warned Cumming in 1855, yet no assistance or clarification of his authority was forthcoming, perhaps because the Indian Department thought it best to pursue—at least for the time being—a wait-and-see policy.[20]

[17] U.S. Statutes at Large, X, 312.
[18] Andrew H. Reeder to B. H. Twombly, January 22, 1855, cited in "Governor Reeder's Administration," TKSHS, V (1889–96), 167, 233.
[19] George W. Clark to Cumming, November 7, 1854, Christopher Columbia to Clark, December 15, 1854, David Hall—"For the Information of All Concerned, Council Grove"—December 20, 1854, Clark to Cumming, January 4, 1855, Clark to Cumming, May 8, 1855, LR, OIA, Potawatomie Agency.
[20] Clark to Cumming, January 10, 1855, LR, OIA, Potawatomie Agency.

At Council Grove, Thomas Huffaker was in a particularly advantageous position to use his influence on the side of Clark and the Kansas. But the former missionary-teacher cast his lot with the opposition when he testified that Columbia was "an honest citizen who really [deserved] a chance to stay in Kansas Territory."[21] For his efforts on behalf of the Kansas, "a lawless band of speculators" charged Clark with "pro-slave broils." His family was threatened, his cabin at the Potawatomie Agency was burned, and his effectiveness as an Indian agent was severely compromised. Completely disillusioned and fearing for his personal safety, he fled with his family to Missouri. The Kansa problem was left in the hands of his superiors.[22]

Meanwhile, portions of the Upper Neosho Reservation were also being overrun by squatters, speculators, and town promoters. According to a census taken in early 1855, at least thirty families had located claims in the vicinity of Council Grove.[23] Obviously the Indian Department could no longer ignore the problem. Thus on March 3, 1855, John Montgomery was appointed as the first official Indian agent for the Kansas, with headquarters at Council Grove. Upon his arrival a few weeks later, Montgomery's reaction to the situation was anything but optimistic. The Kansas were sick and starving. Their drought-stricken corn was "exposed and uncultivated." They were availing themselves of every opportunity to steal, "not only from other people, but from each other." Their annuities were largely spent for whiskey, and their general condition was such that they had "lost all confidence in each other." Writing to Superintendent Cumming in St. Louis, Montgomery complained:

I am constrained to say that the Kansas are a poor, degraded, superstitious, thievish, indigent, tribe of Indians; their tendency is downward, and, in my opinion, they must soon become extinct, and the

[21] Huffaker to Clark, December 18, 1854, LR, OIA, Potawatomie Agency.
[22] Clark to George W. Manypenny, December 5, 1856, LR, OIA, Potawatomie Agency.
[23] James R. McClure, "Taking the Census and Other Incidents in 1855," *TKSHS*, VIII (1903–1904), 234; William E. Unrau, "The Council Grove Merchants and Kansa Indians, 1855–1870," *KHQ*, XXXIV (1968), 270–72.

sooner they arrive at this period, the better it will be for the rest of mankind.[24]

Accompanying Montgomery's dismal report was a statement that smallpox had broken out at the villages in June, 1855.

Taken in the context of Huffaker's recent failure as missionary-teacher and Agent Clark's unfortunate experiences with the land jobbers, the latest tragedy was more than enough to cause Indian Commissioner George W. Manypenny to rebuke Montgomery and to instruct him more precisely concerning the nature of his official responsibilities. Manypenny told Cumming:

I have to direct that you will apprise Agent Montgomery of the nature and extent of his duties to those untutored wards of the government; that instead of designing their extermination, he should employ the best means within his reach calculated to promote their welfare and improvement, and that language such as that above quoted [Montgomery's report] is as improper and inconsistent with his relation and obligations to the Indians as it is unacceptable to this office.[25]

Manypenny's memo scored with telling effect. Following the reprimand, Montgomery conducted himself in a more responsible manner. Apparently he had at least a latent interest in preventing the Kansas from being exploited, for in August, 1855, he ordered the eviction of certain squatters on the half-blood lands in Jefferson County but dropped the matter while awaiting further instructions from his superiors.[26] He reported to Cumming that a legal survey of the reservation was mandatory, since its outer limits "were not known precisely."[27]

Actually, the rough boundaries staked by Indian Department officials a decade earlier, which unfortunately had been certified by Manypenny in 1854, were for the most part based on the "geo-

[24] Montgomery to Cumming, August 31, 1855, LR, OIA, Kansas Agency; *Report of the Commissioner of Indian Affairs* (1855), 34 Cong., 2 sess., *House Executive Document No. 1* (Serial 840), 433–34.

[25] *Report of the Commissioner of Indian Affairs* (1855), 435; Secretary of the Interior to Commissioner of Indian Affairs, September 29, 1855, LR, OIA, Kansas Agency.

[26] Montgomery to Cumming, August 20, 1855, LR, OIA, Kansas Agency.

[27] Montgomery to Cumming, April 26, 1855, LR, OIA, Kansas Agency.

graphical position of the Indian reservations respectively,"[28] not on scientific data. As expected, and despite some evidence to the contrary,[29] the squatters and town promoters argued that the claims at Council Grove and the mouth of Rock Creek (on the Neosho southeast of Council Grove) were outside the reservation and thus legally open to settlement. It was indeed an anomalous situation, as Montgomery recognized when he said: "Where a certain class of people assume to themselves the right to judge . . . matters pertaining to Indian country, it is very difficult for an Indian agent to perform with promptness the duties of his office."[30]

Montgomery had ample experience to back up his words. On October 8, 1855, Commissioner Manypenny issued to all Indian agents general instructions calling for the removal of all intruders on Indian lands.[31] Less than a month later Montgomery tried to comply by serving notice that the half-blood reservation was to be cleared of all squatters, with military force if necessary.[32] The order was ignored in the most blatant manner. Taking advantage of the political turmoil in the Territory, as well as the reluctance of federal military officials to take firm action, "lawless men" who were interested only in "filthy speculation" continued to clear timber while waiting for their claims to appreciate in value. At Fort Riley, Colonel Philip St. George Cooke refused to send troops as requested by Montgomery; he asked for "more information" and suggested that Montgomery contact the equally evasive command at Fort Leavenworth.[33]

Following his initial setback, the Kansa agent resorted to delaying tactics. He requested additional instructions from Washington and spent the winter "collecting more evidence" in Jefferson

[28] Montgomery to Cumming, October 5, 1855, LR, OIA, Kansas Agency.
[29] R. W. Cummins to W. H. Harvey, July 27, 1847, William Medill to William L. Marcy, October 18, 1847, LR, OIA, Fort Leavenworth Agency.
[30] Report of the Commissioner of Indian Affairs (1856), 34 Cong., 2 sess., House Executive Document No. 1 (Serial 893), 681–82.
[31] Ibid., 670.
[32] Montgomery to Commandant, Fort Riley, November 30, 1855, LR, OIA, Kansas Agency.
[33] Colonel [Philip St.] George Cooke to Montgomery, December 3, 1855, LR, OIA, Kansas Agency.

County and at Council Grove.[34] Orders for more direct action finally came from Commissioner Manypenny the following spring.[35] On the evening of June 23, 1856, Montgomery, ostensibly supported by Captain Walker and ten cavalrymen from Fort Leavenworth, burned twenty cabins the squatters had erected on the half-blood lands. Immediately a storm of protest swept through the squatters' ranks. While Walker and his men retired to a more hospitable environment at Topeka, claiming that Montgomery had exceeded his authority, the intruders threatened violence, "confident that the military would support them." They arranged for the Douglas County sheriff to arrest the beleaguered agent on an arson charge (which was later dropped) and even suggested that the territorial government provide them with muskets so that they might "defend their lands."[36] To President Pierce they sent a petition demanding "protection" on grounds that "the laws of nature and Kansas Territory" were being circumvented.[37]

With the squatters and speculators firmly in control, Montgomery angrily wrote Captain Walker: "I now call upon you to state, are you ready to move against these intruders?"[38] Walker was not, nor was Attorney General Andrew J. Isaacs, who with certain other territorial functionaries was personally interested in some of the half-blood land.[39] Montgomery had had enough; he washed his hands of the affair and returned to his agency headquarters at Council Grove. Here he penned his second annual report, saying in part:

Although everything has occurred on the part of the people of Kansas Territory that would tend to excite the passionate feelings of the totally uncivilized red man . . . and although the Kansas have seen

[34] Montgomery to Cumming, December 5, 1855, and March 28, 1856, LR, OIA, Kansas Agency.

[35] Montgomery to Commandant, Fort Leavenworth, June 5, 1856, LR, OIA, Kansas Agency.

[36] Montgomery to Cumming, June 30 and July 8, 1856, Montgomery to Captain Walker, July 1, 1856, Montgomery to E. V. Sumner, July 5, 1856, LR, OIA, Kansas Agency.

[37] Petition of twenty-seven Jefferson County "settlers" to President Franklin Pierce, n.d., 1856, LR, OIA, Kansas Agency.

[38] Montgomery to Captain Walker, July 1, 1856, LR, OIA, Kansas Agency.

[39] Montgomery to Cumming, July 8, 1856, LR, OIA, Kansas Agency.

their country taken from them . . . they have remained quiet and peaceable, for which they deserve credit. . . . The larger portion of the half-breed Kansas reserve now quietly rests in the possession of the intruders . . . in defiance of all law and authority. . . .[40]

The squatter victory in Jefferson County did not go unnoticed in the Neosho Valley, as Montgomery soon learned. His earlier request for a legal survey of the Kansas' Council Grove reservation prompted no action, probably because Manypenny had inadvertently certified the vague Seth Eastman map of 1854.[41] Acting largely on the basis of information provided by individuals who had already located the most desirable claims, Montgomery again requested a survey in February, 1856.[42] Whether the squatters were incorrectly informed or whether they simply chose to ignore the boundaries staked by Cummins and Harvey in 1846 is difficult to determine. Whatever the case, they took a position calculated to further their own interests by arguing that the entire 256,000-acre reservation was southwest of Council Grove—that is, south of the Santa Fe Trail and west of the Neosho River and Rock Creek settlements. With little else to go on, Montgomery (who then was preoccupied with the land question in Jefferson County) was inclined to agree. However, when his sentiment and its obvious implications were reported to the Indian Department, Manypenny quickly authorized the official survey.[43]

Using as much information as was available, including the calculations Cummins and Harvey made in 1846 and the new boundaries established by the Shawnee cession treaty of 1854,[44] the

[40] *Ibid.*; Montgomery to Cumming, October 11, 1856, cited in *Report of the Commissioner of Indian Affairs* (1856).

[41] For a copy of the Eastman map, see Robert W. Baughman, *Kansas in Maps*, 26.

[42] Montgomery to Cumming, November 1, 1855, and February 27, 1856, LR, OIA, Kansas Agency.

[43] Map of the Kansas Tribe of Indians Reserve, Map No. 149, Tube 30, Cartographic Branch, NA; Manypenny to Cumming, May 5, 1856, Manypenny to R. McClelland, May 9, 1856, Montgomery to Cumming, June 11, 1856, LR, OIA, Kansas Agency.

[44] A "Committee of the People" contended that Council Grove was only six miles east of the eastern border of the Kansa Reservation and that most of the settlements were on land ceded by the Shawnees in 1854. See C. Columbia, G. Goddard, George Reese, A. I. Baker, and Aaron Dow to Manypenny, July

official survey, completed by Oliver Short in early July, 1856, clearly indicated that Council Grove was located well within the Kansa Reservation. It meant, of course, that most of the white claims along the Neosho River, Rock Creek, and Big John Creek were on unceded land.[45] While a "Committee of the People" angrily gathered "evidence" to challenge the survey, Montgomery wrote Cumming: "Shall I proceed against the settlers in accordance with the general instructions of October 8, 1855?"[46] Cumming was more than willing to authorize decisive action. He gave his approval, and on October 9 Montgomery posted eviction notices that allowed the squatters (and the Council Grove merchants) no more than twenty days to abandon their claims and "retire from [the] reservation."[47]

However, the intruders were encouraged by the confusing circumstances resulting from more than one map and the ease with which the Jefferson County squatters had defied Montgomery. They ignored the order, as did Columbia, who had been trading without a license for nearly two years. Montgomery waited for nearly a month; then, on November 25, he sent a curt note to Columbia informing him that he had exactly three days to remove himself and his belongings from the reservation. Three days later the squatters received a similar directive.[48] In this manner the land issue was joined and the setting was established for a direct and possibly violent confrontation. While Montgomery and his superiors weighed the consequences of requesting military assistance to clear the reservation, Columbia and the squatters seized the initia-

12, 1856, LR, OIA, Kansas Agency, and Kappler, *Indian Affairs*, 618.

[45] Plat [of the Exterior Lines of the] Kansas Reservation, Approved [by] John Montgomery, July 4, 1856, Manuscript Map No. 116, Tube 405, Cartographic Branch, NA; Survey of 1856, Received by the OIA September 20, 1856, LR, OIA, Kansas Agency.

[46] "Committee of the People" to Montgomery, July 17, 1856, "Committee of the People" to Manypenny, July 19, 1856, Montgomery to Cumming, July 26, 1856, LR, OIA, Kansas Agency.

[47] Cumming to Manypenny, August 12, 1856, "Notice of Eviction," signed by Agent John Montgomery, October 9, 1856, LR, OIA, Kansas Agency.

[48] Montgomery to Columbia, November 25, 1856, LR, OIA, Kansas Agency; "Executive Minutes of Governor John W. Geary," *TKSHS*, IV (1886–88), 655–56.

tive by sending a petition to Territorial Governor John W. Geary. He was informed that the Neosho Valley residents had selected claims "in good faith," using a map certified by Commissioner Manypenny as their guide. According to them, the reservation was actually south and west of the Neosho or beyond the area of settlement. Thus the boundaries established by the latest survey could not be correct; Short had made a serious error, and time was needed to settle the question "in a just and lawful manner."[49]

The squatters' strategy worked, even though the logic of their argument was of dubious merit. With little more than a cursory consideration of the Kansas' rights or the Indian Department's boundary decision, Geary informed Secretary of State William L. Marcy:

[T]he statements of the petitioners seemed so equitable and reasonable, and the season of the year so inclement for their removal [that] I advised the Indian agent to permit the settlers (who claim my protection as citizens of Kansas) to remain undisturbed until I could lay the matter before the Government; having satisfactory assurance from the settlers that they would peacefully acquiesce in a decision from that quarter.[50]

While Geary's action brought some temporary relief to the squatters, it was perhaps largely illusory, especially when compared to the situation Montgomery had encountered in Jefferson County. There it was a matter of determining whether the Kansa half-bloods could possess and/or alienate certain clearly defined plots;[51] in the Neosho Valley it was a matter of determining precisely the reservation boundaries. It was not inconceivable, for example, that

[49] "Executive Minutes of Governor John W. Geary"; Columbia to Governor John W. Geary, December 5, 1856, LR, OIA, Kansas Agency.

[50] Geary to William L. Marcy, December 8, 1856, cited in "Executive Minutes of Governor John W. Geary," 641–42.

[51] On September 26, 1857, Attorney General J. S. Black ruled that the half-blood Kansas had "a perfect right to enjoy the peaceful occupation of their lands." See Black to Secretary of the Interior Jacob Thompson, September 26, 1857, LR, OIA, Kansas Agency. Later, on May 26, 1860, a law was passed providing that "all interest" in the twenty-three sections was vested in the reservees or their heirs. Those reservees or heirs who wished to alienate their claims would be issued the necessary patents, with the proceeds of a given sale going to the reservees, their heirs, or the tribe in general, in that order. See *U.S. Statutes at Large*, XII, 21–22.

Geary had been too easily swayed by the squatters and that Montgomery's eviction order would be upheld in the not too distant future.

The possibility of such a decision caused the squatters and merchants to reexamine their predicament and press for a new treaty that would place their land claims beyond the bothersome tampering of the Indian Department bureaucracy. In their view a diminished reservation of small farms granted in severalty to the Kansas was preferable to the tribal practice of common land tenure. It would settle the boundary question once and for all, perhaps to the squatters' advantage, and force the Kansas to live a more orderly life. But to accomplish this it was necessary to convince the government that the Kansas were indeed ready (and willing) to enter the yeoman stage of civilization.

It was at this decisive juncture that Thomas Huffaker, with his credentials as a former Kansa missionary-teacher, was able to use his influence on behalf of the squatters. On March 1, 1857, without consulting Agent Montgomery, he informed President Buchanan that a delegation of "real [Kansa] leaders" was coming to Washington to negotiate a treaty that would allow the Kansas "to give up the chase and settle down to farming."[52] A bold move, it caught Montgomery off guard. Also unbeknown to the Kansa agent, Huffaker arranged for Northrup and Chick to issue a letter of credit to cover the delegation's expenses to Washington.[53] As the general intent of the scheme became known, others became involved, including a "Mr. C. E. Mix," who claimed to be a government official with instructions to accompany the Kansas to Washington but who was actually a Lecompton land jobber who had offered Hard Hart two thousand dollars if he would "help" with the half-blood lands.[54]

The Kansa chiefs held their Washington conference with Commissioner Denver in late July, 1857, turning the tables on

[52] Huffaker to Buchanan, March 1, 1857, LR, OIA, Kansas Agency.
[53] Northrup and Chick to Cumming, May 9, 1857, LR, OIA, Kansas Agency.
[54] Montgomery to J. W. Denver, June 30, 1857, Talk—July 22, 1857, with Kaw Indians in Washington, D. C., LR, OIA, Kansas Agency.

Huffaker by displaying unexpected awareness of what was really going on.[55] They exposed "Mr. Mix" as the imposter he was;[56] they complained that the squatters were robbing them of their timber; and they demanded more precise information about the boundaries of the land granted to them in 1846 by the government. Before the legal survey it had been relatively easy to placate the Kansas with a few gifts and ambiguous promises of a better life, but now, with some of their leaders assuming a more aggressive posture, it appeared the government would have to choose between expelling the squatters or arranging yet another land-cession treaty.[57]

Meanwhile, Montgomery tried to maintain some semblance of order in the Neosho Valley. On March 30, as soon as he learned that the Kansa delegation had left for Washington, he informed Superintendent Cumming in St. Louis:

Huffaker, I might say *Missionary*, does all in his power consistent with personal interest to get the Indians to leave their country . . . for . . . he expects to *"reap a benefit"* when the Indians are treated with, as he later told me.[58]

Apparently Huffaker was confused about his confidants, for he later denied saying this, claiming to be interested only in the Kansas' welfare. Yet he solicited the support of those territorial officials he thought would promote a new treaty and, in spite of Montgomery's warning not to do so, played an aggressive role in organizing "claim meetings" among the squatters.[59] By now Montgomery's patience was exhausted. He revoked Huffaker's license to continue as the Northrup and Chick agent at Council Grove and demanded a full-scale investigation of the former missionary's relationship with the Kansas.[60]

[55] See Chap. 7, pp. 167–70, 190–93.
[56] Talk—July 22, 1857, with Kaw Indians in Washington, D. C., LR, OIA, Kansas Agency.
[57] Appeal of Kansas Tribe of Indians, July 23, 1857, LR, OIA, Kansas Agency.
[58] Montgomery to Cumming, March 30, 1857, LR, OIA, Kansas Agency.
[59] J. W. Polk to J. W. Denver, May 12, 1857, Huffaker to Cumming, May 17, 1857, Montgomery to Simcock and Conn, S. M. Hays, and T. S. Huffaker, June 12, 1857, Montgomery to Denver, June 14, 1857, LR, OIA, Kansas Agency.
[60] B. A. James to Denver, July 15, 1857, LR, OIA, Kansas Agency.

If Montgomery thought an investigation would result in the termination of Huffaker's influence in the Council Grove area, he was bound to be disappointed. The problem was that the Kansa leaders who were prepared to testify against Huffaker were the very ones who had gone to Washington. Upon discovering this, Montgomery wrote to B. A. James, the Sac and Fox agent who had been assigned to collect evidence for the Indian Department, requesting a postponement of the investigation until the Indians returned. James refused on the seemingly arbitrary grounds that the Indians under consideration were "a very lame source to establish anything in dispute."[61] Yet in a private note written four days before James's refusal to Montgomery, Huffaker admitted to the Sac and Fox agent that Montgomery's charges were essentially correct. He (Huffaker) had indeed encouraged the Kansas to push for a new treaty, since "under the circumstances it was the best thing they could do."[62] Why Agent James failed to report this incriminating statement to Montgomery, Cumming, or Commissioner Denver was not explained, nor was the Indian Department's failure to continue the investigation after the Kansa delegation had complained about Huffaker's operations.

It is possible, of course, that James had been bought off by the speculators. On the other hand, the Kansas' complaints may have been ignored because they came from a minority faction interested in getting more than their share of the tribe's annuity largess. Even Montgomery was not above suspicion, for he was eventually accused (but not convicted) of stealing two thousand dollars from the Kansas in the four years he served as their agent.[63] Although other individuals or cliques may have been involved, it was almost certain that the squatters and speculators as a group were beginning to command a dominant position in the valley and that another treaty was the easiest solution to the land question. Agent James said as much when he told Commissioner Denver that "big trouble

[61] Montgomery to Cumming, June 30, 1857, James to Denver, July 15, 1857, LR, OIA, Kansas Agency.
[62] Huffaker to James, July 11, 1857, LR, OIA, Kansas Agency.
[63] Hiram W. Farnsworth to William Dole, April 23, 1862, and January 24, 1863, LR, OIA, Kansas Agency.

[would] soon break out between the Indians and the settlers, unless something [was] done."[64] He was joined by Marcus J. Parrott, a prominent Free State politician who was elected Kansas territorial delegate to Congress in the fall of 1857. Shortly after his election Parrott reminded Denver that a number of the Neosho Valley settlers had taken up their claims at least thirty months before the official survey of 1856; moreover, he noted, it had always been the government's intention to have the Kansas locate their villages at least twenty-five miles from Council Grove and the immoral influence of the Santa Fe freighters.[65]

Parrott spoke with authority, his timing was excellent, he knew the rules of the political game, and his involvement in the matter made it easier for the squatters to consider Montgomery's eviction notice a meaningless and empty threat. Montgomery received no support from the land-hungry half-bloods, who complained that their agent was "guilty of many things."[66] He received little support from Commissioner Denver, who simply observed that the "neglect of the Indian Department" had allowed the settlers to "completely overrun the 20 sq. mi. reservation."[67] And he received little or no cooperation from tribal leaders at the main villages near Council Grove, who by the spring of 1858 were demanding to know whether they were going to be moved again. With many of their people starving, they saw no point in planting corn that would be taken by the government or destroyed by the squatters' stock.[68]

While the Indian Department officialdom deliberated the kind of treaty that might be acceptable to all parties concerned, relation-

[64] James to Denver, July 15, 1857, LR, OIA, Kansas Agency.

[65] Marcus J. Parrott to Charles E. Mix, December 20, 1857, LR, OIA, Kansas Agency.

[66] Eight Half-Bloods to the Commissioner of Indian Affairs, April 8, 1857, LR, OIA, Kansas Agency.

[67] Denver to Charles E. Mix, March 20, 1858, LR, OIA, Kansas Agency.

[68] Huffaker to Denver, March 19, 1858 (?), Thomas H. Stanley to Mix, August 23, 1858, LR, OIA, Kansas Agency. In February, 1855, 1,040 pounds of wire were shipped to Council Grove for fencing the Kansas' corn fields, but Agent George W. Clark advised that "it will never be used." Apparently the wire was sold at auction to the white settlers, either at Council Grove or Westport. See Clark to Cumming, February 19, 1855, LR, OIA, Potawatomie Agency.

ships between the squatters and the Kansas continued to deteriorate. In September, 1858, the badly mutilated body of a Mr. Helm was found near Council Grove. Without investigating the matter, the squatters naturally concluded that the Kansas were responsible. A "conference was quickly had with the Indians," who were informed "that if they were again known to imbrue their hand in the blood of a white man, the white people would exterminate their tribe."[69] Events of this kind constituted the background for an incident the following spring which revealed just how determined the white intruders were to rid themselves of the Kansas.

A few days before June 17, 1859, a Kansa raiding party stole two horses from the Mexican freighting firm of R. Otise, whose business, of course, was absolutely essential to the Council Grove merchants. Immediately a white citizens' committee ordered that the horses be returned. To this the Kansa leadership agreed, even though they considered stealing from Mexicans no less honorable than stealing from the Pawnees. Fearful that the responsible individuals would be "shaved and whipped," as had been the experience of a party of white horse thieves a short time earlier, a force of nearly one hundred Kansas escorted the contraband animals to Council Grove.

According to one white account, the Indians' behavior was "bantering and insolent"; another described the large body of white men that gathered as "perfectly bloodthirsty." Seth M. Hays, a prominent Council Grove merchant, confronted the Kansas in front of his store and "imprudently" fired two pistol shots into the air, apparently hoping to frighten the Indians into leaving. In the confusion that followed, a Kansa arrow struck Charles Gilky, wounding him slightly; another warrior discharged a gun and seriously wounded William Park. Then the Kansas quickly retreated to a point some four miles southeast of town, where they held a council and decided to send a peace delegation back to Council Grove. However, on entering town a short time later, they were driven back because they had come "for no good purpose." At this point the white citizens' committee decided to send a four-

[69] *Kansas Press* (Cottonwood Falls), July 11, 1859.

man delegation to the Kansas, demanding that they either "turn over the two [guilty] Indians . . . or give up their whole year's annuity." By sunset the delegation returned with the two Indians, one of whom was a minor chief. H. J. Espy, a leader of the citizens' committee, told the crowd that "they were at liberty to do with the two Indians as they saw fit." Shouts of "Hang them!" rang through the evening air, and contrary to Huffaker's later claim that the sentence was carried out only after "mature deliberation," the two Indians were immediately executed. Not until the following evening were their bodies cut down.[70]

That the Kansas were interested in settling their differences with the white man was evident in the stoic manner with which they accepted this arbitrary form of frontier justice. Fool Chief, whose son was one of the two Indians executed, vowed personal revenge,[71] but the tribe as a whole voiced no complaint. Three days later they returned the stolen horses and requested a parley with the citizens' committee "to see if the two parties could not come to some conclusion by which they could both live on the same land."[72] It was a futile effort. Indeed, the June affair only strengthened the intruders' belief that the Kansas were a worthless and barbaric lot. In near-by Cottonwood Falls (about twenty miles south of Council Grove) the local editor, Samuel N. Wood—who would soon move his paper to Council Grove—printed a letter signed "Fessor." The contemptible correspondence stated in part:

Sense yu wor up hear [at Council Grove] times hev ben poorty brisk, we hev haid one hangen, but the material warent good—nuthen but Cau Injens, you ort to hev bin here to witnessed that. They gen them ar Caus one of thee jewhilicanest stretchens ever you sou. They hung em tel they war ded ded, if yu call a day and nite anything.[73]

By the early summer of 1859 it appeared that the cards had been carefully stacked against the Kansas and that the various white

[70] *Ibid.*, June 27, August 11, 1859; Huffaker to Milton C. Dickey, August 8, 1859, Dickey to A. M. Robinson, August 10, 1859, LR, OIA, Kansas Agency.
[71] Matt Thomson, *Early History of Wabaunsee County, Kansas.*
[72] *Kansas Press* (Cottonwood Falls), June 27, 1859.
[73] *Ibid.*, July 11, 1859. Wood brought his paper to Council Grove on September 26, 1859, and renamed it the *Council Grove Press* on July 1, 1860.

interests in the Neosho Valley constituted a united front against the Indians. Milton C. Dickey, who replaced Montgomery as Kansa agent on March 3, 1859,[74] took the position that it would be impossible to evict the settlers and that the Kansas would have to be removed.[75] Editor Wood asserted that "800 squatters are not to be trifled with"; all of the Kansa lands had to be ceded and appraised "at their *cash value in a* STATE OF NATURE."[76] Nevertheless, there were indications that Wood, Huffaker, Hays, and the Council Grove merchants were primarily concerned with their own interests and only incidentally with those of their countryside friends.

An important key to understanding the gulf that was beginning to divide the merchants and squatters was the town mania that gripped the people of territorial Kansas. Wood could complain about the "drunken Indians" preventing good Neosho Valley yeomen from enjoying the fruits of their labors, but he and his associates were more interested in promoting the future of Council Grove, which in his opinion was "a *business* place . . . destined to be one of the most important places in Kansas."[77]

What may have appeared as a rather typical confrontation between the white men and the Kansas was in fact turning into a much more complicated struggle, one that involved at least four fairly distinct groups: the local merchant-speculator group, the absentee (and better-financed) land jobbers, the squatter-farmers, and, of course, the Indians. Although the lines of demarcation were not always precise and loyalties occasionally shifted, the intruder groups vied for control in such a determined manner that they tended to checkmate one another. As a consequence, the Kansas were able to retain at least some control of their Neosho Valley reservation much longer than might otherwise have been possible.

Fearful, perhaps, that the anticipated treaty might result in the eviction of *all* intruders or that it might be engineered to give outside interests the advantage, Thomas Huffaker, Seth M. Hays, Christopher Columbia, Malcom Conn, and others obtained from

[74] "Kansas Agencies," 733.
[75] *Kansas Press* (Cottonwood Falls), June 13, 1859.
[76] *Kansas Press* (Council Grove), October 17, 1859.
[77] *Ibid.*, September 26, 1859.

the Kansas Territorial Legislature on February 9, 1859, a charter of incorporation for the "Council Grove Town Company" on land "not to exceed 640 acres."[78] Four months later they paid Hiram M. Northrup and Joseph S. Chick two thousand dollars for a quit-claim deed to the Council Grove townsite and certain improvements built by William Mitchell sometime after 1846.[79] However, these arrangements did not guarantee an absolute title to the townsite, since this could be secured only through a new treaty or specific action by the federal government. On the basis of Oliver Short's official survey of 1856, Northrup and Chick may have congratulated themselves on having unloaded a white elephant, but Huffaker, Hays, and the Council Grove clique had some good reasons for believing they had obtained a real bargain.

For one thing, Sam Wood, their fiery editor and principal spokesman, was busy promoting a profitable relationship with Robert S. Stevens, a well-connected land jobber and Indian contractor who from his Washington office divided his attention among Congress, the Indian Department, and the frontier.[80] The activity of Stevens, whose previous involvement in the Kansa half-blood lands established his alignment with the speculators, not the squatters,[81] was matched by the machinations of the former Kansas attorney general, Andrew J. Isaacs. In 1858 Isaacs had obtained direct Senate approval for his purchase of the Munsee (or Christian) Indian Tract near Leavenworth, thereby establishing a precedent that was of considerable interest to the Council Grove promoters.[82] Apparently this nefarious transaction marked the first time an important Indian tract in Kansas went directly into private hands without first becoming a part of the public domain, and the possible application of the same procedure in the Neosho Valley helps to

[78] *Private Laws of the Territory of Kansas*, 207–208.
[79] Deed Record, Vol. B., 7, Morris County (Kansas), Office of the Morris County Register of Deeds, Council Grove, Kansas.
[80] Robert S. Stevens to Samuel N. Wood, April 2, 1860, Samuel Newitt Wood Papers, Manuscript Division, KSHS; Gates, *Fifty Million Acres*, 41–42, 96–99, 234.
[81] Gates, *Fifty Million Acres*, 41–42.
[82] Paul Wallace Gates, "A Fragment of Kansas Land History: The Disposal of the Christian Indian Tract," *KHQ*, VI (1937), 228, 233–40.

explain the somewhat guarded confidence with which Huffaker, Hays, and their associates viewed the future. With Stevens' assistance, they could perhaps deal directly with the Indian Department, secure their townsite, and let the squatters fend for themselves. Otherwise they would have to work more closely with the squatters and help promote a treaty that would be acceptable to both groups.

As it turned out, neither the merchants nor Stevens had the necessary influence (at least then) to grab the townsite on their own terms. By the late spring of 1859 it was rumored that the government was determined to evict the intruders as Montgomery had threatened.[83] Even as late as April 2, 1860—fully five months after the government had negotiated with the Kansas—Stevens warned Wood that the Commissioner of Indian Affairs was "inclined to carry out the view of the Senate and clear the reserve."[84] Since this would have been disastrous for every white man in the valley, it is not difficult to understand why Wood advised the squatters to "watch and pray."[85]

The much discussed treaty was finally negotiated at the Kansa villages by Commissioner of Indian Affairs Alfred B. Greenwood on October 5, 1859, and ratified, with amendments, the following June 27. As proclaimed on November 17, 1860, the treaty allowed the Kansas to keep only about 80,000 acres of land. The diminished tract, located in the southwest corner of the original 256,000-acre reservation, was to be subdivided into at least one 40-acre plot for each family head, each family member, and each single male twenty-one years of age or older. The remaining 176,000 acres were to be ceded in trust to the government, to be sold to bidders who paid the highest cash price on sealed proposals. As a concession to those squatters who had "in good faith" taken claims on trust lands before December 2, 1856—the day the legal survey was certified—they were permitted to buy their claims for $1.75 per acre, but only for cash and during a limited time specified by the Secretary of the Interior. It was further allowed that those squatters

83 *Kansas Press* (Cottonwood Falls), May 30, 1859.
84 Stevens to Wood, April 2, 1860, Wood Papers.
85 *Kansas Press* (Council Grove), March 19, 1860.

187

who had settled on the diminished reservation before the same date were entitled to "fair compensation" for their improvements. Fair payment was also authorized for those traders who were "lawfully" living on the reservation. Finally, the proceeds from the anticipated sale of the trust lands were to be used to pay the tribe's depredation claims and commercial obligations and to further the Kansas' agrarian education.[86]

How was the treaty received? Even though the diminished reservation contained little timber, less water, and even less desirable land, Agent Milton Dickey reported that the Kansas seemed "wonderfully interested in the plan adopted . . . to benefit them." They looked with "great favor" on getting their own farms, a new mission school, and a "house for each family."[87] With the merchants and squatters it was otherwise. Few squatters could afford to pay even a relatively low cash price for what they contended were "their" farms; the rest, of course, were at the mercy of unknown speculators and outside-interest groups. Huffaker, Hays, and the Council Grove crowd were equally distressed, since their townsite was no more secure than it had been before the treaty. Angry claim meetings were held, petitions against the Buchanan administration were circulated, and the treaty was characterized as the natural act of blundering politicians and dishonest speculators who were absolutely unconcerned with the rights of the people. With the squatters claiming that "more than one member of the Buchanan dynasty expect[ed] to make money from the hard earnings of the settlers,"[88] editor Wood rose to the occasion by printing his version of "A Kaw Indian's Soliloquy":

Republican very bad party, no Kaw party, no negro party, it be

[86] Kappler, *Indian Affairs*, 800–803. Agent Montgomery reported in 1855 that depredation claims totalling $4,000 had been filed against the Kansas, and by the spring of 1862 it was reported that the tribe owed the various merchants a total of $35,517.72, including $10,032.49 to Northrup and Chick, $6,452.49 to Seth M. Hays, $5,598.69 to Christopher Columbia, and $1,425 to Thomas S. Huffaker. See Montgomery to Cumming, August 31, 1855, Milton Dickey to A. B. Greenwood, October 15, 1859, and Hiram Farnsworth to William Dole, March 22, 1862, LR, OIA, Kansas Agency.

[87] Dickey to Greenwood, December 11, 1860, LR, OIA, Kansas Agency.

[88] *Kansas Press* (Council Grove), December 12, 1859.

only white man's party, me no join Republican party, but me join Democratic party, Great Father loves Kaw Indians, Great Father buy heaps land of Shawnee, whites they jumps on Shawnee lands, and Great Father said they might, but Great Father takes white man's farm and gives it to Superior Race, Great Father very good. Me join Democratic party, Democratic party heap good to Kaw Indian, it be no white man's party; it takes all white man's farms sells em highest bidder, with sealed proposals and give money to Kaw Indians, Democratic party no wants Kaw Indians to go to Smoky Hill, where they no quit drinking, no quit big hunts, no quit stealing no live like white men, no educate Poppooses, no get white man's farm but all die or get killed.

[signed] Kaw Chief[89]

Despite apparent deference to squatter sentiment, Wood and the merchants used tactics that were flexible enough to indicate some concern for the Kansas' welfare. When Commissioner Greenwood was negotiating with the tribal leadership in October, 1859, Wood advised the squatters to "go ahead, sow wheat, take care of our crops [for] the time will come when you will get your homes at or near [the] government price."[90] When the squatters angrily objected to bidding against outside speculators, Wood's advice was: "Go slow, boys."[91] When violence was threatened against Stevens, who in 1861 was awarded a government contract to build permanent houses for the Kansas, the merchants' spokesman told the squatters to "cool off." He even scolded them for failing to realize that the project would contribute a great deal to local economic growth.[92] But when a combination of outside jobbers made a bid for a huge block of trust land in the name of Robert G. Corwin, a Washington attorney and powerful Indian Department lobbyist, Wood cried fraud and predicted that "every man would favor [in Corwin's case] a suspension of the writ of *habeus corpus*." Should Corwin and his gang succeed in stealing no less than twelve thousand prize acres from the squatters, the latter would have no alter-

89 *Ibid.*, October 31, 1859.
90 *Ibid.*, October 17, 1859.
91 *Council Grove Press*, February 23, 1861.
92 *Ibid.*, April 13, 1861.

native but to "go burning up the entire country, improvements and all, and make it a desert in the prairie."[93]

Some squatters were taken in by these glib pronouncements and continued to look to the merchants for leadership; others, however, were beginning to suspect that members of the town company were jobbers in disguise. For example, an unidentified "WHITE MAN" wanted to know in November, 1859, why Huffaker was telling the people to keep quiet about the treaty when "he was in consultation with Greenwood all day at the Agency unbeknown to the people there; is there a secret understanding," he asked, "that Huffaker is to have the Mission farm, if the Treaty is ratified?"[94] Were the merchants more interested in their town enterprise than in the crisis facing the squatters? What did Wood really mean when he asserted that "the true policy for every Kansas man [was] to build and support Kansas towns"? And how would the Indians, who seemed to be showing considerable interest in farming, fit into the scheme of things?

Most squatters undoubtedly faced a dim future after the treaty of 1859 was proclaimed, yet the position of the merchants was not much better. On the basis of Article 4 of the late treaty,[95] it was clearly possible that outsiders might bid on the townsite and seize it from those who had worked so hard to develop its potential. For Huffaker, Wood, and the others, the threat of such an event was exasperating, especially since the future of the area was beginning to look bright. Soon after the firing on Fort Sumter, Wood urged the "quiet people" to flee to the fertile Neosho Valley, where most anyone could "tickle her ribes with a hoe, and she [would] laugh with a harvest."[96] By May, 1861, there were at least fifty houses in Council Grove and more under construction; additional squatters were arriving, business was booming, and railroad talk was in the air. As early as May, 1860, a number of railroad promoters had been extended "the right hand of fellowship," and three years later came the exciting announcement that three lines would connect

93 *Ibid.*
94 *Kansas Press* (Council Grove), November 7, 1859.
95 Kappler, *Indian Affairs*, 801.
96 *Council Grove Press*, May 15, 1861.

Council Grove with the outside world. Irrefutable proof of prosperous conditions—and the fact that the merchants could live with the Kansas as long as the government continued to fund their debts—was the increase in local sales from $22,000 a month in June, 1863, to $64,000 a month by May, 1864.[97]

While the squatters continued to demand that the Kansas be expelled from the valley, it was absolutely essential to the merchants that they obtain clear title to their townsite. Some assurance came from Stevens in August, 1860, when he reported from Washington that he was exerting pressure on the Commissioner of Indian Affairs to grant the merchants "320 acres for a site,"[98] but his efforts brought no immediate results. In the early summer of 1862, after the Senate had rejected a new treaty that would have guaranteed at least some compensation to residents on the diminished reservation, the squatters displayed an "ugly mood" and "threatened violence" unless some specific assurances were made that a similar treaty would be ratified "at a later date."[99] Finally, on March 3, 1863, Congress authorized the executive branch to enter into treaties that would result in the removal of all Indians from Kansas. Nothing was said about compensation for the displaced squatters or when the treaties would be negotiated.[100]

At this point the merchants brought pressure on Kansa Agent Hiram W. Farnsworth[101] to work out a compromise that would placate the squatters and at the same time create an atmosphere more conducive to settling the townsite question. Like the Indians and most of the squatters, Farnsworth admitted that he was "completely confused" concerning the Indian Department's ultimate objectives;[102] nevertheless, with the assistance of Special Commis-

[97] *Ibid.*, April 11, May 11, June 1, August 8, September 9, 1863, and May 28, 1864.

[98] Stevens to Wood, August 6, 1860, Wood Papers.

[99] Hiram W. Farnsworth to William Dole, July 31, 1862, LR, OIA, Kansas Agency.

[100] *U.S. Statutes at Large*, XII, 793.

[101] Hiram W. Farnsworth replaced Milton C. Dickey as Kansa Agent on April 18, 1861; see "Kansas Agencies," 733.

[102] Farnsworth to Samuel C. Pomeroy, July 22, 1861, LR, OIA, Kansas Agency.

sioner Edward Wolcott and the ever present Huffaker, he agreed to meet with some of the Kansas leaders on March 14, 1863. The compromise they worked out provided that squatters who qualified for "fair compensation" under the treaty of 1859 would be issued "certificates of indebtedness" equal to the appraised value of their claims. More important was the provision that authorized the issuance of similar certificates (or land scrip) to squatters who had settled on the diminished reservation after December 2, 1856, but no later than October 5, 1859. In both instances the scrip would be accepted as cash for the purchase of the Kansas' trust lands when these went on sale.[103]

Special Commissioner Wolcott reported that "the main provisions" of the negotiations were acceptable to the squatters, at least for the time being. Not so Article 2, which Wolcott described as an outright "swindle."[104] It read in part:

The Kansas tribe of Indians, being desirous of making a suitable expression of the obligations the said tribe are under to Thomas S. Huffaker, for the many services rendered by said Huffaker as missionary, teacher and friendly counsellor . . . hereby authorize and request the Secretary of the Interior to convey to the said . . . Huffaker the half section of land on which he has resided, and improved and cultivated since A.D. 1851. . . .[105]

The prize half-section was located immediately north of the Council Grove townsite, and "it was easily worth $20 per acre." Worst of all, the Kansas had not the slightest idea of its value for future development. "The whole thing was managed with a great deal of secrecy," complained Wolcott, "and considerable pains were made to keep outsiders away."[106]

Huffaker probably feared that other parties would bid on his claim the moment the trust lands went on sale, which was why he made certain Article 2 was included in the amended treaty. Considering that he had both advised and exploited the tribe since 1851, he should not have been so handsomely rewarded. Nevertheless,

[103] U.S. Statutes at Large, XII, 1221.
[104] Edward Wolcott to Dole, March 19, 1863, LR, OIA, Kansas Agency.
[105] U.S. Statutes at Large, XII, 1221.
[106] Wolcott to Dole, March 19, 1862, LR, OIA, Kansas Agency.

the Senate went along with the proposal. All that was added to the original deal was that Huffaker would have to pay the *appraised value* of the land "at a rate not less than one dollar and seventy-five cents per acre."[107]

While the squatters somberly awaited the outcome of their bids,[108] the merchants won the battle they had fought since 1859. On August 25, 1863, in the name of the Council Grove Town Company, they deposited $977.53 with the Indian Department "in payment of certificates of indebtedness with interest that had accrued thereon" for 560 acres of the townsite.[109] Shortly thereafter, based on an extremely loose (if not illegal) interpretation of Article 4 of the original treaty,[110] the coveted land patent was signed by President Lincoln.[111] In this manner, then, the Council Grove merchants presented themselves to the outside world as the capable speculators they were. For a mere pittance they had obtained a block of real estate worth at least $80,000 on an investor's market at the time and which in the next three months alone would yield well over $4,000 through the sale of subdivided lots.[112] Furthermore, the more influential merchants—especially those who owned shares in the town company—eventually obtained titles to nearly 7,000 acres of the finest reservation land in the valley.[113]

The squatters did not fare as well, for there soon developed a major conflict over the disposal of the trust lands. The Kansas fared worst of all. Like the treaties of 1825 and 1846, the treaty of 1859

[107] *U.S. Statutes at Large*, XII, 1223.

[108] On August 8, 1863, the *Council Grove Press* reported that "no settler, after five months, knows the result of his bid."

[109] Deed Record, Vol. B., 14–15, Morris County (Kansas).

[110] A careful reading of Article 4 suggests that the clause mentioned applied only to the diminished reservation. The townsite was located on the southern edge of the trust lands. See Map of Kansas Indian Lands Drawn and Published by H. D. Preston, Surveyor for the Commission to appraise the Kansas Indian Lands, Council Grove, n.d. (1863?), Manuscript Division, KSHS.

[111] "Patent from the United States of America to the Council Grove Town Company, September 1, 1863," Deed Record, Vol. B., 14–15, Morris County (Kansas).

[112] On August 6, 1860, the *Council Grove Press* reported that one-sixteenth of one share of the Company sold for $5,000; see warranty deeds issued by the Council Grove Town Company, October 2 to December 31, 1863, Deed Record, Vol. B., 24–84, Morris County (Kansas).

[113] Land Books, Ranges 5–10, Townships 14–17, Morris County (Kansas).

did not announce the beginning of a new dispensation. Regardless of their individual differences and objectives, the squatters, the merchants, and the outside interests as a group had scored a major victory, and there was every indication that they would not rest until the entire reservation was theirs. Agent Farnsworth reported that the Kansas wanted to remain in the Neosho Valley, even though "evil white men" were encouraging them to adopt "a negative attitude" toward the future. Unless they immediately received plows, wagons, harness, hoes, shovels, axes, fences, seed, a grist mill, a blacksmith, a carpenter, and a doctor, they would lose faith in the government. But, warned Farnsworth, funds would "have to come from some other source," since the proceeds from the anticipated sale of their trust lands had been "swallowed up by trader claims and house construction . . . for the next twenty years."[114]

[114] Farnsworth to Dole, January 20, 1863, and Farnsworth to H. B. Branch, July 28, 1863, LR, OIA, Kansas Agency.

CHAPTER 8 REMOVAL
TO INDIAN TERRITORY

Wɪᴛʜ the acceptance of the land-scrip amendment and the settlement of the Council Grove townsite question, the Kansas were in a better position to retain at least some of their land. Perhaps one day they would become permanent residents of the Neosho Valley. If the government fulfilled its commitments and if the tribe paid only those debts which had been contracted in good faith, the anticipated income from the sale of 176,000 acres of trust land would be more than enough to provide food, medicine, schools, and comfortable homes. Livestock, seed, agricultural tools, and a badly needed grist mill could also be funded with little difficulty. With government agents dedicating themselves to improving the tribe's economy and morals, traditions of the past would become dim and eventually forgotten. Judged by the white man's standards, the Kansas might then assume their rightful place in white society and play a vital role in making the Neosho Valley a model frontier community.

These objectives, it should be emphasized, were articulated mainly by government planners and "humanitarians" in distant places. They were the goals of men who thought they were doing the right thing but who were either misinformed or unable to understand the tribe's real predicament. They were the ideals of public officials who debated Indian policy with considerable dedication but refused to admit that a tragedy was being perpetuated and who

195

often were prepared to compromise their ideals when pressured by special-interest groups. By 1863 a combination of government ineptitude, frontier land hunger, railroad promotion, intolerance, and Indian warfare on the Great Plains was working against the Kansas. They tried to adjust to these conditions, but it was a losing battle. Within a decade they were forced to relinquish their diminished reservation and move to a distant place in the Lower Arkansas Valley which the white man called Indian Territory.

In accordance with the amended treaty of 1859, the government gave every indication that the Kansas were to remain in the Neosho Valley. Contracts to construct permanent houses, a manual-labor school, and a new agency headquarters were awarded.[1] Agriculture was encouraged,[2] and a contract was negotiated with the Society of Friends of Indiana to promote reading, writing, and regular farm labor.[3] And to placate the squatters and maintain the government's integrity, Secretary of the Interior John P. Usher canceled Robert G. Corwin's bid for seventy-five of the best trust-land claims. Usher wrote Agent Hiram W. Farnsworth:

[Since] some misapprehension existed in the minds of parties making proposals as to the principles which would govern the Department in making awards . . . I have determined to reject all bids received to date and throw the said [trust] land open to competition as before under the . . . Treaty of October, 1859.[4]

New bids were to be taken only "after public advertisement," so that the trust lands would be sold in a manner acceptable to both the actual settlers and the Kansas.[5]

By the fall of 1863 the affairs of the Kansas Agency looked

[1] Hiram W. Farnsworth to William P. Dole, June 18, 1862, Thomas Murphy to D. N. Cooley, March 28, 1866, LR, OIA, Kansas Agency; *Council Grove Press*, April 13, 1863.

[2] Farnsworth to Dole, November 2, 1861, May 20, 1862, LR, OIA, Kansas Agency.

[3] *Ibid.*; Farnsworth to H. B. Branch, September 16, 1863, *Report of the Commissioner of Indian Affairs* (1863), 38 Cong., 1 sess., *Senate Executive Document No. 1* (Serial 1182), 376–77; Addison W. Stubbs to Guion Miller, March 14, 1824, and Chap. I of an untitled history of the Quaker Mission at the Kansa Agency, Stubbs Papers.

[4] John P. Usher to Farnsworth, August 28, 1863, LR, OIA, Kansas Agency.
[5] *Ibid.*

196

more promising than they had for some time. The manual-labor school opened in May with thirty-two boys and three girls in attendance. Superintendent Mahlon Stubbs reported that their learning ability exceeded his "most sanguine expectations" and that their willingness to do most kinds of work was comparable to the efforts of white children of the same ages.[6] A year later Agent Farnsworth reported that crops raised by the Kansas in 1863 "were good, and gave them, with what they derived from hunting, a comfortable support."[7] Even the local editor showed signs of modifying his anti-Kansa bias. "We confess to not being any great friend of the Kaw race, regarding them as a poor miserable race of beings," wrote Samuel N. Wood, "yet frauds have been perpetrated upon them that are not only a disgrace upon those engaged in them, but a disgrace to the [national] Administration."[8]

These apparent changes were short lived. In July, 1863, Is-ta-la-she, the principal chief, wrote an angry letter to Commissioner William P. Dole. He reminded the Great Father that his people had not received the livestock and agricultural implements promised by the government in 1825. He wanted to know what had happened to the money from the sale of the valuable Blue Valley education lands. He accused unscrupulous white men of taking half his grain for milling service, and he wanted to know why his people were receiving a smaller annuity than the twelve thousand dollars Major Harvey had promised in 1845. "White men tell us we will be driven out [of the valley]," was the Kansa leader's most bitter complaint, "but we like this place and want to stay."[9]

Is-ta-la-she's last point was of crucial importance, for it struck at the heart of the government's duplicity in the decade after 1863. Despite the odds that faced them, the most responsible tribal spokesmen refused to concede that removal to Indian Territory was pre-

[6] Mahlon Stubbs to Farnsworth, Ninth Month 17, 1863, in *Report of the Commissioner of Indian Affairs* (1863), 377–78.
[7] Farnsworth to W. M. Albin, September 24, 1864, in *Report of the Commissioner of Indian Affairs* (1864), 38 Cong., 1 sess., *Senate Executive Document No. 1* (Serial 1220), 510.
[8] *Council Grove Press*, April 13, 1863.
[9] *Is-ta-la-she* to My Great Father (translated by Joseph James), July 17, 1863, LR, OIA, Kansas Agency.

requisite to the tribe's survival. Even as late as 1870, after their people had been subjected to additional indignities and suffering, they made it clear that the tribe wanted to remain in the Neosho Valley.[10] Their firm stand on this point was not the result of misguided optimism or native recalcitrance; it was a reasonable reaction to the treaty of 1859 and the government's legal obligation to protect the tribe's remaining holdings on the diminished reservation. What must be understood is that the postponement of Kansa removal for nearly a decade was not so much the result of a commitment to improve the tribe's condition as it was the federal government's desire to resolve the old conflict between squatters and speculators and dispose of *both* the trust lands and the diminished reservation in a manner satisfactory to all concerned, excluding, to be sure, the Kansas.

There were, of course, a variety of factors that made it difficult for the government and private-interest groups to pursue these objectives. Whiskey merchants distributed their illicit commodity in smug defiance of federal statutes. The inevitable consequences were a reckless squandering of annuity funds, a firmer conviction on the part of the squatters that the tribe was hopelessly corrupt, and additional acts of violence. So blatant were the operations of the whiskey peddlers that on one occasion J. L. French, who managed a "grocery" near the diminished reservation, submitted a depredation claim in which he requested government compensation for whiskey stolen during an altercation with a band of about sixty Kansas. French admitted killing one Kansa during the incident, but within a week six additional Indian bodies were found in the timber near his store.[11] Although French was eventually arrested and bound over to U.S. District Court and local opinion held that "the attack by the red-skins was one of the legitimate results of whiskey-selling,"[12] no concerted efforts were made to halt the liquor trade. In 1864 federal and state military authorities sent nearly seven

[10] Enoch Hoag to E. S. Parker, July 19, 1869, Mahlon Stubbs to Hoag, January 6, 1870, LR, OIA, Kansas Agency.
[11] *Emporia News*, February 16, 1860, May 10, 17, 1862; Farnsworth to Dole, July 14, 1863, LR, OIA, Kansas Agency.
[12] *Emporia News*, May 10, 1862.

hundred troops to western Kansas to hunt the "red devils," who allegedly were "under the influence of rebel emmissaries,"[13] but these same authorities would not provide even a small force to shut down a few grog shops that were demoralizing a friendly tribe.

As a matter of fact, the government pursued a policy which added to the tribe's misery. As early as September 13, 1861, Agent Farnsworth reported that enrolling Kansa troops for service in the Union Army would prevent the tribe from making its traditional fall hunt. Food and buffalo robes obtained in this manner, he wrote, were absolutely essential to keep the Kansas from starving and becoming "an added expense to the government."[14] But the advice was ignored. At least seventy young Kansas were forced to serve with Company L of the Ninth Kansas Cavalry and suffer heavy casualties at the very time they were needed by their own people.[15] Meanwhile, relations between the Plains Indians—especially the Kiowas, Comanches, Southern Cheyennes, and Arapahoes—and the military leaders of Kansas and Colorado Territory were deteriorating.

Reacting to unverified reports of a Confederate plan to seize the Santa Fe Trail and anxious to settle personal obligations stemming from his identification with the political faction headed by Senator James H. Lane of Kansas,[16] Major General Samuel R. Curtis, commander of the Department of Kansas, began campaigning in western Kansas in late July, 1864. "[W]ith men and horses taken from the reaper and the mower," the eager Curtis marched a large military force as far west as Fort Larned on a foray described by one participant as "this humbug business of chasing Indians that

---

13 Albert Castel, *A Frontier State at War: Kansas, 1861–1865*, 217; *Smoky Hill and Republican Union* (Junction City, Kansas), August 13, 20, 1864.

14 Farnsworth to H. B. Branch, September 13, 1861, LR, OIA, Kansas Agency.

15 *Is-ta-la-she* to My Great Father (translated by Joseph James), July 17, 1863, LR, OIA, Kansas Agency. Superintendent Thomas Murphy reported that 21 Kansas were killed "in Civil War services." Murphy to Commissioner of Indian Affairs, July 18, 1866, LR, OIA, Kansas Agency.

16 William E. Unrau, "The Civil War Career of Jesse Henry Leavenworth," *Montana Magazine*, XII (1962), 76–83; Castel, *A Frontier State*, 89, 109–10, 154, 164, 187, 216–17.

can't be found."[17] Even though he was unable to engage the foe, Curtis prohibited the Kansas from hunting on the buffalo plains; if found in the Upper Arkansas and Smoky Hill country they—like the Kiowas and Comanches—would be "subject to [military] campaigning." The unfortunate order was issued without regard for a summer drought that had virtually assured the failure of the tribe's meager corn crop or for what Farnsworth described as the Kansas' "absolutely destitute condition."[18]

Under these circumstances some of the Kansa leaders began to modify their views with regard to remaining in the Neosho Valley. On the High Plains a force of impatient Colorado miners and ranchers led by Colonel John M. Chivington put pressure on the Southern Cheyennes and Arapahoes, a move which culminated in the senseless Sand Creek Massacre in November, 1864. Encounters with Pawnees from the north cost the Kansas forty of their best mounts,[19] while at Council Grove the tribe's destitution was matched by the vengeance with which the squatters and speculators tried to subvert the amended treaty of 1859.

While Agent Farnsworth attempted to create the impression that he was primarily concerned with the welfare of his wards, he also "sounded a number of the principal leaders" on the question of their "willingness" to remove to Indian Territory.[20] Interestingly enough, his inquiry was made in October, 1863, not long after it was announced that Council Grove was certain to "get" at least three important railroads: one from Atchison and Topeka to Santa Fe, another from Leavenworth and Lawrence to Council Grove, and a third through the Neosho Valley to Humboldt and Indian Territory.[21] While clearly bombastic, the announcement constituted the logical outcome of the advice offered by Sam Wood in 1859: "If our politicians instead of fighting each other, would unite

[17] Castel, *A Frontier State*, 217; William Mitchell to sister, August 1, 1864, William Mitchell Papers, Manuscript Division, KSHS.
[18] Farnsworth to Dole, August 11, 1864, LR, OIA, Kansas Agency.
[19] Farnsworth to Dole, June 28, 1865, in *Report of the Commissioner of Indian Affairs* (1865), 39 Cong., 1 sess., *Senate Executive Document No. 1* (Serial 1248), 568.
[20] Farnsworth to Dole, October 12, 1863, LR, OIA, Kansas Agency.
[21] *Council Grove Press*, May 11, 1863.

and push forward this great [railroad] enterprise, it would make every man who has an acre of land in this County a rich man."[22] It was a persuasive argument, and its logical implications bade the Kansas no good.

In 1863 Sam Wood was busy promoting the sale of $25,000 worth of Atchison, Topeka & Santa Fe railroad stock in Council Grove, and by February, 1864, he had been made a Santa Fe vice-president. Thus it was logical for him to consider the purchase of at least some of the trust land and diminished reservation in order to attract an important line to the Neosho Valley.[23] Wood could count on the assistance of Alvin N. Blacklidge, later secretary of the Council Grove Town Company and attorney for the Kansas,[24] as well as that of Farnsworth, who on November 11, 1863, reported that Is-ta-la-she (or Is-ta-la-sin), No-pa-my, and Ah-le-ga-wa-ho had changed their minds in favor of moving the entire tribe to Indian Territory. With the right kind of encouragement, these headmen had visited several locations while on hunting trips and, according to Blacklidge, wanted to move their "new house before all the best sites [were] taken by the other tribes."[25] Playing the role that was expected of him, Farnsworth suggested a formal conference with Commissioner Dole, and in May, 1864, six of the most prominent chiefs were escorted to Washington by their agent and Thomas Huffaker.[26] Wood made no effort to disguise his optimism; to all who would listen he predicted that "the Indians would sell out their entire reservation and one of the richest valleys of land in the State would be thrown open to the settlers."[27]

Farnsworth, Huffaker, and the Kansa delegation returned to Council Grove in late June. Immediately it was announced that Is-ta-la-she had visited with President Lincoln and had proudly discussed the valuable service his men were providing in the Union Army. To a larger audience of Washington officials the Kansa

[22] *Kansas Press* (Council Grove), December 5, 1859.
[23] *Council Grove Press*, October 5, 12, 1863, February 15, 1864.
[24] Unrau, "The Council Grove Merchants," 280.
[25] Farnsworth to Dole, November 11, 1863, Alvin N. Blacklidge to Dole, March 14, 1864, LR, OIA, Kansas Agency.
[26] Farnsworth to Dole, June 13, 11, 1863, LR, OIA, Kansas Agency.
[27] *Council Grove Press*, May 21, 1864.

leader said "that it was once his delight to scalp his enemies ... but ... he now endeavored to adopt the ways of the white man. He did not expect to come up to their standard but [did] expect that his children [would]." The most exciting news, however, was that an agreement had been reached whereby the tribe would relinquish all its land in Kansas in return for a considerable amount of money and a new home in Indian Territory.[28]

A victory celebration by either the squatters or speculators at this point would have been premature, for no official action had been taken outside Commissioner Dole's office. Indeed, it was one of the Senate's signal accomplishments that the proposed Kansa treaty of 1864 was not ratified. No matter how well Dole, Farnsworth, and Huffaker adorned the document with promises of land, bacon, and salt, they were unable to disguise the obvious fact that they had brazenly attempted to grab a large part of the trust lands and diminished reservation for a miserly price of between fifty and sixty cents an acre. As proposed, the treaty was a speculator's dream, one that included the usual rhetoric about justice, humanitarianism, and fair compensation for those who would be forced to abandon their claims. And it was made all the more abominable by the inclusion of an article that would have provided fee-simple grants of between 40 and 360 acres to those Kansa headmen who had been parties to the deal.[29]

The abortive land grab was significant for other reasons. Its failure played havoc with Sam Wood's efforts to route the Santa Fe to Council Grove and away from her competitor, Emporia.[30] It provided the ground rules for additional speculative ventures in the area and rekindled the fires of squatter opposition, especially against jobbers who were lobbying for a treaty that would pave the way for them to purchase huge blocks of Kansa land. Anticipating a settlement of this sort, one Boston group purchased $70,000 worth of Kansa land scrip at seventy-five cents on the dollar; by February, 1867, it had increased in value to $1.25.[31] Even Wood

28 *Ibid.*, June 25, 1864.
29 Documents Relating to the Negotiation of an Unratified Treaty of June 11, 1864, with the Kaw Indians, Unratified Treaties, 1821–1865.
30 *Council Grove Press*, March 26, May 21, 28, 1864.

joined in the speculative scramble by announcing that he was prepared to "pay cash for a few thousand dollars of Kaw certificates."[32]

The scrip was issued under the terms of the amended treaty of
1859, the same document which forced the eviction of about eighty-
five squatters from the diminished reservation. Repeated delays in
the awarding of trust-land patents forced many squatters to peddle
at least some of their scrip to the very jobbers who in the end
would be bidding against them. The squatters resented this, especially since they were convinced that the government had paid "less
than one-third the actual cost of their improvements." By the
mid-1860's they were in an ugly mood and were asserting that no
treaty was acceptable unless it included a clause that would return
the diminished reservation to its rightful owners—themselves.[33]
Thus they applauded the failure of the Dole-Farnsworth-Huffaker
treaty, not because it gave the Kansas a temporary stay of removal,
but because it gave the squatters another chance in the struggle to
control the valley.

The conflict became more pronounced with the organization
on September 20, 1865, of the Union Pacific Railway, Southern
Branch. Later known as the Missouri-Kansas-Texas (Katy) Railroad, it was planned as part of a Gulf system that would be built
from Fort Riley, on the line of the Union Pacific Railway, Eastern
Division, "running thence, via Clarke's Creek and the Neosho
River, to a point at or near where the southern boundary-line of
the State of Kansas crosses the said Neosho River."[34] It was hoped
that the line would eventually extend through Indian Territory,
across the Red River, and on to New Orleans. Apart from financ-
ing, the most immediate obstacle to construction through the Neosho Valley and beyond Council Grove was the ten-mile length
across the northeastern corner of the diminished reservation. To
clear the way, a new treaty was mandatory.

[31] Wm. G. Ewing to B. D. Miner, February 20, 1867, William G. and
George Washington Ewing Papers, Manuscript Division, Indiana State Library,
Indianapolis.
[32] *Council Grove Press*, August 8, 1863.
[33] Charles Columbia to Hon. Sidney Clarke, February 1, 1866, LR, OIA,
Kansas Agency.
[34] V. V. Masterson, *The Katy Railroad and the Last Frontier*, 12.

Following a particularly brazen but abortive attempt in early 1866 to buy eighty thousand acres of trust land for an average of eighty-seven and a half cents an acre,[35] the Katy's directors—who until 1869 included Thomas Huffaker—scored a victory by having the federal government name their company the grantee of five alternate sections of land on each side of the proposed roadbed from the starting point at the junction of the Republican and Smoky Hill rivers to the southern boundary of Kansas. The award was made in late July, 1866, after considerable debate in Congress, and the interest displayed by local political hopefuls indicated that even more determined efforts would be made to partition the Neosho Valley Reservation.[36]

Most of the tribe spent the winter of 1865–66 in the buffalo country. According to Agent Farnsworth, they obtained three thousand buffalo robes which brought an average of seven dollars each. They also carried on a considerable trade in horses, which they obtained from the western tribes and sold to the white settlers for a tidy profit. Some progress in farming was also reported. On the other hand, it was announced that the manual-labor school operated by the Society of Friends would soon be closed because the parents of the students refused to support it. "Simultaneous efforts should be made to Christianize the adults," explained Farnsworth. "Otherwise the scholars . . . will return to heathenism with greater capabilities of evil."

Because of the substantial profits involved and the trivial penalties handed down by the local courts to those found guilty, whiskey flowed more freely on the reservation than ever before. Many squatters who complained of the unfair way the government was handling the land question apparently saw nothing wrong with stealing horses and agricultural implements from the tribe. As a result, a number of Kansa chiefs and warriors felt justified in arming themselves with weapons issued to them as Union troops during the Civil War. Candidly summarizing the situation in his last official

[35] Gates, *Fifty Million Acres*, 149–50.
[36] *Congressional Globe*, 39 Cong., 1 sess., Pt. III, 2050, 2664; *ibid.*, Pt. IV 3502; *ibid.*, Pt. V, 4078, 4117; Masterson, *The Katy Railroad*, 25.

report as Kansa agent, Farnsworth wrote: "I am satisfied that the condition of this tribe would be improved if they were moved south, and greater facilities furnished them for farming and stock raising."[37]

Meanwhile, the treaty makers were busy. They were divided into two principal groups: a local one headed by Huffaker, Blacklidge, and those Council Grove merchants who still had some influence in the destiny of the Union Pacific, Southern Branch, and another composed of the more affluent outsiders who wanted to dominate the railroad and profit handsomely by manipulating the value of the scrip they had been purchasing. Unlike the latter group—which included a number of Boston bankers, the Ewing group of Indiana and eastern Kansas, and a combination of northern New York financiers for whom Robert S. Stevens was the principal agent in Washington and Kansas—Huffaker and his associates could, for the most part, count on the support of the squatters. This was a valuable asset, for by 1867 the conflict between contending groups was making it increasingly difficult to negotiate a treaty which would satisfy the squatters, guarantee the desired value of the scrip, and at the same time provide for the removal of the entire Kansa tribe.

Certainly there was no lack of maneuvering after Kansa representatives again visited Washington in early 1867 for the purpose of negotiating another treaty. In a letter to one of his Fort Wayne confidants, William G. Ewing described the nature of the opposition, as well as the problems attendant to land speculation and treaty making:

Ever since my arrival [in Washington] I have been convinced from the difficulty I met with in finding out anything about these certificates [scrip] that there was *something wrong somewhere! !* The day I left here last week for New York it began to "crop out." These certificates formerly sold for 75¢ on the dollar & parties in Boston hold some $70,000—purchased at that figure. They now amount to $1.25 on the dollar, interest & principal & I was told by A. N. Blacklidge (!) today

[37] Farnsworth to Thomas Murphy, September 10, 1866, in *Report of the Commissioner of Indian Affairs* (1866), 39 Cong., 2 sess., *House Executive Document No. 1* (Serial 1284), 274–75.

the parties would be glad to get back their money without interest. I
don't believe a word of it!! *He* also said a party was offered 50¢ for
some & asked his advice yesterday as to selling; thinks 55¢ would have
bought them. Blacklidge afterwards said "it's no use beating around
the bush, & I'll tell you what I'm doing. These [Kansa] Indians are
now here to make a treaty; Huffaker who speaks their language &
has been with them for years is here & they will make any treaty he
advises: *he* will *advise* anything *I say* & *won't* advise them to make
any treaty unless I want it made—&c & &c. He proposes having the
Gov't take their 133,777 acres land & assume pay[ment for] these
certificates; this will make [the] certificates par or nearly so, perfectly good in the end for *face* & *interest, but* the trouble will be to
get the Senate to confirm such a treaty, & it can only be done through
[Edmund] Ross and [Samuel] Pomeroy, Kansas Senators. Ross he
says is too honest to line, but will assist; Pomeroy holds his hand behind his back &c. In short says the agent of the Boston parties was
over last week & he (Blacklidge) proposed to take 20 pr. cent con-
tingent upon success & wants us to do the same!! It may be well to
agree to it, but we must first know who can pull the wires & not get
hold of the wrong man. [Charles] Mix today gave me a punch in the
ribs & *confidentially* informed me of this treaty, & effect of it on the
value of the certificates. Last week I learned W. P. Dole formerly
Com. Ind. Affairs was enquiring who had Kaw Certif's. to sell. When
I cornered Mix & asked square out who were *the* men moving this
treaty he "told me in strict confidence, W. P. Dole." I shall manage
to see Dole in some way & learn if Blacklidge is not a mere hanger-on
I suspect he is.[38]

If Ewing's estimation of Huffaker's influence with the tribe was
correct (and it probably was), then the contending groups may
have reached at least a temporary settlement, for by then Al-le-
ga-wa-ho, Nah-he-gah-wah-tu-in-gah, and Wah-ti-ing-gah had
agreed to a treaty compatible with most of the objectives sought
by the speculators. These included cession of the unsold trust lands
and the entire diminished reservation, recognition that "the legal
rights of railroad corporations [would] accrue thereon," and a
guarantee that the government would fund at face value and
interest $120,805.75 worth of Kansa scrip.[39] However, since the

38 Wm. G. Ewing to B. D. Miner, February 20, 1867, Ewing Papers.
39 Articles of Agreement made and concluded at the City of Washington
on the thirteenth day of February, one thousand eight hundred and sixty seven,

Senate refused to ratify the treaty, Huffaker, Blacklidge, and the Council Grove group may have concluded that they were not getting a fair share of the spoils. Fearful of this, they probably pressured Pomeroy and Ross into withdrawing their support on grounds that acceptance of the treaty would run counter to general settler sentiment in Kansas and was therefore politically inexpedient.

Perhaps the treaty was defeated primarily because the speculative groups "were pulling at cross purposes," with settler pressure operating only as a secondary factor.[40] But the Council Grove schemers had at least one very good reason for siding with the squatters: they wanted to maintain some degree of influence in local railroad development.

While the treaty of 1867 languished in the Senate, plans were being completed for the beginning of Union Pacific construction at Junction City.[41] Even with a federal land grant it would be an expensive and risky enterprise, at least until the diminished reservation was cleared. Under these circumstances the cooperation of all parties concerned was required, including the citizens of Morris County, where Council Grove and most of the Kansa lands were located. Now it was up to Huffaker and Blacklidge, not the promoters who worked out of offices in Boston, Fort Wayne, and New York. At a special meeting on May 27 the Morris County commissioners decided to conduct an election on the question of bonds to support the railroad. Five weeks later citizens agreed in a landslide vote of 170 to 25 to issue $165,000 worth of thirty-year bonds at 7 per cent if the Union Pacific reached Council Grove within two years.[42] The local promoters were understandably elated, for this apparent vote of confidence seemed to assure them a powerful

between Lewis Bogy, Commissioner of Indian Affairs . . . and Chiefs of the Kansas, Unratified Treaties, 1866–1867.

[40] Gates, *Fifty Million Acres*, 150.

[41] Masterson, *The Katy Railroad*, 17–18.

[42] Special Meeting, May 27, 1867, and Meeting, July 1, 1867, Minuts (*sic*), Commissioner's Journal, B, Office of the Morris County Clerk, Council Grove, Kansas.

voice in any future treaty, as well as leverage to contend with the eastern capitalists. For the Kansas, however, it was only additional evidence of the fact that their days in the Neosho Valley were numbered.

While the battle for legal control of the valley was being waged, the squatters defied Kansa Agent E. S. Stover and occupied most of the choice land on the diminished reservation.[43] Such action was easy after October 10, 1867, when the tribe departed for the buffalo plains by way of the Medicine Lodge treaty grounds. But in so doing the Kansas became embroiled in a series of encounters with the Cheyennes and Arapahoes, the consequences of which amounted to another compelling reason for their finding a new home in Indian Territory.

The situation on the plains of western Kansas remained tense in the months and years immediately following the Sand Creek Massacre. Government negotiations at the Little Arkansas in the fall of 1865 brought some relief,[44] but Major General Winfield S. Hancock's ill-conceived and poorly executed demonstration of power west of Fort Larned in the spring of 1867 only agitated the Cheyennes and Arapahoes.[45] Their more aggressive warrior bands continued to harass the outlying settlements and make life miserable for such weaker tribes as the Kansas. Following a raid in the late winter of 1866 that netted the Cheyennes forty-two Kansa ponies and at least one Kansa scalp, the Arapahoes stole an additional thirty-four horses while the Kansas were en route to Medicine Lodge.[46] This left the Kansas short of transportation and

[43] *Emporia News*, April 19, 1867; E. S. Stover to Thomas Murphy, December 5, 1867, LR, OIA, Kansas Agency. Stover replaced Hiram W. Farnsworth as Kansa agent on March 21, 1867. See "Kansas Agencies," 173.

[44] William E. Unrau, "Indian Agent vs. the Army: Some Background Notes on the Kiowa-Comanche Treaty of 1865," *KHQ*, XXX (1964), 150–52.

[45] The literature on the Hancock campaign of 1867 is extensive. For the pro-Hancock position, see Almira Russell Hancock, *Reminiscences of Winfield S. Hancock*, and Winfield S. Hancock, *Reports of Major W. S. Hancock Upon Indian Affairs, With Accompanying Exhibits*. The opposite—and more careful—point of view is found in "Progress of Indian Hostilities," 40 Cong., 1 sess., *Senate Executive Document No. 13* (Serial 1308), especially 83–87, and the correspondence of Jesse H. Leavenworth and Edward W. Wynkoop in LR, OIA, Upper Arkansas Agency (M 234), 1867–1868, NA.

[46] Stover to Murphy, May 14, 1868, LR, OIA, Kansas Agency, and Stover

horses for hunting. After a short stay at the treaty grounds, where they were wrongly accused of stealing horses from the Arapahoes and where General William S. Harney applauded the slaughter of a few "tame" Kansas by the Arapahoes,[47] they proceeded to Plumb Creek, not far from Fort Zarah. Here they established their winter camp, hoping that some game would be available in the immediate vicinity.[48]

It was a costly and tragic decision. In early December a party of Cheyennes visited the Kansa camp, pretending they were prepared to discuss the "difficulties existing between the tribes." After a friendly talk lasting several hours, the Cheyennes left, giving every indication that an understanding had been reached. Minutes later, within a few hundred yards of the Kansa camp, they turned on a lone Kansa herder, whom they killed and swiftly scalped. Having witnessed the cowardly act, a number of enraged Kansas charged the Cheyennes, and within four hours the enemy was driven from the field. Fourteen Cheyennes and two Kansas lay dead, many were wounded, and both sides lost a substantial number of horses. While the Cheyennes rushed to obtain reinforcements, the Kansas fled for their reservation, arriving there on December 25 in a completely destitute condition. At least sixty had died during the retreat, mainly from the terrible cold, hunger, and exposure. More horses were lost, so that they were reduced to about 150 animals for the entire tribe.[49]

A return to the buffalo country after the Cheyenne affair was out of the question. With reports circulating that the Cheyennes would return to gain revenge, the Kansas were confined to their reservation, completely dependent on the government and / or the credit of the Council Grove merchants. Finally, on June 3, 1868, some one hundred Cheyenne warriors appeared at the agency head-

to Murphy, September 10, 1868, in *Report of the Commissioner of Indian Affairs* (1866), 40 Cong., 3 sess., *House Executive Document No. 1* (Serial 1366), 720.

[47] Stover to Murphy, December 20, 1867, LR, OIA, Kansas Agency; Douglas C. Jones, *The Treaty of Medicine Lodge*, 94.

[48] Stover to Murphy, September 10, 1868, in *Report of the Commissioner of Indian Affairs* (1868), 720.

[49] *Ibid.*; Stover to Murphy, December 27, 1868, LR, OIA, Kansas Agency.

quarters south of town. Many of the settlers feared for their lives, while others were certain that they would have an opportunity to witness Indian brutality at its worst. Both groups were wrong. Although a few scattered shots were fired and a considerable amount of shouting and charging with horses occurred, no one was killed.

Although several government officials stood by like spectators at a medieval joust, the confrontation was largely ceremonial. The excitement lasted less than four hours, and after the "aggressors" had departed for Fort Larned, it was learned that the raid had gained them a small amount of plunder from two farms, some sugar and coffee offered as a "sacrifice" by the Council Grove townsmen, some goods from an isolated trading post twenty miles west of Six Mile Creek, seven beefs from the squatters, and eleven more from a party of Texas drovers who happened to be in the vicinity. The authenticity of a report that "a colored woman" was violated was questionable, since the alleged victim admitted the Cheyennes "did not fully succeed." That the objective of the Cheyennes was divided between a desire for supplies and the obtaining of satisfaction from their enemy became apparent when the Cheyennes later informed their agent they wanted to pay for the plunder as soon as their annuities were issued.[50]

Nevertheless, the Cheyenne raid threw the white citizens of the valley into a frenzy, especially after Brigadier General Alfred Sully reported from Fort Harker that "several hundred Arapahoes and Navajoes" were headed for Council Grove.[51] Eight days later, on July 15, a "Mr. Adams" of Council Grove arrived from Fort Zarah with news that eight hundred well-armed Cheyennes, Arapahoes, Kiowas, and Apaches were on their way to fight the Osages "and on their return . . . intended . . . to exterminate the Kaws."[52] Military authorities at Fort Riley were alerted but were told to

[50] Alexander R. Banks to Taylor, May 4, 1868, LR, OIA, Central Superintendency (M 234), 1868, NA; E. W. Wynkoop to Murphy, May 15, 1868, LR, OIA, Upper Arkansas Agency; Albert G. Boone to N. G. Taylor, June 4, 8, 1868, Wynkoop to Murphy, June 12, 13, 1868, LR, OIA, Kansas Agency.
[51] Sully to Colonel English, July 7, 1868, LR, OIA, Kansas Agency.
[52] Stover to Murphy, July 15, 1868, LR, OIA, Kansas Agency.

intervene only under certain circumstances. In an official communication to his temporary camp near the Kansa Reservation, Captain Martin Mullins was ordered: "On *no account* will *you* interfere with the *Indians* so long as their hostility is confined to themselves, but should they attack *white settlers* you will at *once take the aggressive*."[53] Meanwhile, the Kansas were forced to remain on their reservation, completely dependent on food and supplies provided by the local merchants.

The anticipated encounter did not materialize. Indeed, the evidence suggests that rumors of a return engagement between the Cheyennes and Kansas were devised by certain Council Grove merchants who hoped to profit if the Kansas were unable to obtain natural subsistence. In a letter to Commissioner N. G. Taylor in early August, Superintendent Thomas Murphy explained: "Of course, it is well known that Adams' report is not correct—the real factor is the desire of certain parties to keep the Indians confined for the issuing of rations."[54]

Who were these "certain parties"? Several commercial firms were probably involved, but the most important was that of Joab Spencer and James Mead. Spencer, the senior partner, "had quit preaching in 1865 because of ill health" and since then had enjoyed a dominant position in the "order system" at Kansas Agency.[55] In the fall of 1867 he issued beef and flour to the Kansas so that they could make their semiannual hunting expedition. The transaction was on credit, for Spencer and Mead expected to be paid, at least in part, in buffalo robes. But the Plumb Creek battle in December forced the Kansas to return empty handed. Since the tribe's annuities and a small emergency fund were soon exhausted, the traders sought other means of settling their accounts. With the help of the squatters, they spread rumors of an impending Cheyenne attack; they brought pressure on the Indian Department and the military to keep the tribe confined at Council Grove; they continued to supply

[53] Captain M. Howard to Captain Martin Mullins, July 8, 1868, LR, OIA, Kansas Agency.

[54] Murphy to Taylor, August 5, 1868, LR, OIA, Kansas Agency.

[55] Farnsworth to Taylor, May 15, 1867, Murphy to Taylor, March 16, 1868, Stover to Murphy, July 10, 1868, LR, OIA, Kansas Agency.

the Kansas on credit, then waited for Washington to fund the entire operation.

The traders' strategy almost succeeded. On March 3, 1869, Congress authorized an emergency appropriation of $25,000 for the Kansas. Within a few days Spencer and Mead submitted vouchers for $27,718.40 worth of provisions and requested "action thereon, to the extent of $22,000."[56] Despite the fact that the request violated an Indian Department directive of June, 1866, which forbade the issuing of supplies on credit,[57] the traders persuaded Superintendent Murphy and the Kansas congressional delegation to write letters on their behalf.[58] Fortunately for the tribe, Commissioner Taylor and the attorney general's office were not taken in by these tactics; they ruled that the money was specifically for "starving Indians." To obtain a return on their investment, Spencer and Mead were required to wait until money was available from the sale of reservation land.[59]

Consequently, the traders had a good reason to join ranks with the railroad crowd in a final effort to dispossess the Kansas of their reservation. Since it was clear by December, 1868, that the treaty of the previous year would not be ratified,[60] the combination of promoters persuaded Agent Stover and Special Commissioner Walter R. Irwin to call a meeting of the principal tribal leaders at the agency on March 13, 1869. With Huffaker, Spencer, and several Union Pacific dignitaries in attendance, an understanding was quickly reached. The railroad would buy the entire diminished reservation for fifteen cents an acre and the remaining trust lands for eighty-seven and a half cents an acre. Spencer and the traders would be paid "out of the first money received from the sale of lands," up to a maximum of forty thousand dollars. For their part in the deal, the six most distinguished chiefs would each receive a

[56] An Act Making Appropriations to Supply Deficiencies . . . for the Fiscal Year Ending June 30, 1869, J. Spencer and Co. to Taylor, March 18, 1869, LR, OIA, Kansas Agency.
[57] Farnsworth to Murphy, June 8, 1866, LR, OIA, Kansas Agency.
[58] Edmund Ross to Taylor, March 5, 1869, Murphy to Taylor, March 11, 1869, LR, OIA, Kansas Agency.
[59] J. W. McMillan to Taylor, March 11, 1869, LR, OIA, Kansas Agency.
[60] Stover to Murphy, December 10, 1868, LR, OIA, Kansas Agency.

quarter-section of land, while the tribe as a whole would be moved to a twenty-mile-square reservation in Indian Territory. The usual promises concerning annuities, subsistence, and agricultural assistance were included.[61]

In view of the tribe's long history of forced displacement, it was a fitting climax that this unscrupulous attempt at land grabbing failed. Taylor gave it his blessing,[62] but the squatters did not. Neither did Secretary of the Interior J. D. Cox, who charged that it was contrary to the "interests of the settlers upon the public lands."[63] In fact, so pronounced was the opposition that Stevens sought military assistance to prevent the squatters from seizing the reservation.[64] While a local editor noted the existence of a "Circumlocation Office" in Washington where congressmen and Indian agents learned how not to get treaties ratfied,[65] the squatters organized and eventually overran the diminished reservation.[66] The editor immediately executed an about-face and applauded the squatters because their action was "the only way to get the miserable Indians out of the way."[67]

The local press was correct, for in the final analysis the squatters succeeded where the traders and railroad interests had failed. While the Union Pacific directors had to be satisfied with a 100-foot-wide right-of-way, for which they paid twenty-four thousand dollars, and the authority to take timber at twenty cents a tie,[68] it was not long before the settlers were in control of the reservation. Additional bids for large blocks of land by various railroads and speculative groups were rejected, some on technicalities and others

[61] Agreement Made and Concluded at the Kaw Agency, Kansas on the Thirteenth Day of March, One Thousand Eight Hundred and Sixty Nine, Unratified Treaties, 1868–1869.

[62] Taylor to Secretary of the Interior, March 29, 1869, Unratified Treaties, 1868–1869.

[63] J. D. Cox to President of the United States, April 5, 1869, Unratified Treaties, 1868–1869.

[64] Robert Stevens to E. S. Parker, May 22, 1869, LR, OIA, Kansas Agency.

[65] *Emporia News*, June 18, 1869.

[66] *Ibid.*, June 3, 1870.

[67] *Ibid.*

[68] Contract between R. S. Stevens and Enoch Hoag, July 14, 1869, Agreement of J. D. Cox, July 29, 1869, LR, OIA, Kansas Agency.

because of the abrogation of Indian treaty-making power in 1871.[69]

What remained was to convince the Kansas that they had no alternative but to leave the Neosho Valley. Following the rejection of the treaty of 1869, Stover was suspended as the Kansa agent and replaced by Mahlon Stubbs.[70] The latter reported that the construction crews were destroying fences and corn fields on the reservation and that the tribe was very pessimistic about the future.[71] No matter what they did or how often they voiced a preference for the status quo, they were only postponing that inevitable day when they would have to move again. "Permit me to say," wrote Stubbs to Superintendent Enoch Hoag, "that this tribe . . . have been so badly dealt with in former years—that they have but little confidence in white men of any class."[72]

A member of the respected Society of Friends, Stubbs was able to instill a sense of confidence among the Kansas. He presided over a successful peace council between the Kansas and Cheyennes on the North Canadian River in 1870[73] and later that year led a delegation to other parts of Indian Territory to find an acceptable reservation site. The government favored the country west of the Arkansas River, while the tribe preferred the Lower Caney Valley in the eastern part of the Osage Reservation. Since the Kansas feared that the government's choice would result in their being surrounded "by more powerful tribes," a compromise location was arranged through the cooperation of the Cherokee National Council and the Osages. It provided for a 100,137-acre reservation east of the Arkansas River and immediately south of Kansas in present Kay County, Oklahoma.[74]

[69] Gates, *Fifty Million Acres*, 150.

[70] Mahlon Stubbs to E. S. Parker, July 17, 1867, LR, OIA, Kansas Agency.

[71] Stubbs to Enoch Hoag, September 13, October 8, 1869, LR, OIA, Kansas Agency.

[72] Stubbs to Hoag, January 6, 1870, LR, OIA, Kansas Agency.

[73] Stubbs to Hoag, 9th Month 6th, 1870, in *Report of the Commissioner of Indian Affairs* (1870), 41 Cong., 3 sess., *House Executive Document No. 1* (Serial 1449), 738.

[74] Stubbs to Hoag, October 10, December 6, 1870, Hoag to F. W. Walker, April 29, 1872, Stubbs to Hoag, July 22, 1872, Thomas H. Stanley to Uriah Spray, September 22, 1872, LR, OIA, Kansas Agency; "Report with Respect to the House Resolution Authorizing the Committee on Interior and Insular Affairs

An act to provide for the tribe's removal and the sale of the diminished reservation in small tracts was passed on May 8, 1872.[75] Six weeks later, in his last formal speech at Council Grove, Al-le-ga-wa-ho bitterly criticized the Union Pacific executives for their financial duplicity and demanded a fair price for his people's lands. He also made a plea for food, clothing, and schools for his children.[76] Congress appropriated the necessary removal funds on February 14, 1873, and in laws passed in 1874 and 1876 it was decided once and for all that the trust lands would be sold in small quantities to the actual settlers.[77]

Two hundred years after a party of French explorers first recorded their existence, the Kansas began their trek to Indian Territory. What proved to be their last forced migration began on June 4, 1873, and was completed without incident seventeen days later. In a gesture of understanding, the government allowed them to go on a buffalo hunt that fall. Ironically, it was successful, even though it was their last.[78]

The Kansas were on the threshold of a new era. They would continue to encounter the kinds of problems that had plagued them for generations, as well as some that were entirely new. At the same time, they would try to retain at least some of their cultural tradition. This would be difficult, if not altogether impossible. As a powerless minority in an increasingly more complex world, the Wind People were inextricably committed to the white man's way of life.[79]

to Conduct an Investigation of the Bureau of Indian Affairs," 82 Cong., 2 sess., *House Report No. 2503* (1953), 828–29.

[75] *House Report No. 2503, 829.*

[76] Speech of Al-le-ga-wa-ho, June 24, 1872, LR, OIA, Kansas Agency.

[77] *House Report No. 2503, 829.*

[78] Stubbs to Hoag, Ninthmonth 1, 1873, in *Report of the Commissioner of Indian Affairs* (1873), 43 Cong., 1 sess., *House Executive Document No. 1* (Serial 1601), 566–70; Stubbs to Edward P. Smith, Ninthmonth 25, 1874, in *Report of the Commissioner of Indian Affairs* (1874), 43 Cong., 1 sess., *House Executive Document No. 1* (Serial 1639), 526.

[79] For selected phases of Kansa history after 1873, see Berlin B. Chapman, "Charles Curtis and the Kaw Reservation," *KHQ*, XV (1947), 337–51, and Frank F. Finney, "The Kaw Indians and Their Indian Territory Agency," *Chronicles of Oklahoma*, XXXV (1957–58), 416–25.

BIBLIOGRAPHY

MANUSCRIPT MATERIALS
Council Grove, Kansas

Office of the Morris County Clerk
Minuts [*sic*], Commissioner's Journal, B.

Office of the Morris County Register of Deeds
Deed Record, Vol. B.
Land Books, Ranges 5–10, Townships 14–17. 10 vols. 1859–69.

St. Louis, Missouri

Missouri Historical Society
Pierre Chouteau–Maffitt Collection, Chouteau Papers.
John Dougherty Papers.
Indian Papers.
George C. Sibley Papers.

Topeka, Kansas

Kansas State Historical Society
Joseph S. Chick Papers.
W. W. Cone Papers.
John Dougherty Papers.
Hiram W. Farnsworth Papers.
Thomas Sears Huffaker Papers.
Rev. William Johnson Miscellaneous Papers.
Kansas Indian Papers.
John J. Lutz Papers.

Isaac McCoy Papers (microfilm edition).
John C. McCoy Papers.
Jotham Meeker Papers (microfilm edition).
Mineral Resources Papers.
William Mitchell Papers.
George Pierson Morehouse Papers.
William Barclay Napton Papers.
John G. Pratt Papers (microfilm edition).
Addison Woodward Stubbs Papers.
Allen T. Ward Papers.
Samuel Newitt Wood Papers.

Washington, D.C.

Bureau of American Ethnology, Office of Anthropology
James Owen Dorsey Papers.
Kansas Indian Texts and Myths.

National Archives, Cartographic Branch
Connected plat of the survey of the half breed Kansas Indians, A. L. Langham, Surv., 1827. Map No. 94, Tube 60.
Diagram of the Proposed Reserve for Kaw Indians, 1872. Map No. 344, Tube 114.
Map Exhibiting the Territorial limits of Several Nations and Tribes of Indians agreeable to the Notes of A. Chouteau reduced and laid down on a Scale of 80 miles to the inch by R. Paul, February, 1816. Map. No. 884, Tube 702.
Map of Kansas Half-breed Indian Reservation, Kansas River, 1828. Map No. 119, Tube 405.
Map of the Kansas Tribe of Indians Reserve. Map No. 149, Tube 30.
Map of [West]ern Country by Isaac McCoy ... 1832. Map No. 227, Tube 444.
Map Showing Location of the Missouri, Kansas, and Texas Railway through the Trust Lands and Diminished Reserve of the Kansas Tribe of Indians, showing also the Area of Land taken by the Railway in Each Quarter Section. Map No. 62, Tube 982.
Map Showing the Kansas lands in the case of the Kansas or Kaw tribe of Indians vs. the United States, Court of Claims F64, June 1, 1932. Map No. 11321, Tube 1387.
[Plat of lands of] Kaw half-breed Reserves under Treaty of 1825. Map No. 545, Tube 55.
Plat [of the Exterior lines of the] Kansas Reservation, Approved [by] John Montgomery. Map No. 116, Tube 405.

Sketch of Kansas River and Vicinity Relating to Indian Lands. Map No. 88, Tube 55.

National Archives, Records of the Bureau of Indian Affairs

Documents Relating to the Negotiation of Ratified and Unratified Treaties with Various Tribes of Indians, 1801–1869 (RG 75):

Introduction and Ratified Treaties, 1801–1826 (T-494, R 1).

Unratified Treaties, 1821–1865 (T-494, R 8).

Unratified Treaties, 1866–1867 (T-494, R 9).

Unratified Treaties, 1868–1869 (T-494, R 10).

National Archives, Records of the Office of Indian Affairs

Letters Received (M 234):

Central Superintendency, 1868 (R 59).

Fort Leavenworth Agency, 1824–1848 (R 300–302).

Kansas Agency, 1851–1873 (R 364–369).

Kiowa, Comanche, And Apache Agency, 1867–1868 (R 375).

Osage River Agency, 1844–1854 (R 643–644).

Potawatomie Agency, 1853–1856 (R 679–680).

St. Louis Superintendency, 1824–1851 (R 747–756).

Upper Arkansas Agency, 1867–1868 (R 879–880).

Western Superintendency, 1832–1836 (R 921).

Other Depositories

William G. and George Washington Ewing Papers. Manuscript Division, Indiana State Library, Indianapolis.

Rev. W. D. Smith's Letters from the Shawnee Village, 1833. Manuscript Division, Presbyterian Historical Society, Philadelphia, Pennsylvania.

GOVERNMENT DOCUMENTS
Congressional Documents

"Progress of Indian Hostilities." 40 Cong., 1 sess., *Senate Executive Document No. 13* (Serial 1308).

Report of the Commissioner of Indian Affairs. 1855–74.

"Report with Respect to the House Resolution Authorizing the Committee on Interior and Insular Affairs to Conduct an Investigation of the Bureau of Indian Affairs Pursuant to House Resolution 698." 82 Cong., 2 sess., *House Report No. 2503* (Union Calendar No. 790, 1953).

Royce, Charles C. (comp.). *Indian Land Cessions in the United States,* in *Eighteenth Annual Report of the Bureau of American Ethnology, 1896–1897,* Pt. 2. 56 Cong., 1 sess., *House Executive Document No. 736* (Serial 4015).

General Government Documents

Carter, Clarence Edwin (comp. and ed.). *The Territorial Papers of the United States*, Vols. XIII–XV. Washington, 1948–51.

General Laws of the Territory of Kansas Passed at the Fifth Session of the Legislative Assembly, Begun at the City of Lecompton, on the 1st Monday of January, 1859, and Held and Concluded at the City of Lawrence. Lawrence, K.T., Herald of Freedom Press, 1859.

Journal of the Executive Proceedings of the Senate of the United States of America from December 6, 1858, to August 6, 1861, Inclusive. Vol. XI. Washington, 1887.

Kappler, Charles J. (comp. and ed.). *Indian Affairs: Laws and Treaties*. Vols. I and II (Serials 4253 and 4254). Washington, 1903–1904.

Laws of the Territory of Kansas Passed at the Second Session of the General Assembly, Begun and Held at the City of Lecompton, on the Second Monday of January, A. D., 1857. Lecompton, K.T., R. H. Bennett, Public Printer, 1857.

Ninth Census: The Statistics of the Population of the United States, 1870. Vol. I. Washington, 1872.

Population of the United States in 1860: Compiled from the Original Returns of the Eighth Census. Washington, 1864.

Private Laws of the Territory of Kansas Passed at the Fifth Session of the Legislative Assembly; Begun at the City of Lecompton on the 1st Monday of January, 1859 and Held and Concluded at the City of Lawrence. Lawrence, K. T., Herald of Freedom Press, 1859.

U.S. Statutes at Large. Vols. V, X, XII. Washington, 1846, 1855, 1863.

NEWSPAPERS

Council Grove Press (Council Grove, Kansas).
Emporia News (Emporia, Kansas).
Kansas Press (Cottonwood Falls, Kansas).
Kansas Press (Council Grove, Kansas).
Smoky Hill and Republican Union (Junction City, Kansas).

PRIMARY SOURCES

Abel, Annie Heloise (ed.). *Tabeau's Narrative of Loisel's Expedition to the Upper Missouri*. Norman, University of Oklahoma Press, 1939.

Barry, Louise. *The Beginning of the West: Annals of the Kansas Gateway to the American West, 1540–1854*. Topeka, Kansas State Historical Society, 1972.

Biddle, Nicholas (ed.). *The Journals of the Expedition Under the Command of Capts. Lewis and Clark*. New York, The Heritage Press, 1962.

Bieber, Ralph P. (ed.). *Adventures in the Santa Fé Trade 1844–1847 by James Josiah Webb*. Glendale, Calif., Arthur H. Clark Co., 1931.

————. *Journal of a Soldier Under Kearny and Doniphan 1846–1847 by George Rutledge Gibson.* Glendale, Calif., Arthur H. Clark Co., 1935.

————. *Southern Trails to California in 1849.* Glendale, Calif., Arthur H. Clark Co., 1937.

————. *Wah-To-Yah and the Taos Trail by Lewis H. Garrard.* Glendale, Calif., Arthur H. Clark Co., 1938.

Blair, Emma H. (trans. and ed.). *The Indian Tribes of the Upper Mississippi Valley and Region of the Great Lakes as Described by Nicolas Perrot.* 2 vols. Cleveland, Arthur H. Clark Co., 1912.

Boynton, Rev. C. B., and T. B. Mason. *A Journey through Kansas; with Sketches of Nebraska: Describing the Country, Climate, Soil, Minerals, Manufacturing and Other Resources.* Cincinnati, Moore, Wilstach, Keys and Co., 1855.

Brackenridge, Henry Marie. *Views of Louisiana Together With a Journal of a Voyage Up the Missouri River in 1811.* Chicago, Quadrangle Books, 1962.

Bryant, Edwin. *What I Saw in California.* New York, D. Appleton and Co., 1849.

Chittenden, Hiram M., and Alfred T. Richardson (eds.). *Life, Letters and Travels of Father Pierre-Jean DeSmet, S. J., 1801–1873*, Vol. I. New York, Francis P. Harper, 1905.

Coues, Elliott (ed.). *The Expeditions of Zebulon Montgomery Pike, Vol. II.* New York, Francis P. Harper, 1895.

Du Pratz, Le Page. *The History of Louisiana or the Western Parts of Virginia and Carolina, Containing a Description of the Countries that Lie on Both Sides of the River Mississippi.* London, T. Becket, 1774.

Frémont, John C. *Report of the Exploring Expeditions to the Rocky Mountains in the Year 1842 and to Oregon and North California in the Years 1843-'44.* Washington, Gales and Seaton, Printers, 1845.

Gale, George. *Upper Mississippi; or, Historical Sketches of the Mound-Builders, the Indian Tribes, and the Progress of Civilization in the North-West.* Chicago, Clarke and Co., 1867.

Greene, Max. *The Kanzas Region: Forest, Prairie, Desert, Mountain, Dale and River.* New York, Fowler and Wells, 1856.

Hackett, Charles W. (ed.). *Pichardo's Treatise on the Limits of Louisiana and Texas.* Vols. II and III. Austin, University of Texas Press, 1934, 1941.

Hafen, Leroy R., and Ann W. Hafen (eds.). *Rufus B. Sage Letters and Papers, 1836–1847.* Glendale, Calif., Arthur H. Clark Co., 1956.

Hammond, George P., and Agapito Rey (eds.). *Don Juan de Oñate, Colonizer of New Mexico, 1595–1628.* Vols. V–VI in George P. Hammond (ed.). *Coronado Cuarto Centennial Publications, 1540–1940.* Albuquerque, University of New Mexico Press, 1953.

Hancock, Almira Russell. *Reminiscences of Winfield S. Hancock.* N.p., Charles L. Webster and Co., 1887.

Hancock, Winfield S. *Reports of Major General W. S. Hancock Upon Indian Affairs. With Accompanying Exhibits.* Washington, McGill and Witherow, 1867.

Houck, Louis (ed.). *The Spanish Regime in Missouri.* 2 Vols. Chicago, R. R. Donnelly and Sons, 1909.

Irving, John T., Jr. *Indian Sketches Taken During an Expedition to the Pawnee Tribes.* Philadelphia, Carey, Lea and Blanchard, 1835.

Jackson, Donald (ed.). *The Journals of Zebulon Montgomery Pike With Letters and Related Documents*, Vol. II. Norman, University of Oklahoma Press, 1966.

— — —. *Letters of the Lewis and Clark Expedition With Related Documents, 1783-1854.* Urbana, University of Illinois Press, 1962.

Luttig, John C. *Journal of a Fur-Trading Expedition on the Upper Missouri, 1812-1813.* Ed. by Stella M. Drumm. New York, Argosy-Antiquarian Ltd., 1964.

McCoy, Isaac. *History of Baptist Indian Missions.* Washington, William M. Morrison, 1840.

McDermott, John Francis (ed.). *Tixier's Travels on the Osage Prairies.* Norman, University of Oklahoma Press, 1940.

Margry, Pierre. *Explorations of the Tributaries of the Mississippi and Discovery of the Rocky Mountains, 1679-1754.* Part VI of *Discoveries and Establishments of the French Within the West and Within the South of North America, 1614-1754.* Paris, Imprimeric Jouaust et Sejoux Reu Saint-Honorè, 338, 1886. Trans. by Beatrice Paddock, 1936. Copy in Kansas Room, Wichita Public Library, Wichita, Kansas.

Morgan, Lewis Henry (ed.). *The Indian Journals, 1859-1862.* Ann Arbor, University of Michigan Press, 1959.

Nasatir, Abraham P. (ed.). *Before Lewis and Clark: Documents Illustrating the History of Missouri, 1785-1804.* 2 vols. St. Louis, St. Louis Historical Documents Foundation, 1952.

Nichols, Roger L. (ed.). *The Missouri Expedition 1818-1820: The Journal of Surgeon John Gale With Related Documents.* Norman, University of Oklahoma Press, 1969.

Osgood, Ernest S. (ed.). *The Field Notes of Captain William Clark, 1803-1805.* New Haven, Yale University Press, 1964.

Parker, Nathan H. *The Kansas and Nebraska Handbook for 1857-1858.* Boston, John P. Jewett and Co., 1857.

Perrin Du Lac, F. M. *Travels through the Two Louisianas, and Among the Savage Nations of the Missouri.* London, J. G. Barnard for Richard Phillips, 1807.

Redpath, James, and Richard J. Hinton. *Handbook to Kansas Territory and the Rocky Mountains' Gold Region.* New York, J. H. Colton, 1859.

Ruxton, George F. *Adventures in Mexico and the Rocky Mountains.* New York, Harper and Brothers, 1860.

Spaulding, C. C. *Annals of the City of Kansas: Embracing Full Details of the Trade and Commerce of the Great Western Plains.* Kansas City, Van Horn and Abel's Printing House, 1858.

Stoddard, Amos. *Sketches, Historical and Descriptive, of Louisiana.* Philadelphia, Mathew Carey, 1812.

Thomas, Alfred Barnaby (trans. and ed.). *After Coronado: Spanish Exploration Northeast of New Mexico, 1696–1727.* Norman, University of Oklahoma Press, 1935.

Thwaites, Reuben Gold (ed.). *Bradbury's Travels in the Interior of North America.* Vol. V in *Early Western Travels, 1748–1846.* Cleveland, Arthur H. Clark Co., 1904.

———. *Farnham's Travels in the Great Western Prairies, etc., May 21–October 16, 1839.* Vol. XXVIII in *Early Western Travels,* 1748–1846. Cleveland, Arthur H. Clark Co., 1906.

———. *Father Pierre-Jean De Smet's Letters and Sketches.* Vol. XXVII in *Early Western Travels, 1748–1846.* Cleveland, Arthur H. Clark Co., 1906.

———. *James' Account of S. H. Long's Expedition, 1819–1820.* Vols. XIV–XVII in *Early Western Travels, 1748–1846.* Cleveland, Arthur H. Clark Co., 1905.

———. *Josiah Gregg's Commerce of the Prairies, 1831–1839.* Vols. XIX–XX in *Early Western Travels, 1748–1846.* Cleveland, Arthur H. Clark Co., 1905.

———. *Oregon; or, A Short History of a Long Journey from the Atlantic Ocean to the Pacific by Land.* Vol. XXI in *Early Western Travels, 1748–1846.* Cleveland, Arthur H. Clark Co., 1905.

———. *Palmer's Journal of Travels over the Rocky Mountains, 1845–1846.* Vol. XXX in *Early Western Travels, 1748–1846.* Cleveland, Arthur H. Clark Co., 1906.

———. *Thomas Nuttall's Travels into the Arkansas Territory, 1819.* Vol. VIII in *Early Western Travels, 1748–1846.* Cleveland, Arthur H. Clark Co., 1904.

———. *Townsend's Narrative of a Journey Across the Rocky Mountains, to the Columbia River, and a Visit to the Sandwich Islands, Chile, etc.* Vol. XXI in *Early Western Travels, 1748–1846.* Cleveland, Arthur H. Clark Co., 1905.

SECONDARY SOURCES

Baughman, Robert W. *Kansas in Maps.* Topeka, Kansas State Historical Society, 1961.

Beaver, R. Pierce. *Church, State, and the American Indians.* St. Louis, Concordia Publishing House, 1966.

Berkhofer, Robert F., Jr. *Salvation and the Savage: An Analysis of Protestant Missions and American Indian Response, 1787–1862.* Lexington, University of Kentucky Press, 1965.

Blackmar, Frank W. (ed.). *Kansas: A Cyclopedia of State History, Embracing Events, Institutions, Counties, Cities, Towns, Prominent Persons, Etc.* 2 vols. Chicago, Standard Publishing Co., 1912.

Boaz, Franz. *Handbook of American Indian Languages.* Bureau of American Ethnology *Bulletin 40,* Pt. I. Washington, Government Printing Office, 1911.

Bolton, Herbert E. *Coronado: Knight of Pueblos and Plains.* Albuquerque, University of New Mexico Press, 1949.

Brigham, Lalla Maloy. *The Story of Council Grove on the Santa Fe Trail.* N.p., 1921.

Brown, A. Theodore. *Frontier Community: Kansas City to 1870.* Columbia, University of Missouri Press, 1963.

Castel, Albert. *A Frontier State at War: Kansas, 1861–1865.* Ithaca, N.Y., Cornell University Press, 1958.

Chapman, Berlin Basil. *The Otoes and Missourias: A Study of Indian Removal and the Legal Aftermath.* Oklahoma City, Times Journal Publishing Co., 1965.

Cone, William W. *Historical Sketch of Shawnee County, Kansas.* Topeka, Kansas Farmer Printing House, 1877.

Connelley, William E. *A Standard History of Kansas and Kansans.* Vol. I. Chicago, Lewis Publishing Co., n.d.

Coyner, David H. *The Lost Trappers.* Cincinnati, J. A. and V. P. James, 1847.

Douglas, Walter B. *Manuel Lisa.* New York, Argosy-Antiquarian Ltd., 1964.

Folmer, Henri. *Franco-Spanish Rivalry in North America, 1524–1763.* Glendale, Calif., Arthur H. Clark Co., 1953.

Frazer, Robert W. *Forts of the West: Military Forts and Presidios and Posts Commonly Called Forts West of the Mississippi River to 1898.* Norman, University of Oklahoma Press, 1965.

Garraghan, Gilbert J. *Catholic Beginnings in Kansas City, Missouri.* Chicago, Loyola University Press, 1920.

———. *Chapters in Frontier History.* Milwaukee, Bruce Publishing Co., 1934.

223

Gates, Paul Wallace. *Fifty Million Acres: Conflicts over Kansas Land Policy, 1854–1890.* Ithaca, N.Y., Cornell University Press, 1954.

Gray, P. L. *Gray's Doniphan County History.* Benderra, Kan., Roycroft Press, 1958.

Hagan, William T. *The Sac and Fox Indians.* Norman, University of Oklahoma Press, 1958.

Heitman, Francis B. *Historical Register and Dictionary of the United States Army.* 2 vols. Washington, Government Printing Office, 1903.

The History of Jackson County, Missouri, Containing a History of the County, Its Cities, Towns, Etc. Kansas City, Union Historical Co. and Birdsall, Williams and Co., 1881.

Horsman, Reginald. *Expansion and American Indian Policy, 1783–1812.* East Lansing, Michigan State University Press, 1967.

Hotz, Gottfried. *Indian Skin Paintings from the American Southwest: Two Representatives of Border Conflicts Between Mexico and the Missouri in the Early Eighteenth Century.* Trans. by Johannes Malthaner. Norman, University of Oklahoma Press, 1970.

Hyde, George E. *Indians of the Woodlands from Prehistoric Times to 1725.* Norman, University of Oklahoma Press, 1962.

———. *Pawnee Indians.* Denver, University of Denver Press, 1951.

Jones, Douglas C. *The Treaty of Medicine Lodge.* Norman, University of Oklahoma Press, 1966.

Kinnard, Lawrence (ed.). *Spain in the Mississippi Valley, 1765–1794.* 3 pts. Pt. III of *Annual Report of the American Historical Association, 1945.* Washington, Government Printing Office, 1949.

Loomis, Noel M., and Abraham P. Nasatir. *Pedro Vial and the Roads to Santa Fe.* Norman, University of Oklahoma Press, 1967.

Lowie, Robert H. *Indians of the Plains.* Garden City, N.Y., American Museum of Natural History, 1965.

McKenney, Thomas L., and James Hall. *The Indian Tribes of North America,* Vol. III. Edinburgh, John Grant, 1934.

McReynolds, Edwin C. *Missouri: A History of the Crossroads State.* Norman, University of Oklahoma Press, 1962.

Masterson, V. V. *The Katy Railroad and the Last Frontier.* Norman, University of Oklahoma Press, 1952.

Mathews, John Joseph. *The Osages: Children of the Middle Waters.* Norman, University of Oklahoma Press, 1961.

Miller, W. H. *The History of Kansas City.* Kansas City, Birdsall and Miller, 1881.

Nichols, Roger L. *General Henry Atkinson: A Western Military Career.* Norman, University of Oklahoma Press, 1965.

Oglesby, Richard E. "The Fur Trade as Business," in John Francis

McDermott (ed.), *The Frontier Re-examined.* Urbana, University of Illinois Press, 1967.

— — —. *Manuel Lisa and the Opening of the Missouri Fur Trade.* Norman, University of Oklahoma Press, 1963.

Phillips, Paul C. *The Fur Trade.* 2 vols. Norman, University of Oklahoma Press, 1961.

Prichard, James Cowles. *The Natural History of Man,* Vol. II. London, H. Bailliere, 1855.

Prucha, Francis Paul. *American Indian Policy in the Formative Years: The Indian Trade and Intercourse Acts, 1790–1834.* Cambridge, Mass., Harvard University Press, 1962.

Roe, Frank Gilbert. *The Indian and the Horse.* Norman, University of Oklahoma Press, 1955.

Rohrbough, Malcolm. *The Land Office Business: The Settlement and Administration of American Public Lands, 1787–1837.* New York, Oxford University Press, 1968.

Rydjord, John. *Indian Place-Names: Their Origin, Evolution, and Meanings, Collected in Kansas from the Siouan, Algonquian, Shoshonean, Caddoan, Iroquoian, and Other Tongues.* Norman, University of Oklahoma Press, 1968.

Sandoz, Mari. *The Beaver Men: Spearheads of Empire.* New York, Hastings House, 1964.

Sosin, Jack M. *The Revolutionary Frontier, 1763–1783.* New York, Holt, Rinehart and Winston, 1967.

Stearn, E. Wagner, and Allen E. Stearn. *The Effect of Smallpox on the Destiny of the Amerindian.* Boston, Bruce Humphries, Inc., 1945.

Steiger, John W. "Benjamin O'Fallon," in LeRoy R. Hafen (ed.), *The Mountain Men and the Fur Trade of the Far West,* Vol. V. Glendale, Calif., Arthur H. Clark Co., 1968.

Thompson, Matt. *Early History of Wabaunsee County, Kansas.* Alma, Kan., 1901.

Todd, Edgeley W. (ed.). *The Adventures of Captain Bonneville.* Norman, University of Oklahoma Press, 1961.

Unrau, William E., *The Kaw People.* Phoenix, Ariz., American Indian Tribal Series, 1975.

Wedel, Waldo R. *An Introduction to Kansas Archeology.* Bureau of American Ethnology *Bulletin 174.* Washington, Government Printing Office, 1959.

— — —. *Prehistoric Man on the Great Plains.* Norman, University of Oklahoma Press, 1961.

Young, Otis E. *The First Military Escort on the Santa Fe Trail.* Glendale, Calif., Arthur H. Clark Co., 1952.

ARTICLES AND ESSAYS

Abel, Annie Heloise. "Indian Reservations in Kansas and the Extinguishment of their Titles," *Transactions of the Kansas State Historical Society*, Vol. VIII (1903–1904).

Adams, Franklin G. "The Capitals of Kansas," *Transactions of the Kansas State Historical Society*, Vol. VIII (1903–1904).

———. "Reminiscences of Frederick Chouteau," *Transactions of the Kansas State Historical Society*, Vol. VIII (1903–1904).

Anderson, James. "The Methodist Shawnee Mission in Johnson County, Kansas 1830–1862," *Trail Guide*, Vol. I, No. 2 (January, 1956).

Armstrong, R. M. "Sixty Years in Kansas and Council Grove," *Collections of the Kansas State Historical Society*, Vol. XVI (1923–25).

Barnes, Lela (ed.). "Letters of Allen T. Ward, 1842–1851, From the Shawnee and Kaw (Methodist) Missions," *Kansas Historical Quarterly*, Vol. XXXIII, No. 3 (Autumn, 1967).

Barry, Louise (comp.). "Kansas Before 1854: A Revised Annals," *Kansas Historical Quarterly*, Vols. XXVIII–XXXII (Spring, 1962–Spring, 1966).

———. "The Kansa Indians and the Census of 1843," *Kansas Historical Quarterly*, Vol. XXXIX, No. 4 (Winter, 1973).

Baskett, James N. "A Study of Coronado Between the Río Grande and Missouri Rivers," *Collections of the Kansas State Historical Society*, Vol. XII (1912).

Bass, William M., and Donald F. Nelson. "The Identification of an Adult Kansa Male from the Doniphan Site, 14DP2, Doniphan County, Kansas," Kansas Anthropological Association *Newsletter*, Vol. XIII, No. 8 (April, 1968).

Bolton, Herbert E. (ed.). "Papers of Zebulon M. Pike," *American Historical Review*, Vol. XIII, No. 1 (October, 1907).

Brewester, S. W. "Reverend Father Paul M. Ponziglione," *Transactions of the Kansas State Historical Society*, Vol. IX (1905–1906).

Brooks, George R. (ed.). "George C. Sibley's Journal of a Trip to the Salines in 1811," Missouri Historical Society *Bulletin*, Vol. XXI, No. 3 (April, 1965).

Bushnell, David I., Jr. "Villages of the Algonquian, Siouan and Caddoan Tribes West of the Mississippi," Bureau of American Ethnology *Bulletin 83* (1927).

Cass, Lewis. "Indians of North America," *The North American Review*, New Series, Vol. XIII (1826).

Chapman, Berlin B. "Charles Curtis and the Kaw Reservation," *Kansas Historical Quarterly*, Vol. XV, No. 4 (November, 1947).

Chappell, Phil E. "A History of the Missouri River," *Transactions of the Kansas State Historical Society*, Vol. IX (1905–1906).

Coman, Katherine. "Government Factories: An Attempt to Control Competition in the Fur Trade," *Bulletin of the American Economic Association,* Fourth Series, No. 2 (April, 1911).

Connelley, William E. "The Lane Trail," *Collections of the Kansas State Historical Society,* Vol. XIII (1913–1914).

–––. "Notes on the Early Indian Occupancy of the Great Plains," *Collections of the Kansas State Historical Society,* Vol. XIV (1915–18).

–––. "The Treaty Held at Medicine Lodge," *Collections of the Kansas State Historical Society,* Vol. XVII (1926–28).

––– (ed.). "Indian Treaties and Councils Affecting Kansas: Dates and Places, Where Held, Names of Tribes, Commissioners and Indians Concluding Same," *Collections of the Kansas State Historical Society,* Vol. XVI (1925).

Dickson, C. H. "The 'Boy's' Story: Reminiscences of 1855," *Transactions of the Kansas State Historical Society,* Vol. V (1889–96).

Dolbee, Cora. "The Second Book on Kansas: An Account of C. B. Boynton and T. B. Mason's *A Journey Through Kansas; with Sketches of Nebraska,*" *Kansas Historical Quarterly,* Vol. IV, No. 2 (May, 1935).

Doran, Thomas F. "Kansas Sixty Years Ago," *Collections of the Kansas State Historical Society,* Vol. XV (1919–22).

Dorsey, James Owen. "Migrations of Siouan Tribes," *American Naturalist,* Vol. XX, No. 3 (March, 1886).

–––. "Mourning and War Customs of the Kansas," *American Naturalist,* Vol. XIX, No. 7 (July, 1885).

–––. "Siouan Sociology," *Fifteenth Annual Report of the Bureau of Ethnology to the Secretary of the Smithsonian Institution* (1893–94). Washington, 1897.

–––. "A Study of Siouan Cults," *Eleventh Annual Report of the Bureau of Ethnology to the Secretary of the Smithsonian Institution* (1889–1890). Washington, 1894.

Dunbar, Rev. John. "Letters Concerning the Presbyterian Mission in the Pawnee Country, near Bellvue, Neb., 1831–1849," *Collections of the Kansas State Historical Society,* Vol. XIV (1915–18).

Dunn, William E. "Spanish Reaction Against the French Advance Toward New Mexico, 1717–1727," *Mississippi Valley Historical Review,* Vol. II, No. 3 (December, 1915).

"Executive Minutes of Governor John W. Geary," *Transactions of the Kansas State Historical Society,* Vol. IV (1886–88).

"Extracts from the Diary of Major Sibley," *Chronicles of Oklahoma,* Vol. V, No. 2 (June, 1927).

"Ezekiel Williams' Adventures in Colorado," *Missouri Historical Society Collections,* Vol. IV, No. 2 (1913).

Ferris, Ida M. "The Sauks and Foxes in Franklin and Osage Counties, Kansas," *Collections of the Kansas State Historical Society*, Vol. XI (1909–10).

Finney, Frank F. "The Kaw Indians and their Indian Territory Agency," *Chronicles of Oklahoma*, Vol. XXXV, No. 3 (Winter, 1957–58).

Fletcher, Alice C., and Francis La Flesche. "The Omaha Tribe," *Twenty-seventh Annual Report of the Bureau of American Ethnology to the Smithsonian Institution* (1911).

Folmer, Henri. "De Bourgmont's Expedition to the Padoucas in 1724; The First French Approach to Colorado," *Colorado Magazine*, Vol. XIV, No. 4 (July, 1937).

―――. "Étienne Veniard de Bourgmont in the Missouri Country," *Missouri Historical Review*, Vol. XXXVI (October, 1941–July, 1942).

Gates, Paul Wallace. "A Fragment of Kansas Land History: The Disposal of the Christian Indian Tract," *Kansas Historical Quarterly*, Vol. VI, No. 3 (August, 1937).

Gill, Helen G. "The Establishment of Counties in Kansas," *Transactions of the Kansas State Historical Society*, Vol. VIII (1903–1904).

Godsey, Flora Rosenquist. "The Early Settlement and Raid on the 'Upper Neosho,'" *Collections of the Kansas State Historical Society*, Vol. XVI (1923–25).

"Governor Reeder's Administration," *Transactions of the Kansas State Historical Society*, Vol. V (1889–96).

"Governor Walker's Administration," *Transactions of the Kansas State Historical Society*, Vol. V (1889–96).

Gregg, Kate L. "The History of Fort Osage," *Missouri Historical Review*, Vol. XXXIV (October, 1939–July, 1940).

――― (ed.). "The Missouri Reader, Explorers in the Valley, Part II," *Missouri Historical Review*, Vol. XXXIX (October, 1944–July, 1945).

Gritting, W. J. "Committee on Explorations," *Transactions of the Kansas State Historical Society*, Vol. VIII (1903–1904).

Gunnerson, James H. "An Introduction to Plains Apache Archeology: The Dismal River Aspect," Bureau of American Ethnology *Bulletin 173* (1960).

Haines, Francis. "The Northward Spread of Horses Among the Plains Indians," *American Anthropologist*, New Series, Vol. XL (1938).

―――. "Where Did the Plains Indians Get Their Horses?" *American Anthropologist*, New Series, Vol. XL (1938).

Hoffhaus, Charles E. "Fort de Cavagnial," *Kansas Historical Quarterly*, Vol. XXX, No. 4 (Winter, 1964).

Howard, James H. "The Persistence of Southern Cult Gorgets among the Historic Kansas," *American Antiquity*, Vol. XXI (1956).

―――. "The Ponca Tribe," Bureau of American Ethnology *Bulletin 195* (1965).

Hulston, John K. "Daniel Boone's Sons in Missouri," *Missouri Historical Review*, Vol. XLI (October 1946–July, 1947).

"Indian Treaties and Councils Affecting Kansas," *Collections of the Kansas State Historical Society*, Vol. XVI (1923–25).

Jackson, Donald. "Journey to the Mandans, 1809: The Lost Narrative of Dr. Thomas," Missouri Historical Society *Bulletin*, Vol. XX, No. 3 (April, 1964).

"Journals of Capt. Thomas Becknell," *Missouri Historical Review*, Vol. IV, No. 2 (January, 1910).

"Kansas Agencies," *Collections of the Kansas State Historical Society*, Vol. XVI (1923–25).

King, Edward. "The Great South: The New Route to the Gulf," *Scribner's Monthly*, Vol. VI, No. 3 (July, 1873).

"Letters from the Indian Missions in Kansas, by Rev. William Johnson and Other Missionaries," *Collections of the Kansas State Historical Society*, Vol. XVI (1923–25).

"Letters of Rev. James M. Jameson," *Collections of the Kansas State Historical Society*, Vol. XVI (1925).

Lichtenhan, Hartman. "Reminiscences of Hartman Lichtenhan," *Transactions of the Kansas State Historical Society*, Vol. IX (1905–1906).

Lowe, Percival G. "Kansas as Seen in the Indian Territory," *Transactions of the Kansas State Historical Society*, Vol. IV (1886–88).

Lutz, Rev. J. J. "The Methodist Missions among the Indian Tribes in Kansas," *Transactions of the Kansas State Historical Society*, Vol. IX (1905–1906).

McClure, James R. "Taking the Census and Other Incidents in 1855," *Transactions of the Kansas State Historical Society*, Vol. VIII (1903–1904).

McCoy, John C. "Survey of Kansas Indian Lands," *Transactions of the Kansas State Historical Society*, Vol. IV (1886–88).

McGee, W. J. "The Siouan Indians," *Fifteenth Annual Report of the Bureau of Ethnology to the Secretary of the Smithsonian Institution* (1893–94). Washington, 1897.

Madden, John. "Along the Trail," *Collections of the Kansas State Historical Society*, Vol. VIII (1903–1904).

Maier, Ruth Olive. "Literature Pertaining to Kansas Indians: An Evaluation," Kansas Anthropological Association *Newsletter*, Vol. 1, Nos. 2–3 (September–October, 1955).

Marshall, Thomas M. (ed.). "The Journals of Jules De Mun," Missouri Historical Society *Collections*, Vol. V, No. 3 (June, 1928).

Martin, George W. "The Territorial and Military Combine at Fort Riley," *Transactions of the Kansas State Historical Society*, Vol. II (1901–1902).

Mead, James. "The Pawnees as I Knew Them," *Transactions of the Kansas State Historical Society*, Vol. X (1907–1908).

———. "The Saline River Country in 1859," *Transactions of the Kansas State Historical Society*, Vol. IX (1905–1906).

Meeker, Rev. Jotham. "High Waters in Kansas," *Transactions of the Kansas State Historical Society*, Vol. VIII (1903–1904).

"Missions in North America," *Baptist Missionary Magazine*, Vol. XIX, No. 6 (June, 1839).

"Missions in North America," *Baptist Missionary Magazine*, Vol. XX, No. 6 (June, 1840).

Montgomery, Mrs. Frank C. "Fort Wallace and Its Relation to the Frontier," *Collections of the Kansas State Historical Society*, Vol. XVII (1926–27).

Morehouse, George P. "Along the Kaw Trail," *Transactions of the Kansas State Historical Society*, Vol. VIII (1903–1904).

———. "Diamond Springs, 'The Diamond of the Plain,'" *Collections of the Kansas State Historical Society*, Vol. XIV (1915–18).

———. "A Famous Old Crossing on the Santa Fe Trail," *Transactions of the Kansas State Historical Society*, Vol. VIII (1903–1904).

———. "History of the Kansa or Kaw Indians," *Transactions of the Kansas State Historical Society*, Vol. X (1907–1908).

———. "Padilla and the Old Monument Near Council Grove," *Transactions of the Kansas State Historical Society*, Vol. X (1907–1908).

———. "Probably the First School in Kansas for White Children," *Transactions of the Kansas State Historical Society*, Vol. IX (1905–1906).

Morrison, T. F. "The Osage Treaty of 1865," *Collections of the Kansas State Historical Society*, Vol. XVII (1926–27).

Nasatir, Abraham P. "Ducharme's Invasion of Missouri: An Incident in the Anglo-American Rivalry for the Indian Trade of Upper Louisiana," *Missouri Historical Review*, Vol. XXIV, No. 1 (October, 1929).

"Notes of the Early History of the Nebraska Country," *Publications of the Nebraska Historical Society*, Vol. XX (1922).

"Notes on the Missouri River, and Some of the Native Tribes in its Neighborhood," *The Analectic Magazine*, New Series, Vol. I, Nos. 3–4 (April–May, 1820).

Patrick, G. E. "The Great Spirit Spring," *Transactions of the Kansas Academy of Science*, Vol. VII (1879–80).

Patton, Rev. William. "Journal of a Visit to the Indian Missions, Missouri Conference," Missouri Historical Society *Bulletin*, Vol. X, No. 2 (January, 1954).

Pease, Calvin T., and Ernestine Jenison (eds.). "Illinois on the Eve of the Seven Years' War 1747–1755," *Collections of the Illinois State Historical Library*, Vol. XXIX (1940).

Powell, J. W. "Introduction," *Fifth Annual Report of the Bureau of Ethnology to the Secretary of the Smithsonian Institution* (1883–1884).

Quaife, Milo M. (ed.). "The Journals of Captain Meriwether Lewis and Sergeant John Ordway Kept on the Expedition of Western Exploration, 1803–1806," *Wisconsin Historical Publications Collections*, Vol. XXII (1916).

Raber, Charles. "Personal Recollections of Life on the Plains from 1860–1863," *Collections of the Kansas State Historical Society*, Vol. XVI (1923–25).

Remsburg, George J. "Isle Au Vache," *Transactions of the Kansas State Historical Society*, Vol. VIII (1903–1904).

Root, George A. "Reminiscences of William Darnell," *Collections of the Kansas State Historical Society*, Vol. XVII (1926–27).

Rothensteiner, Rev. John. "Early Missionary Efforts Among the Indians in the Diocese of St. Louis," *St. Louis Catholic Historical Review*, Vol. II, Nos. 2–3 (April–July, 1920).

Royce, Charles C. "The Cherokee Nation of Indians," *Fifth Annual Report of the Bureau of Ethnology to the Secretary of the Smithsonian Institution* (1883–1884).

Scholes, France V., and H. P. Mera. "Some Aspects of the Jumano Problem," *Contributions to American Anthropology and History*, Pub. 253, Vol. VI, No. 34 (1940).

Shamleffer, William F. "Merchandising Sixty Years Ago," *Collections of the Kansas State Historical Society*, Vol. XVI (1923–25).

Sharp, Mamie Stine. "Historic Persons and Places Brought to Notice by the Home-Coming Celebration," *Collections of the Kansas State Historical Society*, Vol. XVI (1923–25).

Sheldon, Addison E. (trans.). "New Chapter in Nebraska History—The Battle at the Forks of the Loup and the Platte, August 11, 1720," *Nebraska History and Record of Pioneer Days*, Vol. VI, No. 3 (January–March, 1923).

Shields, Clara M. Fengel. "The Lyon Creek Settlement," *Collections of the Kansas State Historical Society*, Vol. XIV (1915–18).

Skinner, Alanson. "Societies of the Iowa, Kansa and Ponca Indians," *Anthropological Papers of the American Museum of Natural History*, Vol. XI (1915).

Smith, Alice S. "Through the Eyes of My Father," *Collections of the Kansas State Historical Society*, Vol. XVII (1926–28).

Spencer, Rev. Joab. "The Kaw or Kansas Indians: Their Customs, Manners and Folk-lore," *Transactions of the Kansas State Historical Society*, Vol. X (1907–1908).

Stauf, Margaret. "John Dougherty, Indian Agent," *Mid-America*, Vol. XVI, No. 3 (January, 1934).

Stubbs, A. W. "Cheyenne Raid of 1868," *Collections of the Kansas State Historical Society,* Vol. XVI (1923–25).

Tucker, Sara Jones (comp.). "Indian Villages of the Illinois Country," Illinois State Museum *Scientific Papers,* Vol. II, Pt. I (1942), Atlas.

Unrau, William E. "Epidemic Disease and the Impact of the Santa Fe Trail on the Kansa Indians," *Heritage of the Great Plains,* Vol. XVII, No. 2 (Spring, 1984).

— — —. "Charles Curtis and the Politics of Allotment," in L. G. Moses and Raymond Wilson, eds., *Indian Lives: Essays on Nineteenth and Twentieth Century Native American Leaders.* Albuquerque, University of New Mexico Press, 1985.

— — —. "The Civil War Career of Jesse Henry Leavenworth," *Montana Magazine,* Vol. XII, No. 2 (April, 1962).

— — —. "The Council Grove Merchants and Kansa Indians, 1855–1870," *Kansas Historical Quarterly,* Vol. XXXIV, No. 3 (Autumn, 1968).

— — —. "Depopulation of the Dhegiha-Siouan Kansas Prior to Removal," *New Mexico Historical Review,* Vol. XLVIII, No. 4 (October, 1973).

— — —. "Indian Agent vs. the Army: Some Background Notes on the Kiowa-Comanche Treaty of 1865," *Kansas Historical Quarterly,* Vol. XXX, No. 2 (Summer, 1964).

— — —. "Indian Water Rights to the Middle Arkansas: The Case for the Kaws," *Kansas History, A Journal of the Central Plains,* Vol. V, No. 1 (Spring, 1982).

— — —. "Removal, Death, and Legal Reincarnation of the Kaw People," *The Indian Historian,* Vol. 9, No. 1 (Winter, 1976).

— — —. "The Mixed-Blood Connection: Charles Curtis and Kaw Detribalization," in Forrest R. Blackburn, ed., *Kansas and the West.* Topeka, Kansas State Historical Society, 1976.

— — —. "United States 'Diplomacy' with the Dhegiha-Siouan Kansas, 1815–1825," *The Kansas Quarterly,* Vol. III, No. 4 (Fall, 1971).

Voelker, Frederic E. "Ezekiel Williams of Boon's Lick," Missouri Historical Society *Bulletin,* Vol. VIII, No. 1 (October, 1951).

Watkins, Albert (ed.). "Notes on the Early History of the Nebraska Country," *Publications of the Nebraska Historical Society,* Vol. XX (1922).

Way, Royal B. "The United States Factory System for Trading with the Indians, 1796–1822," *Mississippi Valley Historical Review,* Vol. VI, No. 2 (September, 1919).

Wedel, Waldo R. "Culture Sequences in the Central Great Plains," in *Essays in Historical Anthropology of North America, Smithsonian Miscellaneous Collections,* Vol. 100 (Whole Number), No. 3588 (1940).

— — —. "Environmental and Native Subsistence Economics in the Central Great Plains," *Smithsonian Miscellaneous Collections*, Vol. 101, No. 3 (1941).

———. "The Kansa Indians," *Transactions of the Kansas Academy of Science*, Vol. XLIX, No. 1 (June, 1946).

Wilhelm, Friedrich Paul, Duke of Württemberg. "First Journey to North America in the Years 1822 to 1824," trans. by William G. Bek, *South Dakota Historical Collections*, Vol. XIX (1938).

Wilmeth, Roscoe. "Present Status of the Archaeology of the Kansa Indians," Kansas Anthropological Association *Newsletter*, Vol. IV, No. 7 (March, 1959).

Witty, Thomas A., Jr. "Newly Discovered Burials at the Doniphan Site," 14DP1," Kansas Anthropological Association *Newsletter*, Vol. IX, No. 9 (May, 1964).

PAMPHLETS

Lang, John D., and Samuel Taylor, Jr. *Report of a Visit to Some of the Tribes of Indians, Located West of the Mississippi River.* New York, Press of M. Day and Co., 1843. Pamphlet, Special Collections Department, Newberry Library, Chicago, Illinois.

McCoy, Isaac. *Address to Philanthropists in the United States, Generally, and to Christians in the Particular, on the Condition and Prospects of the American Indians.* N.p. Written at Surveyor's Camp, Neosho River, Indian Territory, December 1, 1831. Pamphlet File, Library Division, Kansas State Historical Society, Topeka.

UNPUBLISHED THESES

Folmer, Henri. "French Expansion Toward New Mexico in the Eighteenth Century." Unpublished M.A. thesis, Department of History, University of Denver, 1939.

Fulmer, Gretchen Brook. "An Ethnohistory Study of the Kansa Indians From the Time of First European Contact Until the Present." Unpublished M.A. thesis, Department of Anthropology, Indiana University, 1967.

Keckeisen, Robert Joseph. "The Kansa 'Half-Breed' Lands: Contravention and Transformation of United States Indian Policy in Kansas." Unpublished M.A. thesis, Department of History, Wichita State University, 1982.

COURT CASES

William E. Bowker v. Elisha Higgins. February 17, 1864. District Court of Kansas. 3rd Judicial District, Jefferson County.

Pelagia De Aubri v. Robert S. Stevens. March 2, 1863. District Court of
Kansas. 3rd Judicial District, Shawnee County.
George W. Ewing v. John McManamy. December 10, 1858. Kansas Terri-
torial District Court. 1st Judicial District, Jefferson County.
John McManamy v. George W. Ewing. 1 Kan. 581.
Elizabeth Pechaka v. Andrew J. McHenry. March 19, 1864. District Court
of Kansas. 3rd Judicial District, Jefferson County.
Robert S. Stevens v. Victoria Smith. 77 U.S. (10 Wall.) 321.
Swope v. Purdy. 23 F. Cas. 576.

INDEX

British Illinois: 73
British-Spanish conflict in Upper Louisiana: 55, 74
Bryant, Edwin: 29
Buchanan, James: 188
Buffalo People: 30
Burning Hart (Kansa chief): 92
Burt County, Nebr.: 18

Cabanné, J. P.: 77–78, 84
Cachupin, Don Tómas Vélez (governor of New Mexico): 58, 68
Cahokia, Ill.: 53, 73, 116
Cahola Creek (Kansas): 166
Calhoun, John C. (secretary of war): 95–96, 99
Calvert, Claibourne: 141
Calvo, Casa, Marqués de (governor of Louisiana): 78
Caney River (Kansas): 214
Cantonment Leavenworth: see Fort Leavenworth
Cantonment Martin: 95, 100
Carleton, Lieut. J. Henry: 17
Carleton, Sir Guy: 72
Carondelet, François Luis Hector (governor-general of Louisiana): 76
Cass, Lewis: 117, 150
Catawba Indians: 15
Cavagnial: see Fort Cavagnolle
Cayebasneenzaw ("Little Chief" of the Kansas): 97
Cayegettsazesheegaw ("Old Chief" of the Kansas): 97
Cayezettanzaw ("Big Chief" of the Kansas): 97
Chaupuis, Jean: 68
Cherokee National Council: 214
Cheyenne Indians: 27, 44, 199–200, 208–209, 211
Chivington, Col. John M.: 200
Cholera: 27, 41, 71, 132
Chouteau, Auguste: 71, 73, 75, 85, 96–97, 99, 114, 142–44, 150–51
Chouteau, Cyprian: 115, 130
Chouteau, Francis: 95, 109, 141, 146
Chouteau, Frederick: 115, 130, 143, 150
Chouteau, Gabriel: 95
Chouteau, Jean Pierre (Pedro), Jr.: 81, 84, 86, 143, 165
Christian Advocate and Journal: 129

Christian missionaries: see missionary activity
Chute, Dr. A.: 151
Clamorgan, Jacques (Santiago, St. Yago, Morgan): 76–78, 85
Clark, George W.: 171, 182n.
Clark, Marston G. (Indian agent): 42, 115, 123–24, 128, 141–47
Clark, William (superintendent of Indian Affairs): 17, 21, 41–42, 86, 91, 97, 103, 106, 117, 119, 141, 143, 146, 150–51, 156, 160
Clarke's Creek (Kansas): 203
Collot, Victor: 21
Columbia, Christopher: 171, 177, 185
Columbus, Nebr.: 57n.
Comanche Indians: 149, 162, 199–200
"Committee of the People": 176n.
"Company of the Discoverers and Explorers of the Missouri": 76
Company of the Indies (French): 59–61, 65
Company of the West: see Company of the Indies (French)
Confederacy: 199
Conn, Malcolm: 185
Connelley, William E.: 7
Cooke, Col. Philip St. George: 174
Corn cultivation: 12
Coronado, Francisco de: 53
Corwin, Robert G.: 189, 196
Cottonwood Falls, Kans.: 184
Council Bluffs: see Upper Missouri Agency
Council Grove, Kans.: 26, 32, 43, 157, 162–63, 165–66, 169, 183, 190, 203, 207, 210
Council Grove manual-labor school: 197
Council Grove Town Company: 186, 192–93, 195, 201, 211
Cour de Brule (Kansa chief): 78
Coureurs de bois: 53, 55, 58–59, 61, 72
Cow Island: 100
Cox, Jacob D.: 213
Crawford, T. Hartley (commissioner of Indian Affairs): 139
Crooks, Ramsay: 96
Crow, Dr. (physician to Kansa Indians): 150–51

Macarty, Maj. Mactigue (commandant of Illinois): 67, 69
McCarthy, Dennis: 20
McCoy, Reverend Isaac: *see* missionary activity
McGill, James: 129
McNair, Dunning: 115, 120
Malgares, Lieut. Fecundo: 83
Mallet, Paul: 66
Mallet, Pierre: 66, 68
Man Charles, The (Kansa chief): 50
Mandan Indians: 149
Manhattan, Kans.: 19–20
Manitoba, Canada: 16
Manypenny, George W. (commissioner of Indian Affairs): 173–74, 178
Marain (trader): 65
Marcy, William L.: 178
Marest, Father Gabriel: 55
Marquette, Jacques: 6, 15, 17, 20, 53–54
Martin, Capt. Wyly: 99–100
Mathers, Thomas: 109
Maxent, Laclede and Dee (fur company): 71
Maxwell, Nebr.: 57n.
Mead, James: 211
Medill, William (commissioner of Indian Affairs): 162
Meeker, Jotham: 125
Miró, Esteban Rodriguez (governor-general of Louisiana): 75
Missionary activity: Christian missionaries, 6; James G. Pratt (missionary-printer), 10; Isaac McCoy (Baptist), 10, 17, 25, 37, 40–41, 107n., 122, 160, 162; Thomas Huffaker (Methodist), 32, 166, 168, 173, 179–80, 185–86, 188, 190, 192, 201, 204–207, 212; Rev. William Johnson (Methodist), 72, 123, 128, 131, 144; Roman Catholic, 116–17; Baptist, 118; and Baptist Board of Foreign Missions, 122; Methodist Episcopal, 123, 125, 159, 161, 165; Indian Missionary Society, 123; Rev. Thomas Johnson (Methodist), 123, 129–30, 144; Shawnee Mission, 123, 128; Rev. William D. Smith (Presbyterian), 125–26, 128; Presbyterian, 125–27; and interdenominational conflict, 125, 135; William Bowles (Baptist), 125; Johnston Lykins (Baptist),

125; Harmony Mission, 126; Presbyterian Missionary Board, 127; Indian agents critical of, 128; Rev. G. W. Love (Methodist), 135; Rev. J. T. Perry (Methodist), 136
Mission Creek manual-labor school: 136
Mission Creek villages: 113, 115, 119, 128, 130, 133, 141–42, 151–52, 159
Mississippi River: 6, 12–13, 15
Missouri Company: 78, 113
Missouri Gazette: 23
Missouri Indians: 56–58, 62, 69, 116, 157
Missouri-Kansas-Texas (Katy) Railroad: *see* Union Pacific Railway, Southern Branch
Missouri River: 13, 17–18, 21, 23
Missouri statehood movement: 104–105
Mitchell, William: 186
Monroe, James: 104, 109
Montgomery, John: 167, 172, 177, 179, 180, 182
Montreal, Canada: 53, 59
Morehouse, George P.: 4, 7
Morris County (Kansas) commissioners: 207
Morrison, Col. William: 160
Mullins, Capt. Martin: 211
Munsee (Christian) Indian Tract: 186
Murphy, Thomas (Indian superintendent): 211–12

Nah-he-gah-wah-tu-in-gah (Kansa chief): 206
Navajo Indians: 210
Nebraska aspect: 19
Nemahaw River: 107
Neosho River: 103, 166
Neosho Valley: 24, 162, 164
Neosho Valley Railroad: 200
Nepaholla ("water on the hill," salt spring): 47
New Netherland: 53
New Orleans, La.: 59, 66, 75–76, 203
Ninth Kansas Cavalry: 199
Nodaway (Nodewa) River: 103, 107
No-pa-my (Kansa chief): 201
Northern Indian Agency: 129

O'Fallon, Benjamin (Indian agent): 95, 100–101, 104, 112, 114
O'Fallon, Col. John: 95

Ohio River: 13, 16
Omaha Indians: 7, 11–12, 16, 27, 77–79, 149, 157
Oñate, Juan de: 8
Oneota: *see* Southern Cult
O'Reilly, Alexandro (governor of Louisiana): 73
Osage Indians: 7–8, 12, 23; artifacts of, 20; warfare of, with Kansa Indians, 27, 76–77; physical appearance of, 29; intermarriage of, with Kansa Indians, 33; smallpox among, 41; French fur trade with, 55; Bourgmont's experiences among, 61–62; French trade with, 68, 74; English influence upon, 69; Spain's inability to control, 73; purchase arms from British, 73; Spanish trade with, 74; encouraged to punish Kansa Indians, 75; raid Spanish traders, 76; visit Washington (1806), 83; understanding of, with Kansa Indians (1806), 83; conflict of, with Kansas, 79; serve as guides for Pike, 83; fear Kansa Indians, 83; Little Osages plan attack on Kansas, 83; Chouteaus trade with, 86, 97; Spanish influence on, 86; attack Iowa Indians, 91; pledge peace to Sibley (1811), 92; join Kansas en route to Missouri River, 100; missionary work among, 116; Presbyterian mission among, 126; attack Pawnees (1838), 132; smallpox among (1827), 194
Osage River: 13
Osage River Agency: 167
Otis, R.: 183
Otoe Indians: 27, 56–58, 93–94, 97, 99, 102, 157
Outlas (trader): 65

Padouca Indians (Plains Apache Indians): 60 & n., 62
Pania Republic: *see* Pawnee Indians
Panic of 1819: 95, 104
Papin family: 71
Pappan (Papin), Louis: 34
Park, William: 183
Parrot, Marcus J.: 182
Pawnee Fork: 39
Pawnee Indians: 23, 27; conflict of, with Kansa Indians, 41, 44, 71; small-pox among, 41, 71; and Spanish fur trade, 55; French influence among, 56, 58; role of, in Villasur disaster, 57; Skidi Pawnees, 57; Black Pawnees, 70; cholera among, 71; Kansas move in closer proximity to, 79; visit Washington, D.C. (1806), 83; Pike visits (1806), 83; Republican village of, 83, 88–89; visited by Malgares (1806), 83; conflict of, with Kansas (1809), 88; Republican Pawnees, 88–89, 107, 113, 156–57; Kitkehahkis Pawnees, 88; Grand Pawnees, 88; pledge peace to Sibley (1811), 92; attack Blue Earth village (1812), 92; defeated by Kansas (1812), 92; defeat Kansas (1812), 93; allied with Otoe Indians, 99; attacked by Kansas (1838), 132; attacked by Kansas (1840), 133, 159; war with Kansas (1758), 149; murder Kansas (1829), 157; attacked by Kansas (1831), 157
Peace of Paris (1763): 71
Peace of Ryswick (1697): 54
Peg-gah-hosh-she (Kansa chief): *see* Big John
Peoria Indians: 157
Pérez, Manuel: 75
Perrot, Nicholas: 15
Perry, Rev. J. T.: *see* missionary activity
Philebert, Gabriel: 114, 141
Philip V of Spain: 56
Piankeshaw Indians: 157
Picurís pueblo (New Mexico): 54
Pierce, Franklin: 170
Piernas, Pedro (lieutenant governor of Louisiana): 74
Pike, Lieut. Zebulon M.: 23, 25, 82, 85, 97, 114
Pilcher, Joshua: 113, 139
Plains Woodland culture: 18
Plumb Creek, Kans.: 209
Pomeroy, Samuel: 206–207
Ponca Indians: 9, 12, 16, 78
Portneuf, Louis Robineau de: 67–68
Potawatomie Agency (Kansas): 166–67, 172
Potawatomie Catholic Mission: 153
Potawatomie Indians: 157
Pratt, James G.: *see* missionary activity